A Manual for Writers

Chicago Guides
to Writing, Editing,
and Publishing

On Writing, Editing, and Publishing
Essays Explicative and Hortatory
Second Edition
Jacques Barzun

Writing for Social Scientists
How to Start and Finish Your Thesis, Book, or Article
Howard S. Becker, with a chapter by Pamela Richards

The Craft of Translation
Edited by John Biguenet and Rainer Schulte

Chicago Guide to Preparing Electronic Manuscripts
For Authors and Publishers
Prepared by the Staff of the University of Chicago Press

Getting into Print
The Decision-Making Process
Walter W. Powell

Tales of the Field
On Writing Ethnography
John Van Maanen

A Handbook of Biological Illustration
Second Edition
Frances W. Zweifel

A Manual for Writers of Term Papers, Theses, and Dissertations

Kate L. Turabian

Fifth Edition
Revised and Expanded
by Bonnie Birtwistle Honigsblum

The University of Chicago Press

Chicago and London

KATE L. TURABIAN was editor of official publications and
dissertation secretary at the University of Chicago for over
twenty-five years. BONNIE BIRTWISTLE HONIGSBLUM holds a
Ph.D. from the University of Chicago; she teaches English
and serves as a writing consultant to business and
professional organizations.

Portions of this book have been adapted from *The Chicago Manual
of Style,* 13th edition, © 1969, 1982 by The University of Chicago.

The University of Chicago Press, Chicago 60637
The University of Chicago Press, Ltd., London

Fifth edition, published 1987
Printed in the United States of America
96 95 94 93 92 91 90   10 9 8 7 6

Library of Congress Cataloging-in-Publication Data
Turabian, Kate L.
   A manual for writers of term papers, theses, and dissertations.

   (Chicago guides to writing, editing, and publishing)
   Bibliography: p.
   Includes index.
   1. Dissertations, Academic. 2. Report writing.
I. Honigsblum, Bonnie Birtwistle. II. Title.
III. Series.
LB2369.T8   1982   808'.02   86-19128
ISBN 0-226-81624-9
ISBN 0-226-81625-7 (pbk.)

Contents

Contents

Preface

Kate L. Turabian designed this manual as a guide to suitable style in the presentation of term papers, theses, and dissertations in both scientific and nonscientific fields. The genesis of the manual can be traced to a sentence in the June 1929 edition of the *Handbook of the Graduate Schools* of the University of Chicago, which reads: "Samples of paper and directions concerning the form of the dissertation may be obtained at the Dissertation Desk, in Harper Library." When in 1931 the work of the Dissertation Desk was transferred to a dissertation secretary under the purview of the dean of students, the secretary inherited a one-page set of mimeographed instructions, the first paragraph stating, "In form, the dissertation should follow the style of the University of Chicago Press as exhibited in its publications and set forth in *A Manual of Style*." Students and their typists, therefore, were directed to the Press manual for detailed information needed to bring papers into conformity with accepted thesis style. But this style manual, designed as a guide for typographers, editors, and others dealing with the printed word, required some interpretation if it was to serve as a guide to producing a typescript conforming to its standards. To supplement the Press manual, the dissertation secretary furnished students with a two-page set of mimeographed instructions on such matters as spacing, indention, margins, and underlining. With the flattening of student pocketbooks in the Depression of 1930–35, the need arose to expand those instructions into a small booklet incorporating the materials in *A Manual of Style* that were relevant to the preparation of a typewritten dissertation. The title of the booklet, published in 1937, was essentially the same as the one it bears today. Thus from the beginning the thesis manual has recommended in general the style of the University of Chicago Press as shown in its publications—both books and journals—and as explained in its *Manual of Style*.

The thirteenth edition of the Press manual, *The Chicago Manual of Style*, published in 1982, gave impetus for a fifth edition of the thesis manual. The thesis manual has always followed the Press manual's guidelines for such matters as spelling, punctuation, and distinctive treatment of words. The fifth edition of the thesis manual is also indebted to the thirteenth edition of *The Chicago Manual of Style* for its treatment of parenthetical references and reference lists, footnotes, endnotes, and bibliographies. Significant portions of the Press manual have been adapted here, sometimes verbatim, to chapters on abbreviations, tables, illustrations, and the layout of component parts. Whenever this manual differs from the Press manual, it reflects the needs of a different readership.

Written originally from Kate Turabian's perspective as dissertation secretary at the University of Chicago, the manual has always championed the cause of the individual producing a finished manuscript, often serving as researcher, writer, typist (or now word-processing specialist), graphic artist, proofreader, and printer or photocopier operator, all in one. Having for its model this kind of self-publication, the manual has had to serve as a guide useful in many disciplines and at the same time respond to the expectation that it should set a standard. In coming to terms with rapid, often sweeping advances in publication practices and print technologies, the manual has held its own, proving to be a formidable survivor capable of adapting to new environments. Characteristically, a paragraph from the foreword to the first edition written nearly fifty years ago still pertains:

> As an examination of this manual will reveal, some sections are of interest only to students in certain fields, while some contain information necessary to all writers of dissertations and should therefore be studied in full. Sample pages, sample footnotes, tables, and so forth are provided as supplements to the directions—illustrating and clarifying points of form. They cannot be properly interpreted or safely followed except in conjunction with the rules. It may be observed that familiarity with the requirements during the period when the dissertation is in preparation will greatly facilitate the assembling of materials and the writing of the final draft.

It is, therefore, in the spirit of past editions of the manual that the fifth remains a reference tool designed to help the writer use whatever methods, materials, or technologies may be needed to assemble the final manuscript of a research paper. In other words, the manual is still a "how to" book rather than a consumer guide. As the concept of "use" is limited here to its application in preparing special kinds of research papers, much of what might belong in a general primer to computerized word processing, for example, has been excluded in favor of emphasizing only certain aspects of computerized word processing that seem vital to the task of preparing a finished manuscript. It is not within the scope of this manual to recommend a particular brand of hardware or software, or even to explore fully the process necessary to decide what kind of equipment to bring to the task of preparing a finished manuscript. Chapter 13 does, however, offer a brief overview of the general categories of facilities and materials now available, and it explains how they might be used to prepare research papers. In response to a 1984 survey of over 750 colleges and universities, this edition also introduces a new chapter on parenthetical references and reference lists (chapter 8). In chapter 14, sample pages are brought together, and detailed information on the layout of pages has been added to the samples. Finally, where other resources for the scholarly writer commend themselves, style guides and writing aids are mentioned within the text of the manual. For the writer whose department or discipline recommends an authoritative style guide within its field, a selected bibliography has also been added.

Throughout the making of this revision, Geoffrey C. M. Plampin, editor of official publications and dissertation secretary at the University of Chicago, served as spokesman for those currently committed to the writing of theses and dissertations. Joel J. Mambretti, Ph.D., lead staff analyst in information technologies and new services at the University of Chicago's Computation Center and designer of the University of Chicago's dissertation-formatting program TREATISE, contributed broad experience in academic computing. The editorial staff of the University of Chicago Press advised on matters having to do with the thirteenth edition of *The Chicago Manual of Style*. Many other experts within the University of Chicago community also contributed generously to the process of revising this manual. I should also like to thank the many dissertation secretaries and thesis advisers whose recommendations have reached the Press through personal correspondence and its 1984 survey. In revising and expanding the manual, I have endeavored to address their concerns and meet the needs of the writers they serve.

Bonnie Birtwistle Honigsblum
January 1987

1 Parts of the Paper

1.1 The word *paper* is used throughout this manual to refer alike to term papers, theses, and dissertations except in matters relating specifically to one of these. A term paper fulfills the requirements of a course or an undergraduate major. A thesis fulfills the requirements of a graduate-level course or meets the specifications set for a master's degree. A dissertation meets the requirements for a doctoral degree. Each of these kinds of research paper requires references to works cited within the text, and the manuscript of each must be submitted as finished copy rather than as copy prepared for typesetting. Such research papers must meet specifications set by the degree-granting institutions.

1.2   A paper has three main parts: the front matter, or preliminaries; the text; and the reference or back matter. In a long paper, each of these main parts may consist of several sections (see below).

1.3   With respect to pagination, there are two categories: the front matter, or preliminaries, numbered with consecutive lowercase roman numerals centered at the bottom of pages; and the rest of the work, numbered with consecutive arabic numerals centered at the bottom of pages bearing titles and centered at the top, or in the upper right-hand corner, of all other pages of the text and reference matter.

1.4   Any part of the paper that appears in textual or tabular form may be footnoted, including descriptive paragraphs preceding lists and glossaries.

1.5   Unless specified otherwise by the conventions of a department or discipline, the order given in the above table of contents for this chapter should be observed, regardless of the parts that may be omitted. Not every paper will require each of these parts. In the event that the paper is later published, the organization required by the publisher may differ from that recommended here.

THE FRONT MATTER, OR PRELIMINARIES

TITLE PAGE

1.6   Most universities and colleges have their own style of title page for theses and dissertations, and this should be followed exactly in matters of content, capitalization, centering, and spacing. For term papers, if a sample sheet is not provided, a title page might include the name of the university or college (usually centered at the top of the sheet), the exact title of the paper, the course (including its department and number), the date, and the name of the writer. See sample 14.25 for one style that may be used for theses and dissertations.

BLANK PAGE

1.7   This unnumbered sheet is recommended to prevent the text of the following page from showing through the white space on the title page.

ACKNOWLEDGMENTS

1.8   In the acknowledgments, the writer thanks mentors and colleagues, lists the individuals or institutions that supported the research, and gives credit to works cited in the text for which permission to reproduce has been granted (see 5.1). Although one would wish to acknowledge special assistance such as consultation on technical matters and aid in securing special equipment and source materials, one may with propriety omit an expression of formal thanks for the routine help given by an adviser or a thesis committee. The generic heading ACKNOWL-EDGMENTS, which appears only on the first page of the part, is in uppercase and centered over the text. The format of this page should be the same as that of the first page of a chapter that carries only a generic heading. Each page of the acknowledgments is numbered in lowercase roman numerals centered beneath the text.

PREFACE

1.9   In the preface, the writer explains the motivation for making the study, the background for the project, the scope of the research, and the purpose of the paper. The preface may also include acknowledgments if an acknowledgments section is omitted. If a writer has nothing significant to add about the study to what is covered in the main body of the paper and wishes only to acknowledge the various sorts of assistance and permissions received, these remarks should be entitled ACKNOWLEDG-MENTS rather than PREFACE. A preface appears in the same format as an acknowledgments section (see 1.8).

TABLE OF CONTENTS

1.10   The table of contents, sometimes headed simply CONTENTS, lists all the parts of the paper except the title page, blank page, dedication, and epigraph. No page numbers appear on any of these four, and the last three are not included in the counting of the pagination of the front matter, or preliminaries. If the chapters are grouped in parts, the generic headings (e.g., PART I) and titles (e.g., EARLY FINDINGS) of the parts also appear in the contents. Subheadings within the chapters are frequently included in one of various ways (see 14.26–27), or they may be omitted entirely from the table of contents.

1.11 In preparing a table of contents for a paper containing subheadings of one or more levels (see 1.36), there is great latitude in choosing both the amount of information included and the method of presenting it. At one extreme, the contents may provide what is essentially an outline by including all the levels. At the other extreme, the contents may omit the subheadings—even though the paper may carry subheadings of one level or more than one—showing only the generic headings and titles of chapters. For many papers, both those with only one level and those with more than one level of subheading, the table of contents includes the first-level (principal) subheadings, with or without the page numbers (sample 14.26). Note that when more than one level of subheading is included in the contents, each must appear in order of its rank; that is, it is not permissible to begin with any but the first-level subheading, or to skip from the first and go to the third or fourth level (see sample 14.27).

1.12 If the subheading of any level is longer than one line, the second line of the subheading must be indented three spaces, and the page number should follow the period leaders after the last word of the subheading, as shown in sample 14.27. Double-space between items, and single-space runovers.

1.13 If more than one level of subheading is included in the contents, each level is indented three spaces below the preceding higher level (sample 14.27). If only the first level is shown, each subheading may be indented three spaces below the chapter title (sample 14.26) or, if the subheadings are short, the first one in each chapter may be indented three spaces below the chapter title and the following ones of the same level run in. Run-in subheadings may be separated by semicolons, dashes, or periods. For page numbers with subheadings, see 1.17.

1.14 Capitalization and wording of the titles of all parts, chapters, and sections should agree exactly with the way they appear in the body of the paper.

1.15 Capitalization of titles in the table of contents should be as follows: For the titles of all major divisions (acknowledgments, preface, contents, list of illustrations, list of tables, list of abbreviations, glossary, editorial method, abstract, introduction, parts, chapters, appendix, notes, bibliography, or reference list), capitalize all letters (e.g., PREFACE). In subheadings, use headline style (see 4.6–8), that is, capitalize the initial letter of the first and last words and of all words except articles, prepositions, and coordinate conjunctions (sample 14.26); or use sentence style (see 4.9), that is, capitalize only the initial letter of the first subheading under the chapter and of proper nouns and proper adjectives (see sample 14.27).

1.16 Numbers designating parts and chapters should be given as they are in the text. Part numbers may be uppercase roman numerals (PART I, PART II, etc.) or spelled-out numbers (PART ONE, PART TWO, etc.). The generic heading may precede the part title and be separated from it by a period (sample 14.26), or it may be centered above the title and thus need no punctuation (sample 14.27). Chapter numbers may be arabic or uppercase roman numerals, or spelled-out numbers. The word ''Chapter'' may precede or be placed over the chapter number (samples 14.26–27). Do not use the word ''Chapter'' in the contents if the sections of the paper are not so designated.

1.17 Page numbers in a table of contents are always justified right following a line of periods one space apart (period leaders) separating the title from the page number on which the part of the paper begins (see sample 14.27). Note that only the *beginning* page number of each chapter or other section is given. Page numbers for parts may be omitted if they are all identical with the beginning page number of the first chapter under each part. Note that if the page number is given for one part, it must be given for all of them. Page numbers for subheadings may also be omitted (see sample 14.26). When they are included with run-in subheadings, page numbers are best placed within parentheses immediately following the subheadings.

List of Illustrations

1.18 In a list of illustrations, sometimes headed simply ILLUSTRATIONS, the figure numbers are given in arabic numerals followed by a period; the captions start two spaces after the period;

and the page numbers (in arabic) are separated from the caption by period leaders. Double-space between captions, single-space within.

1.19   The figure numbers in the list are aligned by their periods under the word "Figure," and page numbers are listed flush right under the word "Page," as in sample 14.28.

1.20   Figures must not be numbered "1a," "1b," etc. A figure may, however, have lettered parts to which its legend, or descriptive statement, may refer:

```
Fig. 1. Digitalis. (a) cross-section of stem, (b)
enlargement of a seed.
```

Do not, however, refer to the lettered parts in the list of illustrations.

1.21   The captions in the list of illustrations should agree with those given beneath illustrations, unless the latter are long (more properly, then, called *legends*), in which case it is best to give them in shortened form in the list. For a thesis or dissertation, however, consult the dissertation office. Even if a descriptive or explanatory statement follows the caption under an illustration, do not include such a statement in the list of illustrations (see sample 14.28).

1.22   In this list, captions are capitalized headline style, as in sample 14.28.

List of Tables

1.23   In a list of tables, the table numbers (in arabic, followed by a period) are placed in a column flush left under the heading "Table," and the page numbers are listed flush right under the heading "Page." The table titles should begin two spaces after the period following the table number and should agree exactly with the wording of the titles as they appear above the tables themselves. The titles are capitalized in either sentence or headline style (see 6.27–28), as in sample 14.31, and runover lines are indented three spaces. Double-space between items, single-space within.

List of Abbreviations

1.24   A list of abbreviations is desirable only if the writer has devised abbreviations instead of using those that are commonly accepted, such as standard abbreviations of titles of professional journals within a given field. A list of abbreviations should be arranged alphabetically by the abbreviation itself, not the spelled-out term. Under the centered generic heading in uppercase, list abbreviations on the left in alphabetical order and leave two to four spaces between the longest abbreviation and its spelled-out term. Align the first letter of all other spelled-out terms and any runover lines with the first letter of the spelled-out term following the *longest* abbreviation, and use the longest line in the column to center the list on the page(s). Double-space between items, single-space within, as in sample 14.39. A list of abbreviations should help the reader who wishes to read only a portion of the whole paper instead of reading it from beginning to end. Even when a paper includes a list of abbreviations, the spelled-out version of a term should be given the first time the term appears within the paper, and it should be followed by the abbreviation in parentheses.

GLOSSARY

1.25   A paper that contains many foreign words or technical terms and phrases not likely to be familiar to the reader should include a list of these words, followed by their translations or definitions. The words should be arranged alphabetically. Each word should be typed flush left and followed by a period, a dash, or a colon. The translation or definition follows, with its first word capitalized and with a terminal period, unless all definitions consist only of words or phrases, in which case no final punctuation should be used. If a definition extends to more than one line, the runover lines should be indented five spaces from the left margin. Double-space between items, single-space within, as in sample 14.40.

1.26   If there is more than one glossary, each should start on a new page.

1.27   A glossary placed in the reference matter rather than in the front matter may precede an appendix, if any, and the bibliography or reference list.

EDITORIAL METHOD

1.28   Following the same format as do the acknowledgments and preface (see 1.8), a section devoted to editorial method may be included in the preliminaries to explain the writer's editorial practice or to discuss variant texts, particularly if the paper is a scholarly edition. In practice, however, this discussion is usually a part of the introduction. Short, uncomplicated remarks about editorial method—such as a note that capitalization and punctuation have been modernized—may be included in the preface or placed in a note after the first quotation drawn from the edited work.

ABSTRACT

1.29 An abstract, which may or may not be required, briefly summarizes the thesis and contents of the paper. Like the title of the paper, it may be used by information services to create lists of papers, organized by subject matter. Since each department or discipline has its own requirements, the thesis adviser or dissertation secretary should be consulted regarding the content, style, and format of the abstract.

DEDICATION

1.30 Dedications are usually brief and need not include the word *dedicated*. *To* is sufficient:

To Gerald

It is not necessary to identify (or even give the whole name of) the person to whom the work is dedicated or to give such other information as life dates, though both are permissible. Extravagant dedications are things of the past, and humorous dedications rarely stand the test of time. The dedication, typed in uppercase and lowercase, should be centered on the width of a line three inches from the top of the page. There should be no final punctuation. If *To* is used to introduce the dedication, it should begin with a capital. A dedication is not listed in the table of contents. No number appears on its page, and the page is not counted in the pagination of the preliminaries.

EPIGRAPH

1.31 An epigraph, a pertinent quotation, is not underlined, and it does not appear in quotation marks. When an epigraph heads a whole paper, its format is like that of a dedication (see 1.30). For treatment of epigraphs at the beginning of chapters or sections of a paper, see 5.9. The name of the author of the epigraph (sometimes only the last name of a well-known author) appears below the epigraph, flush right in uppercase and lowercase roman, often followed by the title of the work cited, underlined or enclosed in quotation marks in accordance with the guidelines set forth in chapter 4. The location of a quotation should not appear, and an epigraph should not be footnoted. Epigraphs are usually self-explanatory. The explanation of an epigraph, if needed, should be included in the preface or other introductory matter. An epigraph is not listed in the table of contents. No number appears on its page, and the page is not counted in the pagination of the preliminaries.

THE TEXT

1.32   The main body of the paper is usually separated into well-defined divisions, such as parts, chapters, sections, and subsections. The text may also include parenthetical references, footnotes, or superscript numbers keyed to a reference list or list of endnotes.

INTRODUCTION

1.33   The text usually begins with an introduction, which may be called chapter 1. If it is short, the writer may prefer to head it simply INTRODUCTION and reserve the more formal generic heading CHAPTER for the longer sections of which the main body of the paper is composed. Whether it is called chapter 1 or not, the introduction is equivalent to the first chapter and not part of the preliminaries. Thus the first page of the introduction is page 1 (arabic numeral) of the paper.

PART

1.34   A part-title page is a page containing only the generic heading and title of a part. Part-title pages (sometimes referred to as half-title pages) are required if the chapters are grouped under "parts," the part-title page being placed immediately before the first chapter of the group composing the part. Since the introduction is to the *entire* paper, whether the introduction is titled CHAPTER 1 or not, it is not included in PART I. The first part-title page therefore follows rather than precedes the introduction.

CHAPTER

1.35   The main body of the paper is divided into chapters. Each chapter begins on a new page. Each chapter has a generic heading and a title, both centered in uppercase above the text. In a short paper, some writers prefer to omit the word CHAPTER and to use merely numerals—roman or arabic—in sequence before the headings of the several main divisions. The generic heading of a chapter consists of the word CHAPTER followed by a number. The number may either be spelled out, in capital letters, or given in the form of a numeral (arabic or uppercase roman). The entire heading should be centered. The form in which the chapter number is expressed should be different from the form in which the part number is expressed (e.g., PART TWO, CHAPTER I). The title, which describes the content of the chapter, is centered in uppercase below the generic heading (see samples 14.41, 14.43, and 14.51).

SECTION AND SUBSECTION

1.36   In some papers the chapters or their equivalents are divided into sections, which may in turn be divided into subsections, and these into subsubsections, and so on. Such divisions are customarily given titles, called *subheadings,* which are differentiated and designated respectively *first-, second-,* and *third-level* subheadings. The principal, or first-level, subdivision should have greater attention value than the lower (second, third, etc.) levels. Centered headings have greater attention value than side headings, and underlined or boldface headings, centered or side, have greater attention value than those not underlined or in boldface. (Throughout this manual, *underlined* may also be taken to mean *italicized* for those using typewriters and computer systems that can perform this function. In subheadings, however, underlining may be preferable to italicization, even though italicization may be used consistently—for book titles, for example—throughout the text, notes, and bibliography or reference list.) Each subhead should have two blank lines above if it follows text (see sample 14.42) or three blank lines above if it follows a table or a figure (see sample 14.38). A blank line should go beneath each subhead that is not run in. A plan for the display of five levels of subheadings in a typed paper follows:

First-level, centered heading, underlined or in boldface, capitalized headline style:

<u>Traditional Controversy between Medieval
Church and State</u>

Second-level, centered heading, not underlined or in boldface, capitalized headline style:

Reappearance of Religious Legalism

Third-level, side heading underlined or in boldface, capitalized headline style, beginning at the left margin:

<u>Shakespeare's Early Sonnets</u>

Fourth-level, side heading, not underlined or in boldface, capitalized sentence style:

The Gospel as it is related to Jesus

Fifth-level heading run into (at the beginning of) a paragraph and underlined or in boldface, capitalized sentence style:

<u>The gospel legalized in the Church</u>. The gospel that the early Christians preached within the pagan sects was also a product of their experiences.

1.37   If fewer than five levels are required, the style of these levels may be selected in any suitable *descending order,* as indicated above. For the layout of subheadings on a page, see samples 14.38 and 14.42.

THE REFERENCE MATTER, OR BACK MATTER

APPENDIX

1.38   An appendix, although by no means an essential part of every paper, is a useful device to make available to the reader material related to the text but not suitable for inclusion in it. An appendix is a group of related items. Appendixes, for example, may contain tables too detailed for text presentation, a large group of illustrations, technical notes on method, schedules and forms used in collecting materials, copies of documents not generally available to the reader, case studies too long to be put into the text, and sometimes figures or other illustrative materials. Note that if a writer gathers all of the paper's illustrations, they do not go in an appendix but are instead included in a group entitled ILLUSTRATIONS placed just before the reference matter. If some illustrations are placed in the text, however, any that are grouped in the reference matter must be put in an appendix.

1.39 All appendixes go at the end of a paper, never at the end of the chapters to which they may pertain.

1.40 Materials of different categories should be placed in separate appendixes. Where there is more than one appendix, each should be given a number or a letter (APPENDIX 1, APPENDIX 2, etc.; APPENDIX ONE, APPENDIX TWO, etc.; or APPENDIX A, APPENDIX B, etc.).

1.41 If there is only one appendix, the writer may or may not give it a title, like a chapter or part title. If a paper has more than one appendix, however, each must bear a descriptive title, which must appear in the table of contents (see 14.27). The generic heading and the title of an appendix are both centered and in uppercase.

1.42 Whether an appendix should be single- or double-spaced depends upon the nature of the material; spacing need not be the same for each of the appendixes. Documents and case studies may well be single-spaced, whereas explanations of methods and procedures may be double-spaced, as is the text.

1.43 When photocopied documents, such as previously published articles, facsimiles of manuscripts, or questionnaires, appear in appendixes, a page number should be added to each photocopy, using arabic numerals within brackets in the upper right-hand corner. The brackets indicate that the page number is not part of the original document. These bracketed arabic numerals indicate the sequence of the sheet within the pagination of the paper. The photocopied documents within an appendix may or may not contain their own pagination.

1.44 If an appendix contains photocopied material, the photocopies should be of letter quality.

ENDNOTES

1.45 Endnotes are more commonly used in term papers than in theses or dissertations, where footnotes have been traditionally preferred and where parenthethical references are now commonly recommended. Endnotes are numbered consecutively within the text, using superscript arabic numerals that refer to notes placed in the reference matter of the paper in a section with the generic heading NOTES. Endnotes may have the same content as footnotes, but they are arranged in the format that appears in sample 14.45. In papers using parenthetical references and reference lists, endnotes take the form of content notes, which may include parenthetical references (see 8.20).

BIBLIOGRAPHY OR REFERENCE LIST

1.46 The bibliography or reference list is the last part of the paper (except in those rare instances where a paper carries an index, as does a book). Instructions for the layout of these parts are set forth in chapter 14, within samples 14.46–49.

2   Abbreviations and Numbers

ABBREVIATIONS

2.1   Though the use of abbreviations in formal writing was long limited to a few traditionally prescribed circumstances, during the past few decades abbreviations have been used increasingly in writing of all kinds. In tabular matter, notes, bibliographies, illustrations, and lists of all kinds, abbreviations are normally preferred and are formed according to a standard list accepted within any given field. For guidelines on hyphenating and dividing abbreviations, see 3.50. Such forms of address as *Mr., Mrs.,* and *Dr.* are almost never spelled out. The writer who must form new abbreviations for the purposes of a paper should place them in a list of abbreviations within the front matter (see 1.24).

USE OF PERIODS

2.2   The trend now is strongly away from the use of periods, especially in uppercase abbreviations. In the examples that follow, the periods have been left wherever they have traditionally appeared. Periods may be omitted from many of these examples, but it is still common practice to use periods after lowercase abbreviations (e.g., *in., act., no.*) and to use a period and a space after the initials for personal names (e.g., *E. F. Bowman*). In an abbreviation with an internal period (e.g., *N.Y., Ph.D., N.Dak., U.S.*), there should be no space after the internal period.

15

SOCIAL AND PROFESSIONAL TITLES AND SIMILAR TERMS

2.3   Social titles are always abbreviated, whether with full name or last name only (note that after *Mlle* and *Mme* there traditionally is no period):

```
Mr.            Mrs.            Ms.
M.             MM.             Messrs.
Mlle           Mme             Dr.
```

2.4   The abbreviations *Sr., Jr., III,* and *IV* (for *Senior, Junior, Third,* and *Fourth*) follow a full name and are not used with the family name alone, although in informal writing it is permissible to use these terms with given names (e.g., *John, Jr.*). The terms are never spelled out when part of a name. A comma precedes *Jr.* and *Sr.* (and one also follows, if these forms appear within a sentence), but a comma should not be used before *III* and *IV*:

```
Mrs. Joseph P. Turner, Sr., sent her regrets.

Adlai E. Stevenson III announced his candidacy.

Dexter Harrison III, LL.D., was also a graduate.

Rev. Oliver C. Jones, Jr., spoke to the group.

Do you know Ralph Smith, Jr.'s address?
```

2.5   Abbreviations for scholarly degrees and titles of respect, which follow full names, are preceded by a comma and followed by another comma when they are given in text.

```
Leroy S. Wells, Ph.D., belonged to the committee.

The Reverend Jesse E. Thorson, S.T.B., was nominated
by the board of trustees.
```

The following list includes many frequently used abbreviations for scholarly degrees and professional and honorary designations:

A.B., Artium Baccalaureus (Bachelor of Arts)
A.I.A., American Institute of Architects
A.M., Artium Magister (Master of Arts)
B.A., Bachelor of Arts
B.D., Bachelor of Divinity
B.S., Bachelor of Science
D.B., Divinitatis Baccalaureus (Bachelor of Divinity)
D.D., Divinitatis Doctor (Doctor of Divinity)
D.D.S., Doctor of Dental Surgery
D.Min., Doctor of Ministry
D.O., Doctor of Osteopathy

D.V.M., Doctor of Veterinary Medicine
F.A.I.A., Fellow of the American Institute of Architects
F.R.S., Fellow of the Royal Society
J.D., Juris Doctor (Doctor of Law)
J.P., Justice of the Peace
L.H.D., Litterarum Humaniorum Doctor (Doctor of Humanities)
Litt.D., Litterarum Doctor (Doctor of Letters)
LL.B., Legum Baccalaureus (Bachelor of Laws)
LL.D., Legum Doctor (Doctor of Laws)
M.A., Master of Arts
M.B.A., Master of Business Administration
M.D., Medicinae Doctor (Doctor of Medicine)
M.P., Member of Parliament
M.S., Master of Science
Ph.B., Philosophiae Baccalaureus (Bachelor of Philosophy)
Ph.D., Philosophiae Doctor (Doctor of Philosophy)
Ph.G., Graduate in Pharmacy
S.B., Scientiae Baccalaureus (Bachelor of Science)
S.M., Master of Science
S.T.B., Sacrae Theologiae Baccalaureus (Bachelor of Sacred Theology)

2.6   Abbreviate *doctor* (*Dr.*) before a name, but spell it out when it is not followed by a name:

Dr. Shapiro brought about a total recovery.

The doctor was an expert in his field.

2.7   Spell out a civil, military, professional, or religious title when it precedes the family name alone:

Senator Proxmire   General Patton

But use the appropriate abbreviation before a full name:

Sen. William F. Proxmire   Gen. George S. Patton

2.8   Spell out *Reverend, Honorable,* and *Colonel* if preceded by *the;* otherwise abbreviate to *Rev., Hon.,* or *Col.* Never use these titles, either spelled out or abbreviated, with family names alone. Use them only when the title is followed by the person's full name or by *Mr., Mrs., Miss, Ms.,* or *Dr.* with the family name alone, as may be appropriate:

Col. Arthur Charles reviewed the procedures.

The ceremony was in honor of the Reverend Martin Luther King, Jr.'s birthday observance.

Rev. Dr. Wilson gave the address.

17

```
The Honorable Mr. Collins closed the final session of
the conference.
```

Never use:

```
Rev. Bentley
Reverend Bentley
the Rev. Bentley
the Reverend Bentley
```

2.9   *Saint* may be abbreviated when it stands before the name of a Christian saint:

```
St. Thomas Aquinas      SS. Augustine and Benedict
```

But *Saint* is omitted before the names of apostles, evangelists, and church fathers:

Matthew	Mark	Luke	Peter
Paul	Augustine	Ambrose	Jerome

2.10   When *Saint* forms part of a personal name, the bearer's usage is followed:

```
Étienne Geoffroy Saint-Hilaire
Charles-Camille Saint-Saëns
Muriel St. Clare Byrne
Ruth St. Denis
```

ORGANIZATIONS

2.11   The names of government agencies, network broadcasting companies, associations, fraternal and service organizations, unions, and other groups are often abbreviated, even in text, preferably after one spelled-out use. Such abbreviations are set in uppercase with no periods:

AAAS	AFL-CIO	AMA	AT&T	FTC	HOLC
NAACP	NATO	NBC	NFL	NIMH	NSF
OPEC	TVA	UN	UNESCO	VA	YMCA

2.12   Within the text, company names should be given in their full form, without including the terms *Inc.* or *Ltd.* and without capitalizing the word *the,* even when it is part of a company's full name:

```
A. G. Becker and Company was incorporated in 1894.
```

```
The book was published by the University of Chicago
Press.
```

In notes, bibliographies, parenthetical references, and reference lists, etc., the following abbreviations may be freely (but consistently) used:

```
Bro.    Bros.    Co.    Corp.    Inc.    Ltd.    &
```

GEOGRAPHICAL NAMES

2.13 Within the text, spell out the names of countries, states, counties, provinces, territories, bodies of water, mountains, and the like, with the exception of the Union of Soviet Socialist Republics, now commonly referred to as the USSR. In lists, tabular matter, notes, bibliographies, and indexes where abbreviations are called for, the following may be used:

STATES AND TERRITORIES OF THE UNITED STATES

Ala.	AL	Kans.	KS	Ohio	OH
Alaska	AK	Ky.	KY	Okla.	OK
Amer.Samoa	AS	La.	LA	Oreg.	OR
Ariz.	AZ	Maine	ME	Pa.	PA
Ark.	AR	Md.	MD	P.R.	PR
Calif.	CA	Mass.	MA	R.I.	RI
C.Z.	CZ	Mich.	MI	S.C.	SC
Colo.	CO	Minn.	MN	S.Dak.	SD
Conn.	CT	Miss.	MS	Tenn.	TN
Del.	DE	Mo.	MO	Tex.	TX
D.C.	DC	Mont.	MT	Utah	UT
Fla.	FL	Nebr.	NE	Vt.	VT
Ga.	GA	Nev.	NV	Va.	VA
Guam	GU	N.H.	NH	V.I.	VI
Hawaii	HI	N.J.	NJ	Wash.	WA
Idaho	ID	N.Mex.	NM	W.Va.	WV
Ill.	IL	N.Y.	NY	Wis.	WI
Ind.	IN	N.C.	NC	Wyo.	WY
Iowa	IA	N.Dak.	ND		

PROVINCES AND TERRITORIES OF CANADA

Alberta	AB
British Columbia/Colombie-Britannique	BC
Labrador	LB
Manitoba	MB
New Brunswick/Nouveau-Brunswick	NB
Newfoundland/Terre-Neuve	NF
Northwest Territories/Territoires du Nord-Ouest	NT
Nova Scotia/Nouvelle-Écosse	NS
Ontario	ON
Prince Edward Island/Île-du-Prince-Édouard	PE
Quebec/Québec	PQ
Saskatchewan	SK
Yukon	YT

2.14   Spell out the prefixes of geographical names (e.g., *Fort Wayne, South Orange, Port Arthur*) within the text, with the possible exception of names beginning with *Saint,* which may be abbreviated *St.* to save space and must then be abbreviated consistently:

```
Mount St. Helens has erupted several times.

From northeast Paris it is less than an hour to Saint-
Cloud on the Métro.
```

2.15   Within the text, spell out all of the following words. In close-set matter, the abbreviations may be used:

Avenue	Av. *or* Ave.	Street	St.
Boulevard	Blvd.	Terrace	Terr.
Building	Bldg.	North	N.
Court	Ct.	South	S.
Drive	Dr.	East	E.
Expressway	Expy.	West	W.
Lane	La. *or* Ln.	Northwest	NW
Parkway	Pkwy.	Northeast	NE
Place	Pl.	Southeast	SE
Road	Rd.	Southwest	SW
Square	Sq.		

But always use the abbreviations *NW, NE, SE,* and *SW* in city addresses where they follow street names:

```
Lake Shore Drive is safer than the Dan Ryan
Expressway, where there is truck traffic.

He spent several years in Southeast Asia.

The shop is at 245 Seventeenth Street NW.
```

MEASURE

2.16   In nontechnical writing, spell out expressions of dimension, distance, volume, weight, degree, and so on:

```
five miles            150 pounds            14.5 meters
```

2.17   In scientific and technical writing, standard abbreviations for units of measure are used if the amount is given in numerals. Most guides to scientific and technical writing, several of which are included in the bibliography, list standard abbreviations acceptable within a given discipline. For a general introduction to the use of abbreviations for units of measure, consult *The Chicago Manual of Style,* thirteenth edition, 14.36–53. A full explanation of the International System of Units (*Système international d'unités,* abbreviated ''SI'') appears in *Units of Measurement: Handbook on International Standards for Units of Measurement,* texts of standards compiled by the Information Centre of the International Organization for Standardization, first edition (Geneva: International Organization for Standardization, 1979).

SCHOLARSHIP

PARTS OF A WORK

2.18 Spell out and do not capitalize (unless in a heading or at the beginning of a sentence) the words *book, chapter, part, volume, section, scene, verse, column, page, figure, plate,* and so on, except in cases when such a term is followed by a number in a note or parenthetical reference, in which case the following abbreviations should be used: *bk(s)., chap(s)., pt(s)., vol(s)., sec(s)., sc., v. (vv.), col(s)., p. (pp.), fig(s)., pl(s).* The words *act, line,* and *table* should never be abbreviated.

UNPUBLISHED MANUSCRIPTS

2.19 When referring to unpublished manuscripts, spell out the terms used to describe them within the text, but in notes, bibliographies, and reference lists, use the abbreviations listed below. Terms not in this list should always be spelled out. The abbreviations are used by many curators and librarians. See 9.114–15, 11.49–50, and 11.52–55 for examples of notes and reference-list entries using abbreviations listed here or using spelled-out forms, as needed.

Letter	L
Letter signed	LS
Autograph letter signed	ALS
Typewritten letter	TL
Typewritten letter signed	TLS
Document	D
Document signed	DS
Autograph document signed	ADS
Typewritten document	TD
Typewritten document signed	TDS
Autograph manuscript	AMs
Autograph manuscript signed	AMsS

Typewritten manuscript	TMs
Typewritten manuscript signed	TMsS
Card	C
Autograph card	AC
Autograph card signed	ACS
Typewritten card	TC
Typewritten card signed	TCS
Autograph note	AN
Autograph note signed	ANS

This list is reprinted, with minor changes, from *Modern Manuscripts: A Practical Manual for Their Management, Care, and Use,* by Kenneth W. Duckett (Nashville: American Association for State and Local History, 1975), 143–44, by permission of the publisher. © 1975 by the American Association for State and Local History.

BOOKS OF THE BIBLE

2.20   When referring to whole books or to whole chapters of the Bible or the Apocrypha, spell out their names:

Jeremiah, chapters 42–44, records the flight of the Jews to Egypt when Jerusalem fell in 586 B.C.

The Revelation of St. John the Divine, known as "Revelations," closes the New Testament.

2.21   Whenever scriptural passages are cited by verse in a paper, whether in text, parenthetical references, or notes, abbreviate the names of the books, using arabic numerals, when they are numbered; write the chapter and verse numbers in arabic numerals with either a colon or a period between the chapter and verse numbers; and follow the chapter and verse numbers with the abbreviation for the version of the Bible or Apocrypha from which the passage was taken.

1 Song of Sol. 2.1–5 RSV   Ru 3:14 NAB

For alternate styles of standard biblical abbreviations, see *The Chicago Manual of Style,* thirteenth edition, 14.34–35.

CLASSICAL REFERENCES

2.22   In a paper containing many classical references, both the name of the author and the title of the work may be abbreviated after they have been spelled out in full when cited the first time, whether in text or notes. Often the names of well-known periodicals and reference tools are also abbreviated after being spelled out in the first citation. The most widely accepted standard for such abbreviations is the comprehensive list in the front of the *Oxford Classical Dictionary*.

```
Thucydides History of the Peloponnesian War 2.40.2–3
Thud. 2.40.2–3
Homer Odyssey 9.266–71
Hom. Od. 9.266–71
```

GENERAL SCHOLARLY ABBREVIATIONS

2.23   General abbreviations such as *etc.*, *e.g.*, and *i.e.* are preferably confined to parenthetical references within the text. The abbreviations *ibid.*, *cf.*, and *s.v.* are preferably used only in notes and other forms of scholarly apparatus.

2.24   An abbreviation should begin with a capital when it is the first word of a note and whenever the usual rules for capitalization apply.

2.25   The word *sic* is underlined, but not most other Latin words or abbreviations commonly used in footnotes, bibliographies, tabular matter, and so on (see 2.26).

LIST OF ABBREVIATIONS

2.26   app., appendix
art., article (*plural*, arts.)
b., born
bk., book (*plural*, bks.)
c., copyright
ca., *circa*, about, approximately
cf., *confer*, compare (Note that *confer* is the Latin word for "compare"; *cf.* must not be used as the abbreviation for the English "confer," nor should *cf.* be used to mean "see.")
ch., chapter (in legal references only)
chap., chapter (*plural*, chaps.)
col., column (*plural*, cols.)
comp., compiler (*plural*, comps.); compiled by
dept., department (*plural*, depts.)
d., died
div., division (*plural*, divs.)
e.g., *exempli gratia*, for example

ed., edition; edited by; editor (*plural,* eds.)

et al., *et alii,* and others

et seq., *et sequens,* and the following

etc., *et cetera,* and so forth

fig., figure (*plural,* figs.)

fl., *floruit* flourished (for use when birth and death dates are not known)

ibid., *ibidem,* in the same place

i.e., *id est,* that is

id., *idem,* the same (used to refer to persons, except in law citations; not to be confused with ibid.)

infra, below

l. (el), line (*plural,* ll.) (Not recommended because the abbreviation in the singular might be mistaken for "one" and the plural for "eleven.")

n., note, footnote (*plural,* nn.)

n.d., no date

n.p., no place; no publisher

no., number (*plural,* nos.)

n.s., new series

o.s., old series

p., page (*plural,* pp.; these abbreviations always precede the numbers; when "p." follows a number, it can stand for "pence.")

par., paragraph (*plural,* pars.)

passim, here and there

pt., part (*plural,* pts.)

q.v., *quod vide,* which see (for use with cross-references)

sc., scene

sec., section (*plural,* secs.)

[*sic*], so, thus

supp., supplement (*plural,* supps.)

supra, above

s.v., *sub verbo, sub voce,* under the word (for use in references to listings in encyclopedias and dictionaries)

trans., translator, translated by

v., verse (*plural,* vv.)

viz., *videlicet,* namely

vol., volume (*plural,* vols.)

vs., *versus,* against (v. in law references)

2.27   In quoting from constitutions, bylaws, and the like within the text, the words *section* and *article* are spelled out the first time

they are used and abbreviated thereafter, always in full uppercase:

```
SECTION 1. The name of the . . .
SEC. 2. The object of the . . .
ARTICLE 234. It shall be the . . .
ART. 235. It shall be the duty . . .
```

Standard abbreviations used by many law reviews appear in *A
Uniform System of Citation,* thirteenth edition (Cambridge: Harvard Law Review Association, 1981).

For Further Reference

2.28   *Webster's Ninth New Collegiate Dictionary* includes a great
many abbreviations from all fields in the body of the work, arranged in strict, letter-by-letter alphabetical order. To identify a
rare or unfamiliar abbreviation, consult the *Reverse Acronyms,
Initialisms, and Abbreviations Dictionary,* edited by Ellen T.
Crowley, sixth edition (Detroit: Gale Research Company, 1978),
available at most libraries.

NUMBERS

General Rule

2.29   In scientific and statistical material, all numbers are expressed in
figures. In nonscientific material, numbers are sometimes spelled
out and sometimes expressed in figures, according to prescribed
rules. The general rule followed by many writers and by the
University of Chicago Press is to spell out all numbers through
one hundred (e.g., *sixty-five, ninety-eight*) and all round numbers that can be expressed in two words (e.g., *one hundred, two
hundred, five thousand, forty-five hundred*):

```
At that time the population of the district was less
than three million.
```

All other numbers are written as figures.

```
There are 514 seniors in the graduating class.
```

2.30   The general rule applies to ordinal as well as cardinal numbers:

```
On the 122d and 123d day of his recovery, he received
his eighteenth and nineteenth letters from home.
```

Note that the preferred figure form of the ordinals *second* and
third adds *d* alone (i.e., *2d, 3d*), not *nd* and *rd* (i.e., *2nd, 3rd*).

SERIES

2.31   The general rule requires modification when numbers above *and* below one hundred appear in a series, or group, of numbers, each of which applies to the same kind of thing. Here all are expressed in figures:

```
Of the group surveyed, 186 students had studied
French, 142 had studied Spanish, and 36 had studied
Latin for three years or more.
```

INITIAL NUMBERS

2.32   A <u>sentence should never begin with a figure</u>, even when there are figures in the rest of the sentence. Either spell out the first number or, better, recast the sentence:

```
Two hundred and fifty passengers escaped injury; 175
sustained minor injuries; 110 were so seriously hurt
that they required hospitalization.
```

Or better:

```
Of the passengers, 250 escaped injury, 175 sustained
minor injuries, and 110 required hospitalization.
```

2.33   To avoid confusion, you may spell out one set of figures in an expression that involves two or more series of figures:

```
In a test given six months later, 14 children made no
error; 64 made one to two errors; 97 made three to
four errors.
```

2.34   Although a round number occurring in isolation is spelled out (see 2.29), several round numbers occurring close together are expressed in figures:

```
They shipped 1,500 books in the first order, 8,000 in
the second, and 100,000 in the third; altogether there
were now about 1,000,000 volumes in the warehouse.
```

2.35   Very large round numbers are frequently expressed in figures and units of millions or billions:

```
This means that welfare programs will require about
$7.8 million more per day compared with $3.2 million
spent each day at the current rate of inflation.
```

PERCENTAGES AND DECIMALS

2.36   Figures should be used to express decimals and percentages. The word *percent* <u>should be written out</u>, except in scientific and statistical writing, where the symbol % may be used:

With interest at 8 percent, the monthly payment would
amount to $12.88, which he noted was exactly 2.425
times the amount he was accustomed to put in his
savings monthly.

Grades of 3.8 and 95% are equivalent.

NUMERALS, SYMBOLS, AND ABBREVIATIONS

2.37   Use the symbol for *percent* (%) only when it is preceded by a
figure. Note that *percentage,* not *percent* or *%,* is the correct
expression to use when no figure is given:

The September scores for students enrolled in summer
school showed an improvement of 70.1% [or "70.1
percent" if the writer prefers to use the word rather
than the symbol] over test scores recorded in June.
Thus the percentage of achievers in the second test
indicated that summer school had resulted in higher
scores in a majority of cases.

2.38   The figure preceding either *percent* or *%* is never spelled out:

15 percent   55%

FRACTIONS

2.39   A fraction standing alone should be spelled out, but a numerical
unit composed of a whole number and a fraction should be expressed in figures:

Trade and commodity services accounted for nine-tenths
of all international receipts and payments.

Cabinets with 10½-by-32¼-inch shelves were
installed.

CURRENCIES

UNITED STATES CURRENCY

2.40   The general rule (see 2.29) applies in isolated references to
amounts of money in United States currency. If the amount is
spelled out, so are the words *dollars* and *cents;* if figures are
used, the dollar symbol ($) precedes them:

Rarely do they spend more than five dollars a week on
recreation.

The report showed $135 collected in fines.

Fractional amounts of money over one dollar appear in figures,
as do other decimal fractions ($1.75). When both fractional

amounts and whole-dollar amounts are used in the same sentence (and only in such circumstances), the whole-dollar amounts are shown with a decimal point and ciphers:

```
The same article is sold by some stores for $1.75, by
others for $1.95, and by still others for $2.00.
```

2.41   The expression of very large amounts of money, which may be cumbersome whether spelled out in full or written in figures, should follow the rule for expressing large round numbers (see 2.35), using units of millions or billions with figures preceded by the dollar sign:

```
Japan's exports to Taiwan, which averaged $60 million
between 1954 and 1958, rose sharply to $210 million in
1965 and $250 million in 1966.
```

```
The deficit that year was $120.4 billion.
```

BRITISH CURRENCY

2.42   British currency is expressed in pounds and pence, very like dollars and cents:

```
two pounds                 twenty-five pence
£3.50                      55 p.
```

Before decimalization in 1971, British currency was expressed in pounds, shillings, and pence:

```
two shillings and sixpence
```

```
£12 17s. 6d
```

Or:

```
£12.17.6
```

The term *billion* should not be used for British sums, since *billion* as employed by the British means what *trillion* means in United States terminology.

OTHER CURRENCIES

2.43   Most currencies follow a system like that of the United States, employing unit symbols before the figures. They do vary, however, in their expressions of large numbers and decimals. For papers that deal with sums of money in currencies other than those of the United States or Great Britain, consult the table "Foreign Money" in the March 1984 *U.S. Government Printing Office Style Manual* on pages 238–40, or its latest edition.

NUMBERED PARTS OF WRITTEN WORKS

2.44   With few exceptions (see 9.69, 9.110, and 12.25), all the numbered parts of printed works are cited in arabic numerals. If,
however, a reference is made to the preliminary pages of a work
that designates those pages with lowercase roman numerals, the
reference should also employ that style.

2.45   Citations to public documents and unpublished manuscript material should use exactly the kind of numerals found in the
source.

2.46   In biblical, classical, and many medieval references in text as
well as in notes, bibliographies, and reference lists, the different
levels of division of a work (book, section, line, etc.) are set in
arabic numerals and separated by periods (no spaces should precede or follow these periods). Note that in biblical references
either a colon or a period is acceptable:

```
Heb. 13:3
2 Kings 11.12
Ovid Amores 1.7.27
Augustine De civitate Dei 20.2
```

In a paper, commas are used between several references to the
same level, and a hyphen is used between continued numbers:

```
1 Thess. 4:1,5
Gen. 25.19–37.1
Cicero De officiis 1.33,140
Beowulf 11.2401–7
```

2.47   Fragments of classical and biblical texts (some only recently discovered) are often not uniformly numbered or may have no numbering whatsoever. The same may be true of some modern manuscripts. In citing such materials, indicate any ordering of pages
that has been added, whether by an individual or by an institution holding the collection, by setting added numbering in the
exact style in which it is written on the original manuscript (letters, arabic or roman numerals, upper- or lowercase, subscript
or superscript, etc.) and by enclosing this notation in brackets.
Put a space after the final bracket, and then give the full name
of the person or institution that ordered the text. In subsequent
references this name may be abbreviated.

2.48   If unpaginated fragments or manuscripts are published in collections, the numbering of the material will be unique to a particular edition. In citing published fragments and other documents

unpaginated in the original, do not use brackets around the numbers imposed by an editor or institution. Instead, the first time a collection is referred to, give the editor's name immediately after the fragment number. In subsequent references, initials only should be used:

```
Empedocles frag. 115 Diels-Kranz
Hesiod frag. 239.1 Merkebach and West
Empedocles frag. 111 D.
Hesiod frag. 220 M.-W.
```

DATE AND TIME

DAY, MONTH, YEAR

2.49 One of the two permissible styles for expressing day, month, and year should be followed consistently throughout a paper. The first, in which punctuation is omitted, is preferred:

```
On 28 June 1970, the Convocation Pacem in Maribus was
held.
```

If the alternate sequence month-day-year is used, the year is set off by commas:

```
On June 28, 1970, the Convocation Pacem in Maribus was
held.
```

2.50 Note that when the day, month, and year are mentioned as in the foregoing examples, *st, d,* or *th* does not appear after the day. When the day alone is given, without the month or the year, or when the number of the day is separated from the name of the month by one or more words, the preferred style is to spell out the day of the month:

```
The sequence of events of 10 June is unclear.

The sequence of events of the eleventh of June is
unclear.

The date set was the twenty-ninth.
```

2.51 When month and year alone are mentioned, the preferred style is to omit punctuation between them:

```
She was graduated in December 1985.
```

2.52 In informal writing, it is permissible to abbreviate references to the year:

```
The corporation holds a lease that will expire in
December '95.
```

CENTURY

2.53 References to particular centuries should be spelled out, uncapitalized. Hyphenate such references only when they serve as adjectives, as in the first example below. See also 4.7.

```
seventeenth-century literature
the eighteenth century
the twenty-first century
the mid-twentieth century
```

DECADE

2.54 References to decades take two forms. The context sometimes determines the one chosen:

```
The 1890s saw an enormous increase in the use of
manufactured gas.

During the thirties, traffic decreased by 50 percent.
```

WEEKDAY AND MONTH

2.55 Spell out the names of months and of weekdays when they occur in text, whether alone or in dates. In notes, bibliographies, tables, and other closely set matter, the following designations are permissible if used consistently: Jan., Feb., Mar., Apr., May, June, July, Aug., Sept., Oct., Nov., Dec.; Sun., Mon., Tues., Wed., Thurs., Fri., Sat.

ERA

2.56 For era designations use the abbreviations B.C., A.D., B.C.E., or C.E. ("before Christ," "anno Domini," "before the common era," "common era"). A.D. should precede the year number, and the other designations should follow it:

```
Solomon's Temple was destroyed by the Babylonians in
587 B.C. Rebuilt in 515 B.C., it was destroyed by the
Romans in A.D. 70.
```

TIME OF DAY

2.57 Except when A.M. or P.M. is used, time of day should be spelled out in text matter. Never add *in the morning* after A.M. or *in the evening* after P.M., and never use *o'clock* with either A.M. or P.M. or with figures:

The train was scheduled to arrive at 7:10 A.M.

The meeting was called for 8:00 P.M.

The meeting was called for eight o'clock in the evening.

Where the context makes clear whether morning or evening is meant, these terms need not be expressed.

The breakfast meeting was set for eight o'clock.

The night operator takes calls from eleven to seven.

Midnight is written as 12:00 P.M., noon as 12:00 M. ("meridian").

NUMBERS AND NAMES

MONARCHS, ETC.

2.58 Emperors, sovereigns, or popes with the same name are differentiated by numerals, traditionally capital roman:

Charles V	Henry VIII	Elizabeth II
Napoleon III	Louis XIV	John XXIII

FAMILY NAMES

2.59 Male members of families with identical names are sometimes differentiated in the same way as monarchs:

Adlai E. Stevenson III

See also 2.4.

GOVERNMENT DESIGNATIONS

2.60 Particular dynasties, governments, governing bodies, political divisions, and military subdivisions are commonly designated by an ordinal number before the noun. Numerals of less than one hundred should be spelled out and capitalized; those over one hundred, written in figures:

Nineteenth Dynasty
Eighty-First Congress
107th Congress
Fifth Republic
First Continental Congress
Third Reich
Eleventh Ward

CHURCHES, LODGES, UNIONS

2.61 Numerals standing before the names of churches or religious organizations should be expressed as spelled-out ordinals and should be capitalized:

```
Eighteenth Church of Christ, Scientist
Seventh-Day Adventists
```

2.62 Local branches of fraternal lodges and of unions bear numbers, which should be expressed in arabic numerals following the name:

```
Typographical Union No. 16

American Legion, Department of California, Leon Robert
Post No. 1248
```

STREET ADDRESSES, HIGHWAYS, TELEPHONE NUMBERS

2.63 It is preferable to spell out the names of numbered streets under one hundred for the sake of appearance and ease of reading, but street (as well as building) addresses, highway numbers, and telephone numbers should be expressed in figures:

```
The address is 500 East Fifty-Eighth Street, Chicago,
Illinois 60637. The telephone number is (312) 321-
6530.

The meeting took place at the 1040 First National Bank
Building.

The state will have to repave California 17,
Interstate 80, and Route 30 [or "U.S. 30"].
```

SCIENTIFIC USAGE

2.64 Scientific papers call for the use of numbers and units of measurement expressed in numerical values, making figures, symbols, and abbreviations more common in scientific writing than they are in nonscientific writing. Aside from a few rules here set down, the writer must settle on the scheme to use—preferably when working on the first draft—and maintain the same usage throughout the paper.

2.65 In mathematical text, the demands for the use of symbols and abbreviations, particularly in equations, are so complicated and vary so much from one paper to another, that no suggestions can be given here. Students in this field should receive training in correct usage as part of their study of the science. Editors of some mathematical periodicals have prepared manuals for writers, which give useful suggestions (see the bibliography). See also the chapter "Mathematics in Type" in *The Chicago Manual of Style,* thirteenth edition. For a brief discussion of equations and formulas in papers prepared on computer systems, see also 13.25 in this manual.

COMMAS WITHIN NUMBERS

2.66 For the most part, in numbers of one thousand or more, the thousands are marked off with commas:

1,500	12,275,500	1,475,525,000

No comma is used, however, in page numbers, street address and telephone numbers, zip codes, four-digit year numbers, decimal fractions of less than one, and chapter numbers of fraternal organizations and the like:

The bibliography is on pages 1012–20.

In the coastal district the peel thickness plus the pulp diameter of the Eureka lemon was 0.1911 for fruit from the top of the tree and 0.2016 for fruit from the bottom.

The Leon Robert Post No. 1248 was established in 1946.

Note, however, that in year dates of more than four figures, the comma is employed:

10,000 B.C.

CONTINUED NUMBERS

2.67 The term *continued numbers* (sometimes also called *inclusive numbers*) refers to the first and last number of a sequence of numerical designations, such as pages or years. Continued numbers are separated by a hyphen in a paper and expressed according to the following scheme, which is based on the way one normally speaks these numbers. The table is taken from *The Chicago Manual of Style,* thirteenth edition, page 244:

FIRST NUMBER	SECOND NUMBER	EXAMPLES
Less than 100	Use all digits	3–10; 71–72
100 or multiple of 100	Use all digits	100–104; 600–613; 1100–1123

101 through 109 (in multiples of 100)	Use changed part only, omitting unneeded zeros	107–8; 505–17; 1002–6
110 through 199 (in multiples of 100)	Use two digits, or more as needed	321–25; 415–532; 1536–38; 11564–68; 13792–803
	But if numbers are four digits long and three digits change, use all digits	1496–1504; 2787–2816

The principal use of the foregoing scheme is for page numbers and other numbered parts of written works, and for inclusive year dates:

These cities were discussed on pages 2–14, 45–46, 125–26, 200–210, 308–9.

He lost everything he owned in the years 1933–36 of the Great Depression.

This chapter covers the Napoleonic victories of 1800–1801.

PLURALS OF NUMBERS

2.68   Plurals of numbers expressed in figures are formed by the addition of *s* alone (i.e., not apostrophe and *s*):

Many K–70s were being driven on West German roads in the 1970s.

Pilots of 747s undergo special training.

There was a heavy demand to trade 6½s for the new 8¼s.

2.69   Plurals of spelled-out numbers are formed like the plurals of other nouns:

There were many more twelves and fourteens than thirty-twos, thirty-fours, and thirty-sixes on sale.

Most of the women were in their thirties or forties.

NUMBERS IN ENUMERATIONS

ENUMERATIONS IN TEXT

2.70   Numbers (or letters) used to enumerate items in text stand out better when they are set in double parentheses than when they are followed by periods:

```
He gave two reasons for his resignation: (1) advancing
age and (2) gradually failing eyesight.
```

2.71   When enumerated items appear in text that includes arabic numerals in double parentheses referring to numbered items in a reference list, use underlined letters in double parentheses, rather than arabic numerals, for the enumeration:

```
Haskin's latest theory (2) has several drawbacks: (a)
it is not based on current evidence, (b) it has no
clinical basis, and (c) it has a weak theoretical
grounding.
```

NUMBERS BEGINNING A NEW LINE OR PARAGRAPH IN ENUMERATIONS

2.72   When numbered items in an enumeration without subdivisions begin each on a new line, they are most often indicated by arabic numerals followed by a period. The items may be treated like the paragraphs of the text, that is, given paragraph indention and the runover lines begun at the margin:

```
        1.  The nature of the relationship between
library quality and library use
```

Or they may be set flush with the margin, and the runover lines aligned with the first line of substantive matter:

```
    9.  Selective initial dissemination of published
        material--a direct responsibility of the library

    10. Arrangement and organization of the collection
```

In both styles, the periods immediately following the numerals must be aligned. Periods should be omitted at the ends of items, unless the items are composed of complete sentences or whole paragraphs (see 3.57).

NUMBERS IN OUTLINES

2.73   For an outline or other enumeration in which there are subdivisions, the following scheme of notation and indention is recommended. It is not necessary to use a capital roman numeral for the first level when there are fewer divisions than shown in the example. The first level may well begin with A or with 1 (arabic one):

I.   Wars of the nineteenth century

   A.   United States

      1.   Civil War, 1861–65

         a)   Cause

            (1)   Slavery

               (a)   Compromise

                  i)   Missouri Compromise

                  ii)   1850 compromise . .

         b)   Result

. . . .

II.   Wars of the twentieth century

   A.   United States

      1. First World War . . .

Headings should be capitalized sentence style (see 4.9).

3   Spelling and Punctuation

SPELLING

3.1   Spelling in a paper should agree with the best American usage
and must be consistent—except, of course, in quotations, where

the original must be followed exactly. The authority recommended for spelling and for syllabication (for the division of
words at the ends of lines) is *Webster's Third New International
Dictionary* or its most recent abridgment (currently, *Webster's
Ninth New Collegiate Dictionary*), using the first spelling where
there is a choice. The spelling of many biographical and geographical names is given in lists at the back of *Webster's Ninth
New Collegiate Dictionary*, which serves as a convenient reference. For further reference consult *Webster's New Biographical
Dictionary* and *Webster's Geographical Dictionary*.

Spelling of Plurals

PROPER NAMES

3.2 Plurals of the names of persons and of other capitalized names
are formed by the addition of *s* or *es* without the change of a
final *y* to *i* as required for common nouns.

3.3 Add *s* to all names except those ending in *s*, *x*, or *z*, or in *ch* or
sh:

the Andersons	the Costellos	the Frys
the Bradleys	the Joyces	the Pettees

3.4 Add *es* to names ending in *s*, *x*, or *z*, or in *ch* or *sh:*

the Rosses	the Coxes	the Marshes
the Jenkinses	the Rodriguezes	the Finches

CAPITAL LETTERS

3.5 Form the plurals of most single and multiple capital letters used
as nouns by adding *s* alone:

The three Rs are taught at the two YMCAs.

SMALL LETTERS, CAPITAL LETTERS WITH PERIODS, AND OTHER EXCEPTIONS

3.6 Form the plurals of all small letters, of capital letters with periods, and of capital letters that would be confusing if *s* alone
were added, by adding an apostrophe and *s*. Note that the letter
is underlined (or in italic) and the *s* is not underlined (i.e., in
roman):

All the examples were labeled by letter; the a's were
tested first, the b's second, and so on.

```
The B.A.'s and B.S.'s conferred were almost ten times
the number of M.A.'s, M.S.'s, and Ph.D.'s.
```

```
The A's, I's, and S's in the directory were checked by
one group.
```

POSSESSIVES

3.7 Form the possessive of a proper name in the singular by adding an apostrophe and *s:*

```
Jones's book            Marx's ideology
Stevens's poems         Diaz's revolt
Kinross's farm          Finch's candidacy
```

But see the exceptions noted below (3.8–9).

3.8 The possessive case of the names of Jesus and Moses, and of Greek (or hellenized) names of more than one syllable ending in *es*, is formed by adding an apostrophe alone:

```
Jesus' ministry         Aristophanes' plays
Moses' leadership       Xerxes' victories
```

3.9 For some common nouns as well, a regard for euphony sets aside the rule for forming the possessive by adding an apostrophe and *s*, and instead adds only an apostrophe:

```
for conscience' sake
for appearance' sake
for righteousness' sake
```

3.10 Form the possessive case of a plural proper name (the Bradleys, the Costellos, etc.) by adding an apostrophe to the accepted form of the plural of the name (see 3.3–4):

```
the Bradleys' house     the Rodriguezes' mine
the Costellos' ranch    the Finches' yacht
```

PLURALS AND POSSESSIVES OF PREPOSITIONAL-PHRASE COMPOUNDS

3.11 The plurals of prepositional-phrase compounds are formed according to the rule governing the first noun of the compound:

```
brothers-in-law    commanders-in-chief    men-of-war
```

The possessives of the same compound words are formed as follows:

```
my brother-in-law's business
the commander-in-chief's dispatches
the man-of-war's launching
```

Compound Words

3.12 The hyphen is used in many compound words. Which should be hyphenated, which left open, and which spelled as one word is a difficult question. The unabridged Webster's dictionary gives the answer for most noun forms and for many adjective forms. Nevertheless, there are still some noun forms and a good many adjective forms that are not included in the dictionary. Principles of hyphenation for some of these are given in the following paragraphs.

3.13 Compounds made up of a word of relationship plus a noun should be spelled as separate words:

```
brother officer          mother church
father figure            parent organization
foster child             sister ship
```

3.14 Compounds made up of two like nouns of equal importance should be hyphenated:

```
author-critic            artist-inventor
composer-director        architect-painter
city-state               scholar-poet
```

3.15 Compounds made up of unlike nouns are generally left open:

```
information technologies    dissertation adviser
```

3.16 Compounds spelled as one word may be found in most unabridged dictionaries:

```
dogcatcher          bookkeeper          bathtub
```

3.17 Compounds ending with *elect* should be hyphenated except when the name of the office is in two or more words:

```
president-elect
```

But:

```
county clerk elect
```

3.18 Word combinations that include a prepositional phrase and describe an aspect of personal character should be hyphenated:

```
stay-at-home          stick-in-the-mud
```

3.19 When spelled out, the numerator and denominator of a fractional number should be separated by a hyphen unless either numerator or denominator already contains a hyphen:

```
two-thirds          one-half
```

But:

```
one thirty-second          sixty-five hundredths
```

3.20   Many compounds ending with *book* have been accepted into the general English vocabulary as single words and are to be found in Webster so spelled; others are treated as two words:

```
checkbook                  textbook
```

But:

```
telephone book             pattern book
```

3.21   The same applies to compounds ending in *house:*

```
clubhouse                  greenhouse
```

But:

```
business house             rest house
```

3.22   Spell as separate words adjective forms composed of an adverb ending in *ly* plus an adjective or a participle:

```
highly developed species   barely breathing bird
newly minted coins          easily seen result
```

3.23   Compounds with *better, best, ill, lesser, little, well,* and related comparative forms, should be hyphenated when they precede the noun:

```
better-paid job            little-expected aid
best-liked teacher         well-intentioned man
ill-advised step           lesser-known evil
```

But:

```
a very well intentioned man
```

As predicate adjectives, they are generally spelled as two words:

```
The step was ill advised.
```

```
It was clear that the man was well intentioned.
```

3.24   An adjective form composed of a present participle preceded by its object, or a past participle preceded by a related word, should be hyphenated:

```
emotion-producing language
thought-provoking commentary
dissension-arousing speeches
vote-getting tactics
foreign-made products
computer-formatted copy
```

Noun forms similarly constructed are generally treated as two words:

```
decision making        problem solving
coal mining            food gathering
```

3.25 Chemical terms used as adjectives are spelled as two or more words, unhyphenated:

```
boric acid solution        hydrogen sulfide gas
sodium chloride crystals    tartaric acid powder
```

3.26 Compounds with *all* should be hyphenated whether they precede or follow the noun:

```
all-encompassing aim       all-round leader
all-powerful ruler         all-inclusive title
all-pervasive evil         the team went all-out
```

3.27 Hyphenate phrases used as adjectives before a noun:

```
six-to-ten-year-old group   matter-of-fact approach
on-the-job training         wage-price controls
catch-as-catch-can effort   fringe-benefit demands
```

3.28 Most adjectival compounds made up of an adjective plus a noun to which the suffix *ed* has been added should be hyphenated before the noun they modify and spelled as two words after the noun:

```
rosy-cheeked boy          fine-grained powder
straight-sided dish       open-handed person
```

But:

```
A spot of pink made the boy appear rosy cheeked.

The president of the firm was known to be extremely
open handed.
```

3.29 Adjective forms ending with the suffix *like* should be spelled as one word except when they are formed from proper names, word combinations, or words ending with *ll* (double el):

```
barrellike             mouselike
camplike               umbrellalike
museumlike             lacelike
```

But:

```
Cinderella-like    doll-like    kitchen-cabinet-like
```

3.30 An adjectival compound composed of a cardinal number and the word *odd* should be hyphenated before or after the noun:

```
forty-odd              twenty-five-hundred-odd
175-odd                fifteen-hundred-odd
```

3.31   An adjectival compound composed of a cardinal number and a unit of measurement should be hyphenated when it precedes a noun:

```
twelve-mile limit              eight-space indention
two-inch margin                hundred-yard dash
```

But:

```
10 percent increase
```

3.32   Adjectival compounds with *fold* are written as one word, unless figures are used:

```
tenfold                        multifold
```

But:

```
20-fold
```

3.33   Noun compounds with *quasi* should be spelled as two words:

```
quasi promise                  quasi honor
```

Adjectival compounds with *quasi* should be hyphenated whether they come before or after the noun:

```
quasi-religious                quasi-political
```

3.34   The trend in the spelling of compound words has for some years been away from the use of hyphens. Nowhere is this more evident than in words with such common prefixes as *pre, post; pro, anti; over, under; intra, extra; infra, ultra; sub, super; re; un; non; mini, maxi; micro, macro; multi; semi; pseudo; supra:*

```
prenuptial                     understaffed
postoperative                  intramural
prowar                         extramural
antirevolutionary              infrared
oversupplied                   ultraviolet
subatomic                      nonfunctional
supersonic                     semiconscious
reenact                        pseudoreligious
unconcerned                    supramundane
```

Adjectives with these prefixes are spelled as one word—unless the second element is capitalized or is a figure:

```
pro-Arab         un-American              pre-1900
```

Or unless the second element consists of more than one word:

```
non-food-producing people
pre-nuclear-age civilization
```

It is also necessary to distinguish homonyms:

```
re-cover                       recover
```

DIVISION OF WORDS

GENERAL RULES

3.35   Divide words at the ends of lines according to their syllabication as shown in a reliable dictionary (use *Webster's Third New International Dictionary* or *Webster's Ninth New Collegiate,* as suggested in 3.1). If you use a dictionary other than these, you may find that though the syllables are separated with a dot, as in *Webster's,* an accent mark is used after the accented syllable to serve the dual purpose of indicating syllabication and stress in pronunciation: *syl·lab·i·ca'tion.* In the two *Webster's* dictionaries, the accent mark appears *before* the stressed syllable in the phonetic transcription.

3.36   Avoid placing two or more hyphens in a row at the right margin.

3.37   Word-processing programs that produce justified lines hyphenate automatically, sometimes responding to cues set in the copy to indicate preferred breaking points. Do not assume that automatic hyphenation programs always produce correct results. Most are not context sensitive and therefore cannot distinguish between *rec-ord* and *re-cord,* for example. Large spaces between words, or "rivers," in formatted copy that has been justified by a computer must be closed up in the process of adjusting the hyphenation. Since an uneven, or "ragged," right margin is acceptable for most research papers, it is best to avoid justification programs, which require special proofreading and checking of automatic hyphenation. If a research paper is to be submitted for publication, the publisher will no doubt prefer unjustified copy for editing and typesetting.

3.38   Divide according to pronunciation, rather than derivation. This means that when a word is divided after an accented syllable, the consonant stays with the vowel when the vowel is short:

```
signif-icant        param-eter          hypoth-esis
philos-ophy         democ-racy          pres-ent
```

But the consonant goes with the following syllable when the preceding vowel is long:

```
stu-dent            Mongo-lian                  divi-sive
```

The consonant goes with the accented syllable, however, in such cases as the following:

```
philo-sophical          pre-sent            demo-cratic
```

3.39 Never divide a combination of letters pronounced as one syllable:

```
pro-nounced          ex-traor-di-nary                    passed
```

3.40 When *ing* or *ed* is added to a word whose final syllable contains the liquid *l* (e.g., *cir·cle, han·dle*), the final syllable of the parent word becomes a part of the added syllable:

```
cir-cling    bris-tling    chuck-ling    han-dling
cir-cled     bris-tled     chuck-led     han-dled
```

3.41 In words where an end consonant is doubled before *ing* and *ed*, the division comes between the double consonants:

```
set-ting              con-trol-ling
per-mit-ting          per-mit-ted
```

Note that this rule does not apply to words originally ending in a double consonant:

```
add-ing                    in-stall-ing
```

EXCEPTIONS AND SPECIAL RULES

3.42 Some divisions, although syllabically correct, should never be made.

3.43 Never make a one-letter division:

Wrong:

```
a-mong        u-nite        e-nough        man-y
```

3.44 Never divide the syllables *able* and *ible:*

Wrong:

```
inevita-ble          permissi-ble          allowa-ble
```

Right:

```
inevi-table          permis-sible          allow-able
```

3.45 Never divide the following suffixes:

```
ceons    ceous    cial    cion    cions
geons    geous    gial    gion    gions     gious
                  sial    sion    sions
                  tial    tion    tions     tious
```

3.46 Avoid two-letter divisions, especially when the division would give a misleading appearance:

Wrong:

```
wo-man     of-ten     pray-er     mon-ey     loss-es
```

3.47   Avoid division of hyphenated words except at the hyphen:

Wrong:

```
self-evi-dent    gov-er-nor-elect    well-in-ten-tioned
```

3.48   Avoid division of a proper name unless it is one in which the correct division is obvious:

Right:

```
Wash-ing-ton    Went-worth    Bond-field    John-son
```

A biographical dictionary such as *Webster's* should be consulted before risking division of most proper names.

3.49   Never divide initials used in place of given names. It is best to write given names or initials on the same line as the family name, but it is allowable to place all the initials on one line and the family name on the next:

Wrong:

```
T. / S. Eliot                 J. / B. S. Haldane
```

Allowable:

```
T. S. / Eliot                 J. B. S. / Haldane
```

3.50   Never divide capital letters used as abbreviations for names of countries or states (U.S., N.Y.); for names of organizations (YMCA, NATO); or for names of publications or radio or television stations (*PMLA,* KKHI, KQED); but two sets of initials separated by a hyphen, e.g., KRON-FM, may be divided after the hyphen. Similarly, never divide the abbreviations for academic degrees (B.A., M.S., LL.D., Ph.D., etc.).

3.51   Never divide a day of the month from the month, and never divide any such combinations as the following:

```
£6 4s. 6d.          A.D. 1895          6:40 P.M.
245 ml.             435 B.C.           10%
```

3.52   Never end a line with a divisional mark, such as (*a*) or (1), or with a dollar sign, an opening quotation mark, an opening parenthesis, or an opening bracket; and never begin a line with an ending quotation mark, an ending parenthesis, or an ending bracket.

3.53   For rules on the division of words in foreign languages, consult *The Chicago Manual of Style,* thirteenth edition, chapter 9.

PUNCTUATION

3.54 Punctuation in some of its specialized uses is treated elsewhere in this manual, in the chapters on abbreviations and numbers (2), quotations (5), tables (6), illustrations (7), parenthetical references and reference lists (8), notes (9), and bibliographies (10). Here, the general use of the various marks of punctuation in the text is dealt with briefly, the primary aim being to provide answers to questions that frequently puzzle writers. The rules are based on those set forth in *The Chicago Manual of Style*, thirteenth edition.

PERIOD

3.55 A period is used at the end of a complete declarative sentence, a moderately imperative sentence, and a sentence containing an indirect question.

3.56 A period denoting an abbreviation and coming at the end of a sentence may serve also as the closing period of the sentence. If the sentence ends with a question mark or an exclamation point, the abbreviation period is retained:

```
The meeting adjourned at 5:30 P.M.
Was the committee meeting called for 8:00 P.M.?
```

3.57 Periods are omitted at the ends of items in a vertical list or enumeration, unless the items are whole sentences or paragraphs.

```
The report covers three areas:
    1.  The securities markets
    2.  The securities industry
    3.  The securities industry in the economy
The course has three goals:
    1.  Emphasis is on the discovery of truth.
    2.  Emphasis is on the useful.
    3.  Emphasis is on love of people, especially the
        altruistic and philanthropic aspects of love.
```

3.58 Periods are omitted at the ends of all the following: (1) display headings for chapters, parts, etc.; (2) titles of tables; (3) captions of figures, unless the caption consists of more than one sentence; (4) any subheading that is typed on a line by itself; and (5) address and date lines in communications, and signatures.

3.59   Periods in series (ellipsis points) are used to mark omissions in quoted matter (see chapter 5), and occasionally to guide the eye in relating items in one column of a table to relevant items in opposite columns (period leaders). Those who use computer formatting should be aware that certain programs which justify lines by altering the size of spaces between characters or words on a line may require special steps to create ellipsis points and period leaders with uniform spaces between periods. Such programs may also introduce two spaces after periods that are at the end of lines in the unformatted copy, whether these periods end sentences or not.

QUESTION MARK

3.60   A question mark is used at the end of a whole sentence containing a query or at the end of a query making up part of a sentence:

> Would the teacher–transplant idea catch on in countries other than Germany? was the question the finalists were asking.

> The question put by the Board was, Would the taxpayers vote another bond issue that would raise taxes?

The first word of the sentence that asks the question is capitalized, even though it is included in another sentence.

3.61   Courtesy disguises as a question such requests as the following, which should end with a period rather than a question mark:

> Will you please submit my request to the appropriate office.

3.62   A question mark may be used to indicate uncertainty:

> The Italian painter Niccolo dell'Abbate (1512?–71) assisted in the decorations at Fontainebleau.

EXCLAMATION POINT

3.63   An exclamation point is used to mark an outcry or an emphatic or ironical comment (avoid overuse of this device). Like the question mark, it may occur within a declarative sentence:

> What havoc was wrought by hurricane Agnes!

> "Incredible!" he exclaimed.   "I could hardly believe my senses. Both houses actually passed major bills on the opening day!"

3.64 Do not use an exclamation point to call attention to an error in a quotation, but place the word *sic* enclosed in square brackets after the error (see 2.25, 2.26).

3.65 Although the comma indicates the smallest interruption in continuity of thought or sentence structure, when it is correctly used it does more for ease of reading and ready understanding than any other mark of punctuation.

3.66 In sentences containing two or more independent clauses joined by a coordinating conjunction (*and, but, or, nor, for*), a comma is placed before the conjunction. This is not a hard-and-fast rule, however; where the sentence is short and clarity not an issue, no comma is needed.

```
Most young Europeans spend their holidays in other
European countries, and many students take vacation
jobs abroad.

This silence is not surprising, for in those circles
Marxism is still regarded with suspicion.

John arrived early and Mary came an hour later.
```

3.67 A comma is omitted before a conjunction joining the parts of a compound predicate (i.e., two or more verbs having the same subject):

```
The agencies should design their own monitoring
networks and evaluate the data derived from them.

They do not self-righteously condone such societies
but attempt rather to refute them theoretically.
```

3.68 A series of three or more words, phrases, or clauses (like this) takes a comma between each of the elements and before a conjunction separating the last two:

```
Dishes had been broken, cutlery lost, and carpets
damaged.
```

3.69 No commas should be used, however, when the elements in a series are all joined by the same conjunction:

```
For dessert the menu offered a choice of peaches or
strawberries or melon.
```

3.70 A series of three or more words, phrases, or clauses ending with the expression *and so forth* or *and so on* or *and the like* or *etc.*

should have commas both preceding and following the expression:

```
The management can improve wages, hours, conditions,
benefits, and so on, as part of the settlement
package.
```

3.71   When commas occur within one or more of the elements of a series, semicolons instead of commas should be used to separate the elements:

```
Three cities that have had notable success with the
program are Hartford, Connecticut; Kalamazoo,
Michigan; and Pasadena, California.
```

3.72   Commas are used to set a nonrestrictive dependent clause off from an independent clause. A clause is nonrestrictive if its omission will not alter the meaning of the independent clause:

```
These books, which are placed on reserve in the
library, are required reading for the course.
```

The dependent clause is nonrestrictive, since its omission does not affect the meaning of the main clause, "These books are required reading for the course." But in the following sentence, the dependent clause identifies the books placed on reserve as "required reading for the course," and the clause is therefore restrictive. No commas should be used:

```
The books that are required reading for the course are
placed on reserve in the library.
```

3.73   A word, phrase, or clause in apposition to a noun may also be restrictive or nonrestrictive. When one of the above is nonrestrictive, it is set off by commas:

```
His brother, a Harvard graduate, transferred to
Princeton for a program in theology.
```

```
A one-time officer in the foreign legion, the man
hoped to escape further military duty.
```

If, however, the appositive limits the meaning of the noun and is therefore restrictive, no commas should be used:

```
The Danish philosopher Kierkegaard asked, "What is
anxiety?"
```

```
The motion picture Becket was adapted from the play by
Jean Anouilh.
```

3.74   The name of a title or position following a person's name should be set off with commas:

Norman Cousins, former editor of the <u>Saturday Review</u>, wrote the editorial "Lunar Meditations."

3.75 The individual elements in addresses and names of places are set off with commas, except for zip codes:

The address is 340 Forest Avenue, Palo Alto, California 94023.

The next leg of our trip was to take us to Springfield, Illinois, and promised to be the most rewarding.

3.76 Interjections, conjunctive adverbs, and the like, are set off with commas when they cause a distinct break in the flow of thought:

Nevertheless, it is a matter of great importance.

It is, perhaps, the best that could be expected.

But note that when such elements do not cause a break in continuity and do not require a pause in reading, the commas should be omitted:

It is therefore clear that no deposits were made.

3.77 In using commas to set off a parenthetical element in the middle of a sentence, the writer must remember to include both commas:

The bill, you will be pleased to hear, passed at the last session.

3.78 A comma follows *namely, that is, for example, i.e.,* and *e.g.* There must be a punctuation mark before each of these expressions, but the kind of mark varies with the nature and complexity of the sentence:

Many people feel resentful because they think they have suffered an unjust fate; that is, they look upon illness, bereavement, or disrupted domestic or working conditions as being undeserved.

Restrictions on the sulfur content of fuel oil are already in effect in some cities (e.g., Paris, Milan, Rome, and Stockholm), and the prospect is that limits will be imposed sooner or later in most cities.

3.79 When a dependent clause or a long participial or prepositional phrase begins a sentence, it is followed by a comma:

If the insurrection is to succeed, the army and the police must stand side by side.

After spending a week in conferences, the commission was able to write a report.

```
Having accomplished his mission, he returned to
headquarters.
```

But a comma is usually unnecessary after a short prepositional phrase:

```
For recreation the mayor fishes or sails.
```

3.80 When each of several adjectives preceding a noun modifies the noun individually, the adjectives should be separated with commas:

```
It was a large, well-placed, beautiful house.

We strolled out into the warm, luminous night.
```

However, if the last adjective *identifies* the noun rather than merely modifying it, no commas should precede it:

```
His is the large brick house on the corner.
```

3.81 Use commas to set off contrasted elements and two or more complementary or antithetical phrases or clauses referring to a single word following:

```
The idea, not its expression, is significant.

The harder we run, the more we stay in the same place.

She both delighted in, and was disturbed by, her new
leisure and freedom.

It is a logical, if harsh, solution to the problem.
```

3.82 Use a comma to separate two identical or closely similar words:

```
They marched in, in twos.

Whatever is, had best be accepted.
```

3.83 A comma is sometimes necessary to prevent misreading:

```
After eating, the lions yawned and then dozed.
```

SEMICOLON

3.84 A semicolon marks a greater break in the continuity of a sentence than that indicated by a comma. A semicolon should be used between the parts of a compound sentence (two or more independent clauses) when they are not connected by a conjunction:

```
More than one hundred planned communities are in
various stages of completion; many more are on the
drawing board.
```

53

3.85   If the clauses of a compound sentence are very long and there are commas within them, they should be separated with semicolons even though they are connected by a conjunction:

```
Although productivity per capita in U.S. industry is
almost twice that in West European industry, Western
Europe has an increasingly well-educated young labor
force; and the crucial point is that knowledge, which
is transferable between peoples, has become by far the
most important world economic resource.
```

3.86   When used transitionally between the clauses of compound sentences, the words *hence, however, indeed, so, then, thus,* and *yet* should be preceded by a semicolon and followed by a comma:

```
There are those who think of freedom in terms of
social and economic egalitarianism; thus, reformist
governments of the left are inherently viewed with
greater favor than the regimes of the right.
```

3.87   For the use of the semicolon instead of a comma, see also 3.71.

Colon

3.88   The use of the colon in a sentence indicates a discontinuity of grammatical construction greater than that indicated by the semicolon. Whereas the semicolon is used to separate parts of a sentence that are of equal significance, the colon is used to introduce a clause or phrase that expands, clarifies, or exemplifies the meaning of what precedes it:

```
Europe and America share similar problems: their
labor forces cannot compete with those of Third World
nations, and they depend on the Third World for
critical raw resources.
```

```
People expect three things of their governments:
peace, prosperity, and respect for civil rights.
```

3.89   A colon should be placed at the end of a grammatical element introducing a formal statement, whether the statement is quoted or not. A colon is also used after *following* or *as follows* or *in sum* when they are followed by illustrative material or a list:

```
The qualifications are as follows: a doctorate in
physics; five years' experience in a national
laboratory; and an ability to communicate technical
matter to the lay audience.
```

```
These immigrants all shared the same dream: they
```

thought they could create the City of God on earth in
their own lifetimes.

For the use of numbers to enumerate items in text, see 2.72.

3.90   As noted elsewhere in this manual, a colon is used between
chapter and verse in scriptural references (2.46), between hours
and minutes in notations of time (2.57), between the title and
subtitle of a book or article (9.38 and 4.10), between place and
publisher in footnote and bibliographical references (9.59), and
between volume and page numbers in citations (9.81 and 9.86).

DASH

3.91   The dash, which in printing is an elongated hyphen called an
em-dash, in typescript consists of two hyphens without space
between or on either side of them.

3.92   A dash or a pair of dashes enclosing a phrase may indicate a
sudden break in thought that disrupts the sentence structure:

Rutherford--how could he have misinterpreted the
evidence?

Some of the characters in <u>Tom Jones</u> are "flat"--to
use the term E. M. Forster coined--because they
unfailingly act in accordance with a set of qualities
suggested by a literal interpretation of their names
(e.g., Squire Allworthy).

3.93   Breaks in faltering speech or interruptions may be indicated by
dashes:

Later in chapter 25, Jane Eyre again answers only with
a gesture: "I reflected, and in truth it appeared to
me the only possible one: satisfied I was not, but to
please him I endeavored to appear so--relieved, I
certainly did feel; so I answered him with a contented
smile."

3.94   A dash may be used to introduce an element that emphasizes or
explains the main clause through repetition of one or more key
words:

He asked where wisdom was to be found--"the wisdom
that is above rubies."

One is expected to cram all this stuff into one's
mind--cram it all in, whether it's likely to be
useful or not.

3.95   In a sentence that includes several elements referring to a word that is the subject of a final, summarizing clause, a dash should precede the final clause:

```
The statue of the man throwing the discus, the
charioteer at Delphi, the poetry of Pindar--all show
the culmination of the great ideal.
```

3.96   Use four hyphens (or a 2-em dash) to indicate missing letters (e.g., in citing from a text that is mutilated or illegible), leaving no space between the first and last hyphens and the existing part of the word:

```
We ha---- a copy in the library.

H----h? [Hirsch?]
```

In transcribing from broken texts in languages other than English, it may be the practice to use hyphens to indicate the length of the break and by so doing to indicate with the number of hyphens the number of characters that are missing. In such cases, follow the practice set by scholars and editors within the discipline.

3.97   Use six hyphens (or a 3-em dash) to indicate a whole word omitted or to be supplied:

```
A vessel which left the ------ July.
```

PARENTHESES

3.98   The principal uses of parentheses in the text of a paper are (1) to set off parenthetical elements, (2) to enclose the source of a quotation or other matter when a footnote is not used for the purpose, and (3) to set off the numbers or letters in an enumeration (like that in this sentence). The first use is a matter of choice, since both commas and dashes are also used to set off parenthetical material. In general, commas are used for material most closely related to the main clause, dashes and parentheses for material more remotely connected:

```
The conference has (with some malice aforethought)
been divided into four major areas.
```

```
It is significant that in the Book of Revelation (a
book Whitehead did not like because of its bloody and
apocalyptic imagery), the vision of a new heavenly
city at the end of time has the divine light shine so
that the nations walk by it, and the "kings of the
```

earth shall bring their glory into it" (Rev. 21:22–
26).

Each painting depicted some glorious, or vainglorious,
public occasion of the last hundred years; in each—a
formal diplomatic banquet, a victory parade, the
opening of the Burbank Airport in 1931 (clouded by a
phalanx of tiny Ford Trimotors)—the crowds of people
were replaced by swarms of ants.

BRACKETS

3.99 Brackets are used (1) to enclose any interpolation in a quotation
(see 5.37) and (2) to enclose parenthetical matter within parentheses:

The book is available in translation (see J. R. Evans–
Bentz, The Tibetan Book of the Dead [Oxford: Oxford
University Press, 1927]).

3.100 Brackets may be used to enclose the phonetic transcript of a
word:

He attributed the light to the phenomenon called
gegenschein ['gä–gən–ˌshīn].

OTHER PUNCTUATION MARKS

3.101 The use of quotation marks is described in paragraphs 5.11–17.

3.102 The hyphen, sometimes considered a mark of punctuation, is
discussed in paragraphs 3.12–53 (compound words and word
division) and paragraph 2.67 (continued numbers).

MULTIPLE PUNCTUATION

3.103 The term *multiple punctuation* means the conjunction of two
marks of punctuation—for example, a period and a closing parenthesis. Where such conjunction occurs, certain rules must be
observed concerning (1) whether to omit one mark or the other
(as a period when an abbreviation ends a sentence, see 3.56) or
(2) which mark to put first when both marks are kept.

3.104 A comma is generally omitted following a stronger mark of
punctuation:

If he had watched "What's My Line?" he would have
known the answer.

> She shouts "Where's the beef!" and we cut to a close-
> up of the hamburger.

3.105   Two marks of punctuation fall in the same place chiefly where quotation marks, parentheses, or brackets are involved.

3.106   In American usage, a final comma or period always precedes closing quotation marks, whether it is part of the quoted matter or not. Question marks and exclamation points precede quotation marks if they are part of the quoted matter, follow if they pertain to the entire sentence of which the quotation is a part. Semicolons and colons follow quotation marks. (If the quoted passage ends with a semicolon or a colon in the original, the mark may be changed to a period or a comma to complement the structure of the main sentence.)

> Every public official and every professional person is
> called upon "to join in the effort to bring justice
> and hope to all our people."

> Even this small advance begins to raise the question,
> "What in effect is our true image, our real likeness?"

> Do we accept Jefferson's concept of "a natural
> aristocracy among men"?

> Charged by a neighbor with criminal mistreatment of
> her child and threatened with police action, the woman
> retorted, "Just let you call the police, and you'll
> regret it to your dying day!"

> How dreadful it was to hear her reply--calmly--"We'll
> let the law decide that"!

> He made the point that "in every human attitude and
> choice we make, we are taking an attitude toward
> Everyman"; and then he enlarged upon the point in a
> particularly telling way.

> Rome's planned subcenter, EUR, is "almost a self-
> contained city": it governs itself and provides its
> own services.

3.107   In fields where it is the practice to use single quotation marks (scare quotes) to set off special terms, a period or comma follows the closing quotation mark:

> Some contemporary theologians were proclaiming the
> 'death of God'.

In other uses of single quotation marks, the period or comma is placed within the closing quotation mark (or marks, when both single and double occur together):

The article to which he referred is in the <u>Journal of
Political Economy</u>: "Comment on 'How to Make a Burden
of the Public Debt.'"

3.108 When a complete sentence stands alone and is enclosed in parentheses or brackets, the terminal period for that sentence is placed
within the parentheses or brackets. When elements within a sentence are enclosed in parentheses, the sentence punctuation is
placed outside the parentheses.

We have already noted similar motifs in Japan.
(Significantly, very similar motifs can also be found
in the myths and folktales of Korea.)

Myths have been accepted as literally true, then as
allegorically true (by the Stoics), as confused
history (by Euhemerus), as priestly lies (by the
philosophers of the Enlightenment), and as imitative
agricultural ritual mistaken for propositions (in the
days of Frazer).

3.109 Numbers or letters in an enumeration in the text belong with the
items following them; therefore sentence punctuation precedes
them, and no punctuation mark comes between them and the
item to which they apply:

He gave three reasons for resigning: (1) advanced age,
(2) failing health, and (3) a desire to travel.

3.110 Brackets used to set off words or phrases supplied to fill in incomplete parts of a quotation (5.35–37) or dates supplied in citations (9.67) are ignored in punctuating—i.e., punctuate as if
there were no brackets:

The states have continued to respond to "the federal
stimulus for improvement in the scope and amount of
categorical assistance programs. . . . [Yet] Congress
has adhered to its original decision that residence
requirements were necessary."

FOR COMPUTER USERS

3.111 Punctuation marks may be part of the control language in a
word-processing program. To avoid costly errors, consult the
documentation before entering the text or any other part of the
paper. For example, some programs require control words that
begin with periods, and these control words must often be introduced at the beginnings of lines (see 14.50). When using such
programs, therefore, writers must avoid putting periods in the
first character space in lines (e.g., for ellipses).

4 Capitalization, Quotation Marks, and Underlining (Italics)

CAPITALIZATION

PROPER NAMES

4.1   In all languages written in the Latin alphabet, proper nouns—
the names of persons and places—are capitalized:

John and Jane Doe   Niagara Falls

4.2 In English, proper adjectives—adjectives derived from proper nouns—are also capitalized:

European   Machiavellian

4.3 Proper nouns and adjectives that have lost their original meanings and have become part of everyday language, however, are not capitalized:

french doors   india ink   roman numerals

OTHER NAMES

4.4 Before the final manuscript is prepared, the writer should decide which terms are to be capitalized and which are not. Inconsistency in the matter is a sign of careless writing. Detailed suggestions for capitalization of many terms occurring in the text may be found in chapter 7 of *The Chicago Manual of Style,* thirteenth edition. The following paragraphs discuss the capitalization of titles of written works, the problem encountered most frequently by writers of papers.

TITLES OF WORKS

4.5 In giving titles of published works in text, notes, reference list, or bibliography, the spelling of the original should be retained, but capitalization and punctuation may be altered to conform to the style used in the paper. In most scientific fields, sentence-style capitalization is used (see 4.9). In the humanities and most of the social sciences, however, it is customary to capitalize titles headline style, according to the rules given in 4.6–8.

HEADLINE-STYLE CAPITALIZATION

4.6 In the titles of works in English, capitalize the first and last words and all words except articles, prepositions, the word *to* used as part of an infinitive, and coordinate conjunctions (*and, but, or, nor, for*):

Economic Effects of War upon Women and Children

"What It Is All About"

How to Overcome Urban Blight: A Twentieth-Century Problem

Note that the subtitle, following a colon, is capitalized the same way as the main title.

4.7   Rules for capitalizing compound words vary widely. A rule of thumb that usually proves satisfactory is (1) always capitalize the first element and (2) capitalize the second element if it is a noun or proper adjective or if it has equal force with the first element:

Twentieth-Century Literature in the Making

Computer-aided Graphics: A Manual for Video-Game Lovers

4.8   The original capitalization of long titles of works published in earlier centuries is retained:

The precedents of general issues, and the most usual special pleas; precedents of replications, rejoinders, demurrers, &c; a synopsis of practice, or general view of the time when the proceedings in an action should be carried on in the Court of King's Bench and Common Pleas.

SENTENCE-STYLE CAPITALIZATION

4.9   In parenthetical references and reference-list entries, titles of books and articles in English are capitalized sentence style, that is, the first word of a title or subtitle is capitalized and only proper nouns and proper adjectives thereafter:

The triumph of Achilles

Seeing and selling America, 1945–55

"Natural crisis: Symbol and imagination in the American farm crisis"

TITLES IN FOREIGN LANGUAGES

4.10   In titles of French, Italian, Spanish, and German works, capitalize only what would be capitalized in a normal sentence. The first word of a subtitle would also be capitalized. As in the title of works in English, a colon should separate title and subtitle. If, as is often the case in foreign language publications, a period separates the title and subtitle, this should be changed to a colon:

Dictionnaire illustré de la mythologie et des antiquités grecques et romaines

Bibliografia di Roma nel Cinquecento

Historia de la Orden de San Gerónimo

Reallexikon zur deutschen Kunstgeschichte

Phénoménologie et religion: Structures de
l'institution chrétienne

Since some romance language departments may have other rules for capitalization of titles, it is well to inquire before preparing a final manuscript.

4.11 In Greek and Latin titles, capitalize the first word and all proper nouns and proper adjectives thereafter:

Iphigeneia hē en Taurois

Speculum Romanae magnificentiae

4.12 An exception is made for modern works with Latin titles, which are capitalized as though they were English:

Acta Apostolicae Sedis   Quo Vadis?

PARTS OF WORKS

4.13 References to such parts of a work as contents, preface, foreword, introduction, bibliography, and appendix should not be capitalized:

A foreword may be included if desired.

The paper should include a bibliography.

The preface to this popular work was written by Lionel Trilling.

"Thinking French" is the title of chapter 6.

The variables within the experiment are listed in table 2.

Copies of supporting documents are in appendix 3.

UNDERLINING AND QUOTATION MARKS FOR TITLES AND NAMES

4.14 Throughout this manual, an example or part of an example that is underlined may be italicized by those using typewriters and computer systems that can perform this function. When italics are used, adjacent punctuation (except parentheses or brackets) must also be italicized.

4.15 In all fields except some of the sciences, titles of published books and some other kinds of works are underlined. Other titles are enclosed in double quotation marks, and still others are capitalized but neither underlined nor enclosed in quotation marks.

The general rule is to underline the titles of *whole* published works and to put the titles of *parts* of these works in quotation marks. Titles of unpublished material are also in quotation marks. Titles of series and manuscript collections, and various kinds of descriptive titles, are neither underlined nor in quotation marks.

BOOKS AND PERIODICALS

4.16 Underline the titles of books, pamphlets, bulletins, periodicals (magazines, journals, newspapers), and long poems (such as *Paradise Lost*). It should be noted that although a published work is thought of as set in type and printed in conventional form, it may be a typewritten script reproduced by mimeograph or one of the photoduplicating processes, or it may be published in microform. *If the work bears a publisher's imprint,* it should be treated as published rather than unpublished material; that is, the title should be underlined wherever it appears.

4.17 Titles of chapters or other divisions of a book, and titles of short stories, short poems, essays, and articles in periodicals are set in quotation marks:

The First Circle, chapter 27, "A Puzzled Robot"

"The New Feminism," Saturday Review

"Amazing Amazon Region," New York Times

"The Demon Lover," Fifty Years: A Retrospective Collection

Part 4 of Systematic Theology, "Life and the Spirit"

"The Dead," the final story in Dubliners

BOOK SERIES AND EDITIONS

4.18 Titles of series and names of editions are neither underlined nor put in quotation marks:

Michigan Business Studies

Modern Library Edition

DISSERTATIONS AND OTHER UNPUBLISHED WORKS

4.19 Titles of unpublished theses, dissertations, and other papers are set in quotation marks:

"Androgen Action and Receptor Specificity" (Ph.D. dissertation, University of Chicago, 1985)

"Costing of Human Resource Development," paper presented at the Conference of the International Economics Association

"One Man's CBI: A Different Kind of War," TMs, Hoover Library, Stanford, Calif.

MANUSCRIPT COLLECTIONS

4.20 Names of manuscript collections and archives and designations such as *diary, autograph, memorandum,* etc., are not capitalized, underlined, or set in quotation marks when they occur in running text. In notes and bibliographical or reference-list entries, however, they should be capitalized sentence style in roman and abbreviated in papers citing many such primary sources (see 2.19, 9.114, and 11.52–55).

SACRED SCRIPTURES

4.21 The titles of books of sacred scripture—Bible, Koran, Talmud, Upanishads, Vedas, etc.—and the names of books of the Bible and of the Apocrypha are neither underlined nor set in quotation marks:

This passage is taken from the King James Version of the Bible.

The Book of Daniel is a part of the apocalyptic literature of the Bible.

LEGAL CASES

4.22 The names of legal cases (plaintiff and defendant) are underlined in text; *v.* (versus) may be in roman or underlined, provided that use is consistent:

Miranda v. Arizona

Green v. Department of Public Works

West Coast Hotel Co. v. Parrish

POEMS

4.23 Titles of long poems are underlined; titles of short poems are in quotation marks:

Milton's <u>Paradise Lost</u>

"Pied Beauty," in <u>The Oxford Book of Modern Verse</u>

Where many poems, both long and short, are mentioned, it is best to underline all titles.

PLAYS AND MOTION PICTURES

4.24 Titles of plays and motion pictures are underlined:

Molière's <u>Le bourgeois gentilhomme</u>

Orson Welles's <u>Citizen Kane</u>

RADIO AND TELEVISION PROGRAMS

4.25 Titles of radio and television programs are set in quotation marks:

CBS's "60 Minutes"

"A Prairie Home Companion" on National Public Radio, WBEZ in Chicago

SHIPS AND AIRCRAFT

4.26 Actual names of ships, aircraft, and spacecraft are underlined. Designations of make, etc., are not:

S.S. <u>Constitution</u>   <u>Spirit of St. Louis</u>
H.M.S. <u>Saranac</u>   <u>Apollo XIII</u>

OTHER NONBOOK MATERIALS

4.27 For treatment of the titles of other nonbook materials, see 9.114–28.

FOREIGN WORDS AND PHRASES

4.28 In running text in English, underline foreign words and phrases that are not part of sentences or passages quoted in full:

Clearly, this . . . leads to the idea of <u>Übermensch</u> and also to the theory of the <u>acte gratuit</u> and surrealism.

4.29 A quotation *entirely* in a foreign language is not underlined. In the following sentence, the words *le pragmatisme* should be underlined within the English text, but the words of the quotation, all in French, should not be underlined:

```
The confusion of le pragmatisme is traced to the
supposed failure to distinguish "les propriétés de la
valeur en général" from the incidental.
```

4.30   In the following foreign-language quotation, the author of the quoted passage has underlined some words used as examples. The person using the quotation in a paper written in English must observe the author's usage, since a quotation must always be reproduced exactly as it appears in the original:

```
Reviewing Mr. Wright's book, Professor Nichols writes:
"Quand j'ai dû analyser le style de Wright . . . j'ai
été frappé par l'emploi ironique de ses prépositions
et conjonctions causales (à cause de, parce que,
etc.)."
```

4.31   Foreign titles preceding and sometimes following proper names, and foreign names of persons, places, institutions, and the like, are not underlined:

```
Père Grou                     the Académie Française
the Puerto del Sol            the Gare du Nord
M. Jacquet, Ministre des      the Teatro real
   Travaux Publics            the Casa de los Guzmanes
the Vienna Staatsoper         Place d'Italie
```

4.32   If foreign words have become sufficiently anglicized to be listed in a good English dictionary, they should not be underlined:

```
de facto           vis-à-vis              milieu
```

4.33   The writer's appreciation of the needs of the audience for which the paper is intended will govern the choice of whether or not to include the definition of a foreign word in text, in a note, or in an appendix. If a definition follows a foreign word or phrase within the text, the definition is enclosed in parentheses or quotation marks:

```
"I would like to eat," or ena tuainu-iai, "I wanted to
eat."
```

```
According to Sartrean ontology, man is always de trop
(in excess).
```

In notes and appendixes, translations into foreign languages should follow 4.28 if they are several words or less in length, and 4.29–30 if they are longer.

5   Quotations

PERMISSIONS

5.1   The use of quotations within a research paper is a way of rep-
resenting the continuity of research within a field and introducing the ideas of others by referring directly to their works.
Lengthy quotations involving more than a few contiguous paragraphs or stanzas at a time, even if scattered, and the use of
anything in its entirety—a poem, an essay, a letter, a section of
a book, an illustration, or sometimes a table—may exceed the

limits of "fair use" as defined by the Copyright Act of 1976. Publishers, libraries, and others who hold the rights to literary works do not interpret fair use uniformly. For example, some publishers and others holding copyright define fair use in terms of length, although the Copyright Act and the courts have defined it more generally, in terms of proper use to illustrate or support a point, accurate transcription, and proper credit given in notes or parenthetical references. Some publishers require permissions for lengthy quotations used in dissertations and some do not. Some librarians consider dissertations forms of publication and some do not. It is advisable, therefore, when a paper contains lengthy quotations, to consult holders of literary rights to unpublished as well as published documents in order to determine whether there is any need to seek or obtain permissions. For a thorough discussion of the subject, see chapter 4 in *The Chicago Manual of Style,* thirteenth edition.

PLAGIARISM

5.2 By definition, a research paper involves the assimilation of prior scholarship and entails the responsibility to give proper acknowledgment whenever one is indebted to another for either words or ideas. This chapter demonstrates how to include the words and ideas of others in a paper by quoting works accurately and attributing quotations and ideas to their authors in notes (chapter 9), parenthetical references and reference lists (chapter 8), and bibliographies (chapter 10). Failure to give credit is plagiarism. *The MLA Style Manual* offers a very useful perspective on the subject (see pages 4–5 and 163).

ACCURACY

5.3 In general, direct quotations should correspond exactly with the originals in wording, spelling, capitalization, and punctuation. Exceptions to the general rule are discussed below.

PROSE

5.4 Short, direct prose quotations should be incorporated into the text of the paper and enclosed in double quotation marks: "One small step for man; one giant leap for mankind." But in general a prose quotation of two or more sentences which at the same time runs to four or more lines of text in a paper should be set off from the text in single-spacing and indented in its entirety four spaces from the left marginal line, with no quotation marks at beginning or end. In this manual, a quotation so treated is called a *block quotation*. Exceptions to this rule are allowable when, for purposes of emphasis or of comparison, it is desirable to set off quotations of less than four lines as block quotations. Paragraph indention in the original text should be indicated by a four-space indention within a block quotation. Double-space between the text and the block quotation, but single-space between the paragraphs of a quotation. However, when including material from different sources in a single block quotation, double-space between separate passages.

5.5 Some word-processing programs use control words for inserting block quotations and assigning note numbering to them. Before preparing the final manuscript, those using computers should consult relevant documentation.

POETRY

5.6 Quotations of poetry two or more lines in length should normally be set off from the text, line for line as in the original and centered on the page without quotation marks. Quotations of poetry may be double- or single-spaced, following the original as closely as possible:

```
              We are not the same you and
    i, since here's a little he
    or is
    it It
    ?    (or was something we saw in the mirror)?

                        e. e. cummings,
                        "here's a little mouse)and"
```

5.7 If the lines of the poem are too long to be centered on the page, all the lines should be indented four spaces, with runover lines indented another four spaces:

```
    A child said What is the grass? fetching it to
        me with full hands;
    How could I answer the child?  I do not know what
        it is any more than he.

    I guess it must be the flag of my disposition, out
        of hopeful green stuff woven.

                    Walt Whitman, Song of Myself
```

5.8 It is sometimes desirable to insert a line or two of verse directly into text. For example, a writer who is making a critical examination of a poem may find this method of quoting well suited to the purpose of the paper. Quotation marks are placed at the beginning and the end of the line or lines quoted, and if there is more than one line, a slash, or virgule (/), with a space before and a space after, is used to separate them. When using the line justification function of a word-processing program, it may be necessary to enter these spaces on the formatted version or treat them otherwise, using special program facilities.

```
In the valley the mariners find life's purposes
reduced to the simple naturalistic proposition, "All
things have rest, and ripen toward the grave; / In
silence, ripen, fall, and cease."
```

EPIGRAPHS

5.9 When used at the heads of chapters, epigraphs are blocked on the right half or two-thirds of the page, and they are not enclosed in quotation marks. The name of the author of the quotation and the title of its source are given below the epigraph, flush right:

```
A storm of mosquitoes may create a noise like thunder.

                                      Old Chinese Saying

Heavy matters!  Heavy matters!  But look thee here,
boy. Now bless thyself: thou met'st with things dying,
I with things new-born.

                          Shakespeare, The Winter's Tale
```

QUOTATIONS IN NOTES

5.10 Prose quotations appearing within notes are enclosed in quotation marks and run in:

```
    1"He leaves a terrible blank behind him and I
have a horrid lonely feeling knowing that he is gone"
(Field-Marshall Lord Alanbrooke, Diary, 18 April 1940
[AMs, Personal Files]).  Writing of Dill somewhat
later, Brooke expressed a strong feeling of admiration
and affection: "I know of no other soldier in the
whole of my career who inspired me with greater
admiration and respect. An exceptionally clear, well-
balanced brain, an infinite capacity for work,
unbounded charm of personality, but, above all, an
```

```
unflinching straightness of character. . . . I owe him
an infinite debt for all I learned from him" (idem,
"Notes on My Life" [AMs, Personal Files], 2:66).
```

Verse quotations are set off as in text.

QUOTATION MARKS

5.11 Direct quotations other than block quotations as described in paragraphs 5.30–34 require double quotation marks at beginning and end. If the quoted passage itself contains a quotation that is set off with double quotation marks, those marks must be changed to single quotation marks (see 5.16). In a block quotation, however, the double quotation marks that appear within the original matter are retained.

5.12 In addition to their use with quotations from other sources, double quotation marks are used to set off titles (see 4.17 and 4.19) and single words, letters, or numbers in certain contexts:

```
Twenty-one papers were prepared under the topics
"Background," "Relation to Card Catalogs,"
"Techniques," "Standards," and "Applications."

The enumerations may be either numbered "1," "2," "3,"
etc., or lettered a, b, c, etc.
```

In some fields—linguistics, theology—it is accepted practice to use single quotation marks to set off words and concepts:

```
kami 'hair, beard'

The variables of quantification, 'something',
'nothing', . . .
```

5.13 If a whole letter is quoted, including address and signature lines, it should all be set off as an indented block quotation, retaining the spelling, punctuation, emphasis, and spacing of the original:

```
              To my Lord the Lord Deputy of Calais

        Pleaseth you to understand that I humbly
    beseech your noble person that it may please you
    to give me leave to set up certain bills and
    notices touching my craft of writing, so that if
    within this town of Calais there be any who should
    desire to have the aforesaid art taught to their
    children, together with the French tongue, that
```

```
the residence of the said your humble servant is
at St. Omer; and thus doing, my lord, I shall pray
God for your good prosperity.
```

```
                    J. Filleul (St. Clare Byrne 1981, 5:738)
```

5.14 In quoting an outline, set it off as an indented block quotation, retaining the spelling, punctuation, emphasis, and spacing of the original:

```
Their outline for the third-year course is as follows:

    III.  Predicate-element concept

        A.  Verb

            1.  Forms and uses of verb 'to be'

            2.  Tense

                a)  Present perfect

                b)  Past perfect[4]
```

In quoting an enumeration, do likewise:

```
    1.  Book selection

    2.  Arrangement and organization of the collection

    3.  Guidance to readers[6]
```

Introduce the quotation of all such material in such a way as to make it clear that it *is* quoted and not the writer's own work. Lengthy material of this nature may belong in an appendix.

5.15 For a quotation that includes headings and subheadings, use a block quotation and retain the spacing, indention, spelling, and punctuation of the original, being careful to cite the source of the quotation with a note or a parenthetical reference:

```
                    CHAPTER II

        THE DEVELOPMENT OF A RACE RELATIONS

                ACTION-STRUCTURE


            Race Relations in the British
        Isles: 1700 to the First World War

    From the defeat of the Spanish Armada in 1588
until the abolition of slavery throughout the
British Empire in 1833, the economy of Britain was
tied, in some measure, to the fortunes of the
African slave trade. . . .
    Conservatives and liberals felt that this
dependency had always been a mistake.[8]
```

5.16   For a quotation within a quotation, single quotation marks are used; for another quotation within that one, double marks are again used; if yet another, single marks, and so on:

> The chairman reported as follows:
>
>> The mayor's representative has replied: "I am authorized by the Chamber of Commerce to make this offer, their provision stating, 'The jobs shall be made available provided that the committee guarantee all the means for receiving applications.' That guarantee has been made and a procedure outlined for taking job applications." Our thanks go to the mayor for his handling of our committee's request (Guthrie Center 1987, 4).

PUNCTUATION WITH QUOTATION MARKS

5.17   Periods and commas should be placed inside quotation marks (even when the quotation marks enclose only one letter or figure); semicolons and colons, outside. Question marks and exclamation marks should be placed outside quotation marks unless the question or exclamation occurs within the quotation itself. In the first example below, the question is not posed within the quotation, but in the sentence as a whole, and the question mark properly belongs after the closing quotation mark. In the other two examples, the question mark in one and the exclamation mark in the other clearly belong within the quotations:

> How does he show "evil leading somehow to good"?

> One may well ask, "Is it really necessary to lose the world in order to find oneself?"

> The cries of "Long live the king!" echoed down the broad avenues.

> "You speak, my friend, with a strange earnestness," said old Roger Chillingworth.

> In Keats's "Ode on a Grecian Urn," the urn says, "Beauty is truth, truth beauty."

See also 3.103–7.

ELLIPSES

5.18   Any omission of words, phrases, or paragraphs in quoted matter is indicated by ellipsis points, which are period dots, not asterisks (stars). There should be a space before each dot, unless the first dot is the period of an abbreviation or sentence, and a space also after the last if a word follows. Since ellipsis points stand for words omitted from the quotation itself, they are always placed *within* quotation marks. When quotation marks either precede or follow ellipsis points, do not leave a space between the quotation marks and the dot. Computer users who rely on word-processing programs that justify lines by adjusting spaces between words may find that ellipsis points require special processing. For example, some programs when formatting automatically add two spaces after periods that occur at the end of lines in the unformatted text, whether or not they end sentences.

OMISSION WITHIN A SENTENCE

5.19   An omission within a sentence is shown by three spaced dots:

```
In conclusion he stated, "What we require . . . is a
new method."
```

5.20   If other punctuation comes immediately before the ellipsis, it is placed next to the word:

```
"We are fighting for the holy cause of Slavdom, . . .
for freedom, . . . for the Orthodox cross."
```

5.21   If other punctuation occurs immediately before a word that is preceded by ellipsis points, that punctuation mark is placed before the word, with the usual intervening space:

```
"All this is not exactly in S's tradition . . . ; and
it was not, as I recall, your style."
```

OMISSION FOLLOWING A SENTENCE

5.22   An omission following a sentence is indicated by four dots. The first, placed immediately after the last word, is the period:

```
"When a nation is clearly in the wrong, it ought to
say so. . . . I am only enunciating principles that we
apply in our own case."
```

If in the original source the sentence preceding the ellipsis ends with a question mark or an exclamation mark, that mark rather than the period is used:

```
"How cold it was! . . . No one could function in that
climate."
```

5.23 How much of an omission may be indicated by a mark of terminal punctuation and three dots? In current practice, the period (or other mark of terminal punctuation) and three spaced dots may indicate the omission of (1) the last part of a quoted sentence, or (2) the first part of a quoted sentence, or (3) the last part of one sentence and the first part of the next sentence, or (4) a whole sentence or more, or (5) a whole paragraph or more. But note the following exceptions.

WHEN TO USE A LINE OF ELLIPSIS POINTS

5.24 In quoting an excerpt of poetry, the omission of one or more complete lines is shown by a full line of ellipsis points, approximating in length that of the line of poetry immediately above it:

```
    Weep no more, woeful shepherds, weep no more,
For Lycidas your sorrow is not dead,
. . . . . . . . . . . . . . . . . . . .
Henceforth thou art the genius of the shore,
In thy large recompense, and shalt be good
To all that wander in that perilous flood.[7]
```

5.25 The use of a full line of ellipsis points may be desirable in quoting portions of an outline or an enumeration. In the following example, the four dots at the end of the first paragraph indicate the omission both of the last part of the item and of items 2 and 3. The full line of dots that follows is necessary to indicate missing lines. The semicolon and the three dots at the end of item 4 indicate the omission of the last part of the paragraph.

```
1.  The paper must include a discussion of the
    moral bases and social effects of the kind of
    ownership which you favor or which you wish to
    attack. . . .

    . . . . . . . . . . . . . . . . . . . .
4.  In form, the paper must be an argument: . . .
```

See also 5.23.

CAPITALIZATION OF FIRST WORD

5.26   Exact quotations should follow precisely the wording, spelling, capitalization, and punctuation of the original (5.3), but long-established scholarly practice makes an exception by altering the capitalization of the first word of a quotation according to the following rule:

> 1. If the text introducing the quotation ends either with terminal punctuation or with a colon, the first word of the quotation is capitalized, even though it is not capitalized in the original:
>
> ```
> The following day Sand reported: "With Pebble
> soliciting members on the side, it was imperative that
> the meeting be no longer delayed."
> ```
>
> In the original of the above, ''With'' occurs inside a sentence and is therefore not capitalized.
>
> 2. If, however, the quotation is joined syntactically to the writer's introductory words, the first word of the quotation is begun with a small letter, even if it is capitalized in the original:
>
> ```
> The Act provided that "the General Counsel of the
> Board shall exercise complete supervision."
> ```
>
> In the original, ''the'' is the first word of the sentence and is therefore capitalized.

WHEN NOT TO USE ELLIPSIS POINTS

5.27   In general, no ellipsis points should be used (1) before or after an obviously incomplete sentence, (2) before or after a run-in quotation of a complete sentence, (3) before a block quotation beginning with a complete sentence or an incomplete sentence that completes a sentence in the text, (4) after a block quotation ending with a complete sentence. If ellipsis points are considered necessary before or after a quoted passage—and sometimes it is desirable to include them—three should precede and four, including the period, should follow the quoted matter if it ends with a complete sentence or if it ends the sentence in the text. But ellipsis points are seldom used at the beginning or end of a quoted passage. After all, unless it is the opening or closing sentence in a work that is being quoted, it is simply understood that something precedes and follows the passage.

INCOMPLETE QUOTED EXPRESSIONS

5.28   When a quotation consists of a few words or an incomplete sentence, obviously a fragment from the original, no ellipsis points should be used either before or after the fragment. If, however, an omission occurs within the fragment, it is noted by three ellipsis points:

```
General Smith wrote that the president had been "very
much impressed" by the State Department's paper that
stressed "developing a major part of the world by
using the economic resources . . . of the super
powers."13
```

OMISSIONS IN FOREIGN-LANGUAGE QUOTATIONS

5.29   Treat omissions in foreign-language quotations as you would those in English. This is in line with the present practice of the University of Chicago Press as well as other publishers. If the paper itself is written in a language other than English, the writer should follow the rules of that language in the matter of omissions (as well as of punctuation). Some of these rules are given in *The Chicago Manual of Style,* thirteenth edition.

BLOCK QUOTATIONS

5.30   When material in a block quotation (5.4) begins with a paragraph in the original, it is given paragraph indention of four spaces and the first word is capitalized. Thus with a block quotation indented four spaces from the left margin, the paragraph indention is eight spaces from the left margin.

```
Goodenough raises questions that Kraeling does not
raise:

        Primarily why did the artist want to put David
    as the tamer just here?  We have seen that the
    original vine or tree growing from the vase was
    changed to make more explicit the symbolic and
    ritualistic implications of the vase. (Goodenough
    1986, 40)
```

5.31   If a block quotation is introduced in text with quoted fragments interspersed with the words of the writer of the paper, the fragments cited must all have quotation marks at beginning and end. It is not permissible to begin a quotation within the text with quotation marks at the beginning, as required, and to continue the quotation in block form, where ending quotation marks are not used. Note the following example of *incorrect usage* in introducing a block quotation:

```
Religion is just "the product of the craving to know
whether these imaginary conceptions have realities
answering to them in some other world than ours."  And
Mill continues, "Belief in a God or Gods
        and in a life after death becomes the canvas which
        every mind . . . covers with such ideal pictures
        as it can either invent or copy.⁶
```

The writer who is aware of this difficulty will avoid introducing in running text a quotation that would have to be completed in block form. A suitable solution, such as the following, is recommended:

```
And Mill continues,
        Belief in a God or Gods and in a life after death
        becomes the canvas which every mind . . . covers
        with such ideal pictures as it can either invent
        or copy.⁶
```

Sometimes the writer must rephrase the text or reconsider the amount to be quoted.

5.32   Two conditions under which a block quotation begins with paragraph indention are considered in 5.30 and 5.33. When those conditions are not present, the first line of the block quotation is indented four spaces from the left marginal line, as shown in the example immediately above. Note that the first (partial) paragraph is the only one in a block quotation of more than one paragraph that may start flush left. All the others must be given paragraph indention, whether the quotation begins with the first sentence of the paragraph or at some point within it.

5.33   If in a quotation of several paragraphs, there is an omission of a full paragraph or more, that omission should be indicated by a period and three ellipsis points at the end of the paragraph preceding the omission. Thus it may be possible that four dots at the end of a paragraph may be followed by three dots at the beginning of the next paragraph, as illustrated in the paragraphs of the following example. This use of two consecutive sets of ellipsis points may occur in a block quotation, but not in a quotation that is run into text:

```
Recalling as an adult the time in his early youth when

a "new conscience" was forming, Merton writes:

        A brand-new conscience was just coming into
     existence as an actual, operating function of a
     soul.  My choices were just about to become
     responsible. . . .
        . . . since no man ever can, or could, live by
     himself and for himself alone, the destinies of
     thousands of other people were bound to be
     affected, some remotely, but some very directly
     and near-at-hand, by my own choices and decisions
     and desires, as my own life would also be formed
     and modified according to theirs.⁷
```

5.34 If it is considered desirable—and one can think of instances in which it would be—to quote in block form fragments of prose which are widely scattered in the original source, a full line of ellipsis points may be used between the individual fragments.

INTERPOLATIONS

5.35 It is sometimes advisable for the writer to insert in a quotation a word or more of explanation, clarification, or correction. All such insertions, or interpolations, must be enclosed in brackets: [ ]. Parentheses may *not* be substituted. Seeing a parenthetic element in a quotation, a reader assumes it was put there by the author of the source quoted. Words enclosed in brackets indicate that the comment was put there by the person quoting the author. If the typewriter has no brackets, insert them in the copy by hand, in black ink.

5.36 To assure the reader that the faulty logic, error in fact, incorrect word, incorrect spelling, or the like, is in the original matter quoted, the Latin word *sic* ("so"; always underlined) may be placed in brackets after the error:

```
Little lizards gambling [sic] in the sun.
```

The use of *sic* should not be overdone. Quotations from sixteenth-century writing, for example, or from obviously archaic or nonstandard writing, should not be strewn with *sic*s.

5.37 Interpolations made for purposes of clarification or correction are illustrated in the following:

"But since these masters [Picasso, Braque, Matisse]
appeared to be . . . rebelling against academic
training, art teaching has itself been discredited."[4]

"The recipient of the Nobel Peace Award for 1961
[1960] was Albert John Luthuli."[5]

UNDERLINING (ITALICS)

5.38 In underlining, or italicizing, words in quotations, follow the guidelines set forth in chapter 4. Words that are not italicized in the original of the matter quoted may be underlined (or italicized) for emphasis desired by the writer of the paper. The source of the change should be indicated to the reader in one of three ways.

1. By a notation enclosed in square brackets and placed immediately after the underlined words:

"This man described to me another large river beyond
the Rocky Mountains, the southern branch [italics
mine] of which he directed me to take."[7]

2. By a parenthetical note following the quotation:

"This man described to me another large river beyond
the Rocky Mountains, the southern branch of which he
directed me to take" (italics mine).[7]

3. By a note. Either a note or the scheme mentioned in (2) is preferable when underlining has been added at two or more points in a quotation.

6   Tables

6.1   Tables efficiently organize and compress data into a standardized form. Because tables must be accurate and easy to read, care is required in spacing, ruling, arrangement of headings, and placing of the tables with respect to the text. Because they supplement the text, tables should be located within the text or in an appendix, unless they occupy a complete apparatus of their own.

6.2   Computer software that includes functions for managing spread sheets, columnar adjustments, and other tabulation formats can be useful for designing tables. Some programs include capabilities for automatic rule generation and insertion of special characters for joining horizontal and vertical lines, such as "corners," although tables designed using software without such features could be treated just as typewritten tables, with vertical rules inserted by hand (see 7.27–32). For more information on the use of software to compose tables and set them in text, see 13.26–27.

PLANNING AND CONSTRUCTING STATISTICAL TABLES

6.3 Most tables constructed to present information in numerical form—percentages, tallies of occurrences, amounts of money, and the like—are known as statistical tables. As a simple example, say that a scholar has completed a survey on smoking among American adults, a survey incorporating information on the respondents' date of birth, sex, income, social background, etc., and wishes to present some of the data in tabular form. The survey has produced responses from 7,308 individuals—3,362 males and 3,946 females, all eighteen or over.

6.4 In any one table, a single category of responses is always at the center of attention. The table is constructed to illustrate the variations in that category of responses (the dependent variable) with respect to some other set or sets of data (independent variables). Here the dependent variable would be whether or not the respondent smoked, and the independent variable could be any of several other categories or facts concerning the respondent, say the person's sex. Classifying responses according to these two variables might then result in the simple array shown in table 1. (The survey, needless to say, is imaginary, and all the data derived from it are entirely hypothetical.)

Table 1.--Smokers and Nonsmokers, by Sex

	Smoke	Don't Smoke	Total
Males	1,258	2,104	3,362
Females	1,194	2,752	3,946
Total	2,452	4,856	7,308

6.5 An array of raw data like this is, however, relatively useless. For purposes of comparison the data must be presented in terms of percentages. This has been done in table 2. In any statistical table employing percentages (or other proportional figures) the compiler should always give the finite number—the *data base,* or *N*—from which the percentages are derived. Here *N* is given in a separate column, but other arrangements are also appropriate (see table 6).

6.6   Table 2 represents an extremely simple statistical situation. Both the independent variable (sex) and the dependent variable (smoke/don't smoke) are *dichotomies*—entities that divide into two mutually exclusive categories. When either variable consists of more than two categories, tabular presentation necessarily becomes more complex.

Table 2.--Smokers and Nonsmokers, by Sex

	N	Smoke	Don't Smoke
Males	3,362	37.4%	62.6%
Females	3,946	30.3%	69.7%
Total	7,308	33.6%	66.4%

6.7   Say the researcher wishes to present the data in terms of age rather than sex. For this purpose birth dates would be grouped by years or spans of years to represent respondents' ages at the time of the survey, and these groups would be divided according to the smoke/don't smoke dichotomy. The results could be presented as in table 3. Here age is broken down into four categories, the first three of which consist of fifteen-year spans, but smaller groupings could be used.

Table 3.--Smoking among American Adults, by Age

Age	N	Smoke (%)	Don't Smoke (%)
18–32	1,722	30.6	69.4
33–47	2,012	37.1	62.9
48–62	1,928	35.2	64.8
63+	1,646	30.5	69.5
Total N	7,308		

6.8   If the writer wishes to present the data by both age and sex, the responses would be subdivided once more. The data might then be presented as in table 4.

Table 4.--Smoking among American Adults, by Age and Sex

Age and Sex	N	Smoke (%)	Don't Smoke (%)
Males			
18-32	792	30.0	70.0
33-47	926	44.9	55.1
48-62	886	34.5	65.5
63+	758	39.3	60.7
Total (males)	3,362		
Females			
18-32	930	31.0	69.0
33-47	1,086	30.4	69.6
48-62	1,042	35.7	64.3
63+	888	23.0	77.0
Total (females)	3,946		
Total (both)	7,308		

6.9   Suppose respondents were asked other questions about smoking—whether they had quit smoking or ever tried to quit and (if they smoked at all) whether or not they smoked cigarettes. Presenting these data in meaningful ways would involve expanding the tabular display and making it more complicated.

6.10   Take the data on quitting smoking. If these statistics are to be presented in connection with age and sex as the independent variables, they might be arranged as in table 5. Here each half of the basic smoke/don't smoke dichotomy has been further split according to whether the respondent has quit smoking or tried to quit. *N* for each age group also must be split between smokers and nonsmokers. Note that each column of *N*s applies to the two columns immediately to the right of it.

6.11   Finally, let us say, the writer wants to present data on cigarette smoking in connection with an element of social background—whether the respondent came from a rural, small-town, or big-city environment—as well as age and sex. (The question eliciting this response would of course have to be a definite one—like ''Which of these categories comes closest to the type of

Table 5.--Smoking History of American Adults, by Age and Sex

	Smoke			Don't Smoke		
	N	Have Tried to Quit (%)	Never Tried to Quit	N	Never Smoked Regularly (%)	Quit Successfully
Males						
18-32	238	15.1	84.9	554	93.9	6.1
33-47	416	28.8	71.2	510	72.2	27.8
48-62	306	60.1	39.9	580	46.6	53.4
63+	298	88.6	11.4	460	38.7	61.3
Total (males)	1,258	48.0	52.0	2,104	63.5	36.5
Females						
18-32	288	18.8	81.2	642	40.3	59.7
33-47	330	28.5	71.5	756	68.5	31.5
48-62	372	62.4	37.6	670	50.4	49.6
63+	204	89.2	10.8	684	41.8	58.2
Total (females)	1,194	47.1	52.9	2,752	62.6	37.4
Total (both)	2,452	47.6	52.4	4,856	45.2	54.8

place you were living in when you were sixteen years old?''—
followed by a listing of various kinds of locales.) Responses are
first sorted by age and sex, as for table 4, and then by background of the respondent—with ''Don't know'' answers omitted. The twenty-four groups created by dividing the responses in
this manner constitute the data bases for the final dichotomy into
those who smoke cigarettes and everybody else, though only the
smokers need to be tabulated (table 6). As before, the total in
each category is expressed as a percentage of *N*. Here it is impractical to show *N*s in columns of their own, and so another

Table 6.--Smoking among Adult Americans, by Type of
Background, Urban or Rural

	Country (%)	Town, Small City (%)	Big City & Suburbs (%)
Males			
18-32	26.5 (98)	29.6 (294)	29.9 (398)
33-47	34.6 (153)	41.2 (306)	43.0 (460)
48-62	28.6 (220)	31.4 (385)	34.1 (270)
63+	34.8 (273)	35.1 (279)	36.5 (189)
Total (males)	31.8 (744)	34.2 (1,264)	36.3 (1,317)
Females			
18-32	28.4 (116)	31.0 (348)	31.5 (463)
33-47	27.9 (179)	30.6 (359)	31.1 (540)
48-62	27.7 (260)	35.8 (450)	42.3 (319)
63+	21.5 (329)	23.1 (325)	25.8 (213)
Total (females)	25.6 (884)	30.6 (1,482)	32.8 (1,535)
Total (both)	28.4 (1,628)	32.2 (2,746)	34.4 (2,852)

Note: Figures in parentheses are base *N*s for the adjacent
percentages. Total *N* = 7,226 (3,325 males, 3,901 females).
Respondents (82) who did not know where they were living at
age 16 have been excluded from the data base.

device has been adopted: the N for each category is shown in parentheses below and slightly to the right of the percentage figure. Other arrangements, like that of table 5, are possible, but this is the one preferred by most people who work with statistics.

ARRANGEMENT OF THE ELEMENTS

6.12 The conventions governing the arrangement of the various elements of a statistical table, though not immutable, are accepted by many who make frequent use of them. Consequently, follow existing fashion when it comes to the basics of tabular presentation.

Numbering

6.13 Every table should be given an arabic number and a title, even though there may be few tables in the paper. (A very simple tabulation—e.g., five or six figures arranged in two columns—introduced in such a way that a caption seems unnecessary need not be given a number or a caption.) The order in which the tables are mentioned in the text determines the numbering. Enumeration of tables continues straight through the text.

6.14 Tables in an appendix should be numbered consecutively with the tables in the text. That is, if the last table in the text is table 52, the first table in the appendix is table 53.

6.15 All text references to a table should be by number, not by an introductory phrase such as "in the following table."

6.16 The most elegant way to refer to a table is by a simple reference helping the reader locate relevant data:

The percentages in table 5 illustrate this margin of error.

A majority of voters was absent during the election (see table 4).

In table 25, the rates increase markedly.

6.17 Numbered references make it possible to set the table at the end of the page or the paragraph, or on a separate page, whatever its size permits.

POSITION

6.18   Ideally, each table should be placed as close to the first reference
to it as possible. If space permits, however, it is best to finish
the paragraph of text in which the reference occurs before inserting the table (see table 13, sample 14.38). If a table cannot
be accommodated in the remaining space available for it on a
given page, continue the text to make a full page and place the
table at the top of the next page.

6.19   If a table appears on a text page, three blank lines should be left
above and three blank lines below each table (i.e., the table
number is typed on the fourth line following the text, and the
text is continued on the fourth line below the bottom rule or the
table's notes, as in table 13, sample 14.38).

SIZE AND SHAPE

6.20   In most tables the columns run the long way on the page. A
table may occupy the full width of the page or, if the number
and width of columns permit, less than the full width. In either
case each table must be centered horizontally upon the page.

LONG AND NARROW

6.21   When a table is long and narrow, space may be saved by dou-
bling up—dividing it in equal parts and placing them side by
side (see table 8, sample 14.33). Note the vertical double line
separating the two parts.

WIDE

6.22   If a table is too wide for the page, it should be turned lengthwise
(broadside table; see table 12, sample 14.37)—that is, the paper
is put in the typewriter sideways, and the table is typed so that
the columns run the short way of the paper, or it is entered using
software that creates broadsides. No text should be placed on a
page containing a broadside table. The page number appears in
its usual place, whether the paper is prepared on a typewriter or
a computer system.

6.23   If too wide to be accommodated broadside, a table may be arranged on two facing pages. This is done physically by turning
the first page over so that the text is on the back and thus faces
the next page (the other side of the first page, now the front,
remains blank). If the paper is to be bound, a note to the binder,

in addition to the correct placement of the pages, will insure accurate results. The parts of the table must be of the same dimensions on both pages, and special care is required to insure that the appropriate figure in each column is exactly in line with the item in the stub (i.e., first column) to which it belongs. Some software will not automatically generate a wide table on facing pages, but it may be possible to generate two tables that could be positioned on opposite pages and then photocopied. A better solution might be to generate the table in smaller type size or to reduce a table photographically once it has been printed in standard pica or elite. This reduction could then be mounted on the page and photocopied, and its page number would then be typed in the upper right-hand corner. The type size in reductions should be large enough to be legible in the microfilm reproduction of a thesis or dissertation.

6.24 Tables too wide to be accommodated on the 8½-by-11-inch page in the ways described above may be typed on a larger sheet and then folded, though this method is less satisfactory for dissertations that must be bound (see 7.44–46).

CONTINUING LONG

6.25 Long tables may be continued from page to page. The table number and the caption are placed at the beginning of the table; the table number only on succeeding pages, written, for example, "Table 2—Continued." Ordinarily, the column headings are repeated on every page, except that in a continued broadside table in which the pages face each other, the headings need not be repeated on the second page (and the fourth, sixth, etc.). In a table that is continued, the bottom rule is omitted except on the last page, at the end of the table.

TITLE

6.26 It is necessary to give each numbered table a title. If a very brief tabulation is introduced in such a way that a title seems unnecessary, the tabulation should not be given a table number (see 6.13).

6.27 Place the table number at the upper left margin of the table; add a period and a dash and continue with the title, giving the first and all succeeding full lines the full width of the table and centering the last, shorter line. The title of the table may be capitalized either headline style (see 4.6–8) or sentence style (see 4.9):

```
    Table 21.--Probable rate of damage per foot-candle
   for thirty light sources expressed in percentage
                relative to zenith day
```

Retain one style of capitalization in table titles consistently throughout the paper.

6.28 In a traditional, alternative style, the number, in arabic numerals, and the word *table,* in uppercase, are centered. A blank line follows this, and the table title is then centered in uppercase, with any subheading centered on the next line and capitalized headline style. If a title is longer than the width of the table, set it in two or more lines, arranged in inverted pyramid form and single-spaced (see tables 7–10 and 12, samples 14.32–35 and 14.37). If table titles contain chemical, physical, or mathematical expressions conventionally expressed in lowercase rather than uppercase, these expressions should remain in lowercase, even though the rest of the title is in uppercase, or follow the style recommended in 6.27, but use one style consistently throughout a paper.

6.29 The title, set above the body of the table, should identify the table briefly. It should not furnish background information or describe the results illustrated by the table. A title like the following:

```
Table 1.--Effect of DMSO on Arthritic Rats and
Nonarthritic Rats after 20, 60, and 90 Days
                of Treatment
```

should be pared down to something like

```
Effect of DMSO on Rats
```

The column headings indicating 20, 60, and 90 days and the horizontal rows for arthritic and nonarthritic rats will give the results. The kind of editorial comment implied by a title like

```
High Degree of Recidivism among Reform School Parolees
```

should be eliminated:

```
Recidivism among Reform School Parolees
```

A table should merely give facts—discussion and comment being reserved for the text.

6.30 Grammatically, the title should be substantival in form. Relative clauses should be avoided in favor of participles. Not

```
Number of Families That Subscribe to Weekly News
Magazines
```

but rather,

`Families Subscribing to Weekly News Magazines`

6.31 A minor point of usage: in conservative practice, *percent* is still not considered a noun, although colloquially it is commonly so used. Accordingly, a title reading

`Percent of cases diagnosed correctly`

should preferably be made to read

`Percentage [or Proportion] of cases diagnosed`
`correctly`

6.32 The table title may carry a subheading, usually enclosed in parentheses:

`Table 36.——Investment in Automobiles since 1900`
`            (In Thousands of Dollars)`

Indication of the number of individuals in a group under consideration (for example, $N = 253$) may be treated as a subheading if it applies to the whole table.

COLUMN HEADINGS

6.33 A table must have at least two columns and usually has more. The columns carry *headings* (or *heads*—the terms are synonymous) at the top, brief indications of the material in the columns. These were formerly called *boxheadings* or *boxheads*, from the fact that in a fully ruled table they were enclosed in rectangles of rules, or *boxes*. The term is occasionally still heard.

6.34 Like the table title, the column headings are substantival in form, and the same grammatical strictures apply to them. If the first column of a table (the *stub*, discussed below) carries a heading, it should be singular in number. The other headings may be singular or plural according to sense.

6.35 Column heads may carry subheadings when they are needed, usually to indicate the unit of measurement employed in the column. Subheadings are normally enclosed in parentheses; abbreviations, if used consistently throughout a series of tables, are acceptable: ($), (lb.), (%), (mi.), (x 100 km), (millions), and so on. If the columns of a table must be numbered for purposes of text reference, arabic numerals are set in parentheses as subheads.

6.36 The nature of tabular matter sometimes demands two or more levels of headings, and then *decked heads* must be used. A decked head consists of a *spanner head* and the two or more column heads to which it applies. A horizontal rule is set between spanner and column heads to show what columns the spanner applies to (see table 9, sample 14.34). Decked heads should seldom exceed two levels, as larger ones are hard to follow down the columns of an unruled table.

6.37 Excessive decking of the heads can sometimes be avoided by using a *cut-in head*—a head that cuts across the statistical columns of the table and applies to all the tabular matter lying below it. For an example of cut-in heads, see table 11, sample 14.36.

6.38 In typing column heads, leave at least two spaces between the longest lines in adjacent headings. The width of the column headings generally determines the total width of a table, so they should be kept as brief as possible. Use either headline- or sentence-style capitalization, and type runover lines flush left. Spanner and cut-in heads, however, must be centered above the columns they pertain to. The column head with the most lines defines the vertical space available for all the heads. In typing, it is simplest to align the last lines of all the other heads horizontally with the last line of the longest one. Any subheads are typed on the line below this one. Rules running the full width of the table are customarily typed or drawn above and below the column heads and any spanners used. The rule below a spanner head is exactly as wide as the column headings spanned, and the rules above and below a cut-in head are exactly as wide as the column heads they apply to (usually just the statistical columns but sometimes the first, or stub, column as well, as in table 11, sample 14.36).

STUB

6.39 The left-hand column of a table, known as the stub, has no column heading unless one is necessary for identification. Items in the stub should be capitalized sentence style, and no periods are used at the ends of items. If items require runover lines, the items are single-spaced and runovers indented three spaces. When an item is subdivided, however, the subdivisions are indented three spaces and any runovers are indented five spaces:

```
Relative to issue
     price
   1923-27  . . .
   1949-55  . . .
```

Another way to show subdivision in a stub is to underline the main entry but not the subdivisions, aligning all at the left (table 10, sample 14.35).

6.40 Consistency within the stub is also important. Items that are logically similar should be treated similarly: Authors, Publishers, Printers, *not* Authors, Publishing concerns, Operates printshop. In a series of tables, the same item should always bear the same name in the stub: the Union of Soviet Socialist Republics, for instance, should not appear as USSR in one table and Soviet Union in another.

6.41 If a *Total, Mean,* or *Average* appears in the stub, the word should be indented two spaces more than the greatest indention above it. If both *Total* and *Grand Total* are given, the latter is indented further.

6.42 If the open space between the end of a line in the stub and the columnar matter to which it refers is such that the eye does not move easily from one to the other, period leaders (spaced periods) may be used to connect the two (see 3.59).

OMISSIONS

6.43 In a long column of figures, zero preceding a decimal point may be omitted from all entries except the first and the last. Degree and dollar signs (°, $) must appear in the entry at the top of each column where relevant and after every break in a column, such as rules above totals and cut-in headings.

6.44 If all the figures in a table are in thousands or millions, space may be saved by omitting the relevant zeroes and noting the fact at the end of the title, as, for example, "(Figures in millions)". (See table 10, sample 14.35.)

6.45 A blank space in a column should be indicated by spaced period leaders, which should be at least three in number and centered with respect to the longest number in the column (see table 9, sample 14.34) or the number necessary to occupy the full width of the column. Two hyphens may also be used. Use one of these styles consistently.

ALIGNMENT

6.46 The items in the stub should be aligned with their related items in the columns. If the stub item occupies more than one line and the column entry one, align on the last line of the stub (see table 9, sample 14.34); if both contain more than one line, align on the first line and omit leaders:

```
Mean water content
    (percent) . . . . . . . . . 69.6
```

But:

```
C2 (35"-50"+) (fresh      Dark grayish brown
    till, slightly          (10 YR 4/2) boul-
    oxidized)               dery loamy sand;
                            massive structure;
                            pH of 6.42
```

6.47 In a column of figures, align all decimal points and commas. Note that every figure of 1,000 or more must use one or more commas (see 2.66) unless the entire table consists of four-digit figures. Align also dollar signs and plus, minus, plus-minus, and equals signs. When the number of digits varies, allow for the longest number. Some word-processing programs will align columns by decimal points.

ABBREVIATIONS AND SYMBOLS IN TABLES

6.48 Although discouraged for the most part in text, abbreviations and symbols are legitimate space-savers in column and cut-in headings and in the main body of tables, but not in titles (except for mathematical and chemical symbols). Standard abbreviations should be used if they exist; if they do not, the writer may devise them, explaining them in a note or key unless they are self-explanatory. Abbreviations must be consistent for all tables.

6.49 Symbols that cannot be made with the typewriter or printer should be inserted by hand, using permanent black ink and a mechanical pen (see 7.27–32).

FOOTNOTES TO TABLES

6.50 Footnotes to a table are of four general kinds and should appear in this order: (1) source notes, (2) other general notes, (3) notes on specific parts of the table, and (4) notes on level of probability.

6.51   If data for a table are not the writer's own but are taken from another source, the writer will wish to include a source note, introduced by the word *Source(s),* followed by a colon:

```
Source: Michael H. Day, Guide to Fossil Man, 3d ed.
(Chicago: University of Chicago Press, 1977), 291-304.
```

6.52   Other unnumbered notes, applying to the table as a whole, follow and are introduced by the word *Note(s),* followed by a colon. These might include remarks on reliability of the data presented or on how they were gathered or handled; when practical, such notes should be gathered into one paragraph. If the entire table is reproduced without change from another source, credit is best given in a general note such as that illustrated in the second of the following examples:

```
Notes: Since data were not available for all items on
all individuals, there is some disparity in the
totals.  This table may be compared with table 14,
which presents similar data for Cincinnati, Ohio.

Note: Reprinted, by permission of the publisher, from
Ana-Maria Rizzuto, "Freud, God, the Devil, and the
Theory of Object Representation," International Review
of Psycho-Analysis 31 (1976): 165.
```

6.53   For notes on specific parts of a table, superior letters, beginning over again in each table with *a,* are usually employed as reference marks. They may be used on the column headings, the stub items, and the body of the table, but not on the table number or title. Any note applying to the number or title would be a general note and should be so treated. The reference marks are placed on the table in whatever order the reader will find easiest to follow, normally beginning at the upper left and extending across the table and downward, row by row. The same mark may be used on two or more elements if the corresponding note applies to them.

6.54   Footnotes to tables must not be numbered in the same series as text notes. A new series of reference numbers, or symbols, is begun for each table.

6.55   For a table consisting only of words, superior numbers could be used as reference marks (though even here letters are quite usual); and for a table that includes mathematical or chemical equations, a series of arbitrary symbols may be used, because of the danger of mistaking letters or figures for exponents. The series is as follows:

* (asterisk or star), † (dagger), ‡ (double dagger),
§ (section mark), ‖ (parallels), # (number sign)

When more symbols are needed, these may be doubled and tripled in the same sequence:

**, ††, ‡‡, §§, ‖ ‖, ##,
***, †††, ‡‡‡, §§§, ‖ ‖ ‖, ###

6.56   In notes to tables, the reference marks—letters, numbers, or symbols—are conventionally placed in superior position, not on the line as numbers may be in endnotes, for example. The reason for this may be not simple conservatism but a desire to avoid the appearance of an enumeration when lettered or numbered notes follow a general note to a table.

6.57   If a table contains values for which levels of probability are given, a fourth type of note is used, following the other specific notes. By convention, asterisks are used for these notes, both on the value in the body of the table and before the note at the foot. A single asterisk is used for the lowest level of probability, two for the next higher, and so on, with the specific levels being given in the notes below:

* $p < .05$.

** $p < .01$.

*** $p < .001$.

6.58   Footnotes are typed below the body of the table, and flush left. Double-space between items, single-space within. Leave a blank line between the rule separating table from notes and the first note. Three blank lines separate notes from the continuation of the text following a table, if any.

RULING

6.59   Since some institutions specify that all tables be ruled, and others allow considerable latitude, it is advisable for the student to consult the appropriate staff member. The following suggestions are for those who must make their own decisions. In general, the fewer vertical rules the better.

6.60   Two-column tables are best left without any rules (see table 7, sample 14.32). In general, all tables of more than two columns may carry vertical rules. It is permissible, however, to omit the rules between columns covered by a spanner heading (see table 9, sample 14.34), provided that the columns are not too close together. In table 9, sample 14.34, omission of a rule between columns 1 and 2 and between columns 3 and 4 is allowable; but in table 11, sample 14.36, the columns of figures are so close together that rules are important for ease of reading, and therefore are not omitted. It is increasingly common to omit all vertical rules, even in very large tables, and this is permissible if columns are appropriately spaced. Such tables are termed "open-style" (see tables 5 and 6).

6.61 Each ruled table should have either a single or a double horizontal rule at the top, above the heading, and a single horizontal rule at the bottom, or end, of the table. There are no vertical rules at the sides of a table.

6.62 Blank space should be left on all sides of a column heading. Never begin a heading on the line immediately below the rule, and never begin a rule on the same line as a heading (thus giving the effect of underlined words).

6.63 A horizontal rule should be typed above totals at the feet of columns, across the columns but not extending through the stub (see table 9, sample 14.34). Subtotals, grand totals, means, and averages are similarly handled.

6.64 Horizontal rules can be made with the underscoring key of the typewriter or computer keyboard. A double rule is typed by turning the knob of the typewriter roller just slightly before typing the second line. If the carriage of the typewriter takes the paper the long way, all the rules may be made with the typewriter. But using the typewriter to make vertical rules requires special care if columns are only one or two spaces apart. Those using computer systems to prepare tables should consult the user's manuals.

6.65 If vertical rules are made by hand, they should first be added to the typed or printed copy in very light, thin pencil and then retraced, using a mechanical pen with black ink and a rule with ink-absorbing edge. Press-apply lines that offer a thin black adhesive line may also be placed along the pencil line. These materials will reproduce without appearing darker than the text or blurring.

7 Illustrations

7.1 Illustrative materials may consist of drawings, paintings, photographs, charts, graphs, and maps. Such illustrations are also called *figures*.

LINE AND CONTINUOUS-TONE COPY

7.2 Artwork containing only black and white, with no shading—a pen-and-ink drawing, for instance, or a bar chart—is known as *line copy*. Artwork that does contain shading—such as a painting, a wash drawing, or a photograph—is known as *continuous-tone copy* or, less accurately, *halftone copy*.

7.3 It is not within the scope of this manual to give advice on the inclusion of illustrative materials or on what types to use or, except in general terms, to give instructions on their presentation. These matters are fully treated in a number of specialized books and manuals. One of the best among them is Frances W. Zweifel's *A Handbook of Biological Illustration* (Chicago: University of Chicago Press, 2d ed., 1988). Although, as the title implies, the emphasis is on biological illustrations, the treatment of many topics is equally helpful in other fields. Some general principles, however, do need to be summarized here to bring the preparation of illustrative materials for a paper into harmony with that of the text.

POSITION

7.4 Illustrations, especially graphs and charts, should be placed as close as possible to their first references in the text. Like tables, they should be referred to by number so that their exact placement is flexible (see 6.13–17). In some papers there may be sound reasons for grouping all the illustrations, if they are of one type, at the end of the paper or in an appendix (see 1.38).

FULL-PAGE ILLUSTRATIONS

7.5 When illustrative materials are too large to be included in the text and are consequently placed on pages by themselves, these pages are numbered consecutively with the textual matter. It is not permissible to give them supplementary numbers (e.g., page 45*a*) after the text has been numbered. A folded map or chart is numbered in the center at the top of the exposed fold (see also 7.44–46).

7.6 Pages of illustrations placed together at the end of the paper should follow the pagination of the text.

MARGINS

7.7 A margin of at least one inch should be allowed on all four sides of a page carrying illustrative material. More is permissible and is required on the left-hand margin for papers that are to be bound, such as theses and dissertations. The number of the illustration and its caption, or legend—everything but the number of the page—must fall within the margins (for margins when mounting material, see 7.41).

Two or More Illustrations on a Page

7.8   Two or more illustrations may appear on the same page, each with its number and legend. Also, two or more related illustrations may be placed on the same page, the group as a whole given a number and a legend, and the individual illustrations identified by letter alone (*a, b,* etc.) or by letter and legend. If space is not sufficient below the individual illustrations for both letter and legend, each illustration may simply be lettered, and letters and legends either grouped at the foot of the page or typed on the opposite page. In the latter instance, the page with the legend is turned over to face the illustration, so that the reader will see illustration and legend on facing pages (see also 6.23). The page facing the illustration is counted in the numbering of the paper but no page number appears on it.

Broadsides

7.9   A wide illustration may be placed broadside on the page, with the top at the binding (left) side. The legend, with its number, should appear below the illustration so that it reads vertically up the page. The page number is in its normal position (see sample 14.30). This same arrangement may be used for a group of illustrations.

Position of Legend

7.10   Some illustrations—maps in particular—carry printed or hand-lettered headings at the top or the side of the illustration. In such a case, only the spelled-out word *Figure* and the number of the illustration is centered below it.

Position of Key or Scale

7.11   A key or scale (of miles, inches, millimeters, etc.), if included, should preferably be placed in a convenient space beside or within the illustration rather than below it.

Position of Number and Legend

7.12   If the space below an illustration is not sufficient to carry the number and legend and still allow the one-inch margin at the bottom of the page, the number and legend may be placed within the illustration. If there is not enough space within the illustration, number and legend may be placed on the opposite page (see 6.23 and 7.8).

FIGURE NUMBERS AND LEGENDS

7.13   Even if a paper contains several types of illustrations, such as maps, charts, diagrams, and graphs, it is desirable to label them all as figures and number them consecutively, using arabic numerals:

Fig. 43   Figure 2

7.14   A legend follows the number; this may be in the form of a title, or caption:

Fig. 2.   Block diagram of Fern Lake

The legend is frequently in the form of an explanation consisting of a sentence or more (not necessarily grammatically complete sentences) of explanation. Here the punctuation and capitalization follow ordinary sentence style:

Fig. 9.   Relationship between number of buds or leaf scars, number of branches subsequently produced, and length of shoots. Small numbers identify multiple observations of same value.

7.15   The legend should be single-spaced and may run the width of the illustration. Short legends are centered.

Identifying Parts of an Illustration

7.16   Such words as *top, bottom, left, right, above, below, left to right, clockwise from left,* and the like, are frequently used in legends to identify individual subjects in an illustration or parts of a composite. These are underlined, or italicized, and usually precede rather than follow the phrase identifying the object or person:

Fig. 4.   <u>Above left</u>, William Livingston; <u>right</u>, Henry Brockholst Livingston; <u>below left</u>, John Jay; <u>right</u>, Sarah Livingston Jay.

If a list follows the introductory tag, a colon rather than a comma is preferred:

<u>Left to right</u>: Dean Acheson, Harry Hopkins, President Roosevelt, Harold Ickes.

7.17 Letters of the Latin alphabet, abbreviations, and symbols are all used as keys for identifying parts of a figure. When such a key is referred to in a legend, the form used in the legend should reflect as closely as possible the form used in the figure itself. If capital letters are used in the figure, capitals should be used in the legend, and so on. In the legend, however, the key should always be underlined, or italicized, whatever emphasis may be employed in the figure:

Fig. 5. Four types of Hawaiian fishhooks: <u>a</u>, barbed hook of tortoise shell; <u>b</u>, trolling hook with pearl shell lure and point of human bone; <u>c</u>, octopus lure with cowrie shell, stone sinker, and large bone hook; <u>d</u>, barbed hook of human thigh bone.

Fig. 6. Facial traits of (<u>A</u>) <u>Propithecus verreauxi verreauxi</u> and (<u>B</u>) <u>Lemur catta</u>, which vary from one individual to the next; <u>ea</u>, ear; <u>ca</u>, cap; <u>cpl</u>, capline; <u>br</u>, brow.

When symbols are used in a figure, use of the same symbols in the legend requires the least effort of the reader:

Fig. 7. Dependence of half-life on atomic weight for elements in the radium-uranium region: ○ = even α-emitters; ● = odd α-emitters; □ = isotopes capable of K-capture or β-decay.

If the symbols are not available, they must then be described:

Fig. 8. Dependence of half-life on atomic weight for elements in the radium-uranium region: <u>open circles</u>, even alpha-emitters; <u>solid circles</u>, odd alpha-emitters; <u>open squares</u>, isotopes capable of <u>K</u>-capture or beta-decay.

In the above example, note also that in a scientific context the names of the Greek letters may usually be substituted for the letters themselves.

CREDIT LINES AND PERMISSIONS

7.18 A brief statement of the source of the illustration may be necessary or appropriate. The only significant exception is an illustration (chart, graph, drawing, photograph, etc.) of the writer's own creation.

7.19   Illustrative material in copyright, whether published or unpublished, may require permission of the copyright owner before it can be reproduced even in a dissertation. It is the writer's responsibility to determine what is in copyright and to obtain permission to reproduce it.

7.20   The credit line may run at the end of the legend, usually in parentheses, or the pertinent facts may be worked into the text of the legend copy. If most or all of the illustrations are from a single source, that fact may be stated in the preface or acknowledgments.

PREVIOUSLY PUBLISHED MATERIAL

7.21   Use of an illustration reproduced from a source protected by copyright may require formal permission from the copyright holder. Consult the publisher or the holder of the rights to the illustration to determine whether to seek or obtain permission (see 5.1). There is no fixed style for such credit lines, but they should be consistent and, for a work of book length, should include a page number, figure number, or the like. A short form is appropriate if the work from which the illustration has been taken is listed in the bibliography or reference list. The person who grants permission to reproduce the illustration may, however, specify a certain form of credit including the full facts of publication and even a copyright notice. The following example shows a credit within the caption for a kinship diagram:

```
Reprinted, by permission, from Wagner, Curse of Souw,
82.
```

A credit within the caption for a portrait engraving:

```
From a drawing by J. Webber for Cook's Voyage to the
Pacific Ocean, 1776-1780, reprinted, by permission of
the writer, from Edwin H. Bryan, Jr., Ancient Hawaiian
Life (Honolulu, 1938), 10.
```

A credit within the caption for a photograph of a lemur:

```
Reprinted, by permission, from Alison Jolly, Lemur
Behavior, pl. 6. Photograph by C. H. Fraser Rowell.
© 1966 by the University of Chicago.
```

7.22   Illustrations may be reproduced from published works without seeking permission if the work is in the public domain. A work is in the public domain if it was never in copyright (as is true of most publications of the United States government) or if the copyright has run full term and lapsed. Even though permission is not required, it is good policy to use a credit line out of deference to the reader as well as the creator of the material.

Illustration by Joseph Pennell for Henry James, English Hours (Boston, 1905), facing p. 82.

Reprinted from John D. Shortridge, Italian Harpsichord Building in the Sixteenth and Seventeenth Centuries, U.S. National Museum Bulletin 225 (Washington, n.d.).

ORIGINAL MATERIAL

7.23   It was mentioned above that any illustrations that are the writer's own do not need credit lines. This is not to say, however, that credit lines should *not* be used, if there is some reason for the inclusion. There are often reasons apart from vanity for appending a credit line to an illustration of the writer's own creation. If, for example, all but a few of the illustrations are from one source and this source is acknowledged in the preliminaries, it would be appropriate to place under a photograph taken by the writer a line reading:

Photograph by the author

Or:

Photo by author

Somewhat different is the case of material commissioned by the writer, usually maps, photographs, or drawings. Here, professional courtesy dictates mention of the creator of the material either in the preliminaries or below each piece, where the credit line might read as follows:

Map by Gerald F. Pyle
Photograph by James L. Ballard
Drawing by Joseph E. Alderfer

If a map or drawing is signed and the signature is reproduced, nothing further is needed, of course.

7.24   For material that the writer has obtained free of charge and without restrictions on its use, a credit line is again seldom legally required but usually appended nonetheless. In such credit lines it is appropriate to use the word *courtesy:*

Photograph courtesy of Ford Motor Company

Or:

Courtesy Ford Motor Co.

If the name of the photographer is well known, or if the supplier of the print requests it, the photographer's name may also be given:

Photograph by Henri Cartier-Bresson, courtesy of the Museum of Modern Art

7.25 Agency material—photographs and reproductions of prints, drawings, paintings, and the like, obtained from a commercial agency—usually require a credit line. The contract or bill of sale will specify what is expected. Typical credits:

Woodcut from Historical Pictures Service, Chicago
Photograph from Wide World Photos

7.26 Sometimes a writer does not directly reproduce another's material but nonetheless is indebted to that person. The writer may, for example, use data from a table in another book to construct a chart, or revise another's graph with fresh data, or redraw a figure with or without significant changes. In such situations, although the writer's material is technically original, a credit line is in order. Again, there is no set form. Thus for a chart based on a table in another work, the credit line might read

Data from John F. Witte, Democracy, Authority, and Alienation in Work (Chicago: University of Chicago Press, 1980), table 10

If the book is fully listed elsewhere in the paper, the citation could be

Data from Witte, Democracy, Authority, and Alienation in Work, table 10

Or:

Data from Witte 1980, table 10

PREPARATION

7.27 Since many colleges and universities retain graphic arts departments for the purpose of preparing dissertation- and publication-quality illustrations, only professional artwork now has a place in theses, dissertations, and the articles for professional journals or other scholarly publications that are drawn from theses and dissertations.

7.28 In the absence of such services or in the event that one is preparing a term paper, for example, artwork can be rendered professionally by using the materials graphic artists now use. Most are available at art supply stores.

7.29   Color should not be used in a thesis or dissertation for a university or college that requires microfilm reproduction of such papers. A large selection of press-apply tones has made color in all research papers, except those in which art, medical, and otherwise color-determined research is involved, unnecessary, impractical, and too costly for many student papers. When microfilm reproduction is not required, color may be used for line drawings if suitable photoduplicating equipment is available, and color photographs may be included when the colors in them are absolutely necessary for the paper. When color or black-and-white photographs are required, they may be mounted individually in each copy of the paper or developed on light-weight photographic paper, leaving a suitable white margin.

7.30   To design linear graphs, charts, and the like, use graph paper with lines that disappear in photoduplication, and draw on it with mechanical pencils and mechanical pens using black ink. Lightly draw in all lines first, using a mechanical pencil. Then draw over these lightly penciled lines with a mechanical pen using black ink, resting it against a double-ink edge (to prevent blurring of lines). Or instead, a press-apply line may be placed over the lightly penciled one. Press-apply tones and lines are available in many varieties. Their advantage over inked tones and lines is that they do not smudge or blur, and they can be easily moved before they are burnished into place.

7.31   Add letters, symbols, curves, and numbers only after the inked or taped lines (and tones, if any) are in place. Templates and adjustable curves may be used with mechanical pens, using black ink, or one of the many press-apply forms of lettering, numbers, and symbols may be used. Templates and press-apply forms are available in many typefaces and a variety of point sizes.

7.32   It is usually better to render a drawing larger than it will be on the page and then reduce it onto acid-free paper (see 13.50 for a description of this paper stock) through either photographic or photoduplicating methods, especially when fine detail must be shown in the illustration.

MAPS

7.33   Many kinds of maps are available ready made, and some may serve satisfactorily with no additions except page and figure numbers and, possibly, a caption (see sample 14.30). Some may be used as base maps, with crosshatching, outlining of specific areas, and figures or letters superimposed. Unless crosshatching of only a small area is required, handwork should not be attempted. Press-apply tones are available in many useful designs. The use of such products, however, presupposes photographic reproduction for presentation in the paper (see 13.51–52).

7.34 Maps often need to be executed entirely by hand. In the fields of geography and geology, where knowledge of maps and map making is an important aspect of the student's training, handmade maps in theses and dissertations are likely to be a requirement.

COMPUTER GRAPHICS

7.35 Computer software that converts raw laboratory data into conventional graphics with corresponding legends is available, and some programs can produce graphs with labeled axes, interval marks, and symbols as well as curves or histograms. Before using such a program to produce an illustration, consult either the user's manual or a computer adviser so that the artwork will have the proper dimensions for the paper or for photoduplication, microfilming, and any reduction needed to bring such an illustration within the specifications set by a department or discipline. Continuous-tone illustrations (color and black-and-white), animations, and three-dimensional subjects may also be technically feasible on computers, and such illustrations would be acceptable if they met the requirements for size and quality of reproduction specified by the institution. In chapter 13, see the following paragraphs for discussions of computer graphics (13.28–30), of printing (13.31–36), and of photoduplicating (13.51–52).

PHOTOGRAPHS

7.36 Photographs should be finished either 9-x-6-inch or smaller and mounted one or more to a page on single-weight, acid-free paper. Matte-surface photographs are preferable to glossy prints, although the latter make sharper illustrations and are therefore a better choice where minute detail must be shown.

MOUNTING

7.37 Color photographs or other color reproductions are the only illustrations that should be mounted within a finished thesis or dissertation (but see 7.29), because black-and-white photographs (except where extremely accurate reproduction of detail is needed), artwork, and color line-drawings should all be reproduced through one of several available means of photoduplication. For example, photographs can be reproduced on single-weight 8½-x-11-inch, acid-free paper, allowing for a suitable white margin, using a screening process readily available in graphic arts departments on many campuses.

7.38 Dry-mounting tissue is the most satisfactory adhesive for mounting illustrations. Properly applied—and correct application is most important—the mounts will remain firm for many years without causing deterioration of the illustrations. The tissue is available in sheets or in rolls, accompanied by complete directions for its use, and can be purchased from photographic and art supply stores.

7.39 Although dry-mounting tissue is the preferred adhesive for mountings designed to withstand use for many years, some kinds of glue stick offer a reasonably satisfactory substitute.

7.40 Before doing the final mountings, it might be well to experiment a bit with positioning, using special tape that is only slightly adhesive and will not mar the illustration as it is positioned on the page.

7.41 Whether the adhesive used is dry-mounting tissue or a glue stick, the area of the paper to be covered by the illustration should be indicated before the mounts are put in place by drawing a very light pencil line at the top or by placing a dot at each upper corner. The illustration, or the composite of illustrations, should be centered on the page. "Centering," in this connection, assumes a slightly wider margin at the bottom of the sheet than at the top, and a half-inch wider margin at the left than at the right (to accommodate binding).

7.42 When using dry-mounting tissue, as each page of mounted material is finished, set it aside to dry for a few minutes (follow precisely the directions for drying mountings) before placing it under a weight for several hours. It is advisable to protect the newly mounted material by putting a piece of plain paper between each two sheets while they are under a weight.

7.43 It cannot be emphasized too strongly that sufficient time should be set aside for this job of mounting illustrations. Unless cautioned beforehand, the inexperienced person is likely to under-estimate the time required to do this work satisfactorily.

FOLDING

7.44   Illustrations larger than the normal page size may usually be re-duced photographically. If reduction is not feasible, as in the case of large maps, for example, the material may be folded, provided that the institution for which the paper is prepared does not prohibit folding.

7.45   To fold, work first from right to left, making the first crease no more than 7½ inches from the left side of the sheet, which should have a 1½-inch margin. If a second fold is necessary, carry the right-hand portion of the sheet back to the right, mak-ing the second crease no more than 6½ inches to the left of the first. Additional folds, if required, should be parallel with the first two. If the folding is done as directed, when the large folded sheet is in place, there will be no danger of the folds at the left being caught in the stitching or of those at the right being sheared off in the process of trimming.

7.46   Folding in more than one direction should be avoided, but when such folding is necessary, the sheet should first be folded from bottom to top, making the first fold no more than 10 inches from the top of the sheet. When this first fold has been made, unfold the sheet and cut a strip 1 inch wide from the left-hand side of the sheet, starting at the bottom and continuing up to the fold. The removal of this strip is necessary to prevent the free portion of the sheet from being caught in the stitching. The sheet may then be refolded and folded from right to left as directed above.

8   Citation I: Parenthetical References and Reference Lists

8.1   Writers of term papers, theses, and dissertations must first of all determine whether a particular method of citation is required by the department or discipline in which research is conducted. In the natural and social sciences, the use of parenthetical references and reference lists is generally preferred. The Modern Language Association has recently set forth its guidelines for a parenthetical documentation style, though citations using footnotes and bibliographies have long been preferred in most fields of the humanities. If a department or discipline specifies a particular method of citation, follow an authoritative manual of style recommended within the field (see the bibliography at the back of this manual). In addition, each institution usually has its own rules governing the style of citations in research papers.

8.2   The style of parenthetical references and reference lists recommended in *The Chicago Manual of Style,* thirteenth edition, is discussed in this chapter, and examples based on this method of citation are included in chapters 11, 12, and 14. For rules governing the use of notes and bibliographies, see chapters 9 and 10, and for examples in this style, see chapters 11, 12, and 14.

PARENTHETICAL REFERENCES IN THE
AUTHOR-DATE SYSTEM

8.3   In the parenthetical reference system recommended in this manual, authors' names and dates of publication are given in parentheses within the running text or at the end of block quotations, and keyed to a list of works cited, which is placed at the end of the paper. This list is arranged alphabetically by authors' family names (see 10.14–32) and chronologically within lists of works by a single author. It may bear the title "Reference List," "Works Cited," "Literature Cited," "Bibliography," or some variation of these, depending on what seems most appropriate.

8.4   *Author* as used in these paragraphs means the name under which the work is alphabetized in the list of works cited and may thus refer to an editor, compiler, organization, or group of authors. The abbreviations "ed." and "comp." are not given in the text reference but do appear in reference-list entries. No comma appears between author and date:

(Buttlar 1981)   (Clarke 1985)

8.5   For works having two or three authors, use the names of each author:

(Haines and Rupp 1987)
(Wynken, Blynkin, and Nodd 1988)

8.6   In a text reference to a work by two family members with the same last name, the family name is repeated:

(Weinberg and Weinberg 1980)

8.7   For works having more than three authors, use the name of the first followed by "et al." or "and others." Thus, for a work by Zipursky, Hull, White, and Israels, the parenthetical reference would read as follows:

(Zipursky et al. 1979)

8.8   If, as sometimes happens, there is another work of the same date that would also abbreviate to "Zipursky et al."—say a paper by Zipursky, Smith, Jones, and Brown—give either the group of names in full for both or a short title in each, identifying the work cited:

(Zipursky, Smith, Jones, and Brown 1983)
(Zipursky, Hull, White, and Israels 1979)

Or:

```
(Zipursky et al., Brief Notes, 1983)
(Zipursky et al., Preliminary Findings, 1979)
```

8.9   Another way sometimes, but rarely, used to distinguish such works is to cite the first two names, followed by "et al.":

```
(Zipursky, Smith, et al. 1983)
(Zipursky, Hull, et al. 1979)
```

8.10   When a book or pamphlet carries no individual author's name, or group of authors' names, on the title page and is published or sponsored by a corporation, government agency, association, or other named group, the name of that group may serve as author's name in text references and in the reference list. Most of these names present no problem and may be used in full:

```
(International Rice Research Institute 1977)
(Federal Reserve Bank of Boston 1976)
```

8.11   Some group names, being lengthy or composed of several parts, are awkward in text references, particularly when these names must be cited frequently within a paper. Abbreviations or shortened forms are desirable for these, but care must be exercised to make the entry in the reference list begin with the element used in the text reference. If, for example, a text reference reads "(Center for Human Resource Research 1977)," but the work appears in the reference list under "Ohio State University, College of Administrative Science," how is an interested reader going to find it? Since the full reference, "(Ohio State University, College of Administrative Science, Center for Human Resource Research 1977)," is clearly too long for more than, at the most, one text reference, it would be advisable to use either "(Ohio State University 1977)" or "(Center for Human Resource Research 1977)" with a cross-reference in the reference list. See also 8.23, 11.2, and 12.2.

```
Center for Human Resource Research. 1977. See Ohio
     State University. 1977.
```

8.12   Works published by the same author(s) in the same year are arranged alphabetically by title in the reference list and assigned the letters *a, b, c,* etc., following the order of the reference list. The parenthetical reference to these should include the letter:

```
(Kelley 1896a, 1896b, 1907)
```

8.13   Several works by the same author are cited by year only and separated by commas. When page numbers are given, the references are separated by semicolons, and the name is repeated:

```
(Kelley 1896a, 10; Kelley 1896b, 4; Kelley 1907, 3)
```

8.14 A specific page, section, equation, or other division of the cited work follows the date, preceded by a comma. Unless confusion would result, "p." or "pp." is omitted:

```
(Rollings 1984, 15, 43)      (King 1987, eq. [57])
(Farley 1987, 74)            (Black 1979, sec. 24.5)
```

8.15 When the reference is to both volume and page of the author's work, a colon will distinguish between the two. A reference to a volume only, without page number, often requires "vol." for clarity:

```
(García 1982, vol. 2)
(Kusnierek 1981, 3:125)
(García 1982, 2:26, 35; 3:50-53)
```

8.16 Citation of a source not in the reference list, such as a personal letter or interview, should give the full name of the letter writer or the person interviewed (unless it appears nearby in the text) and the description and date of the communication:

```
Spieth has indicated that some men they studied who
had taken hypertensive drugs were indeed faster in
psychomotor speed than nontreated hypertensives
(Walter Spieth, letter to the author, June 1962).

Zebadiah Zulch (telephone interview, 1 April 1978) has
maintained that he never agreed with Zipursky in the
matter.
```

8.17 Citations to collections of unpublished manuscripts or archives may be handled by mentioning the specific item and its date, if any, in the text itself and listing the collection and its depository in the reference list:

```
Mary E. Carpenter, a farmer's wife who lived near
Rochester in 1871, listed what she did in one day at
harvesting time: "My hand is so tired perhaps you'll
excuse pencilling," she began a letter to her cousin
Laura on 18 August.
```

One might add "(Carpenter Papers)" at the end of the above, but it is unnecessary if the name mentioned in the text is the same as the name of the collection listed in the reference list, in which case there could be no confusion with another collection. The reference listing would read:

```
Carpenter, Mary E. Lovell, and Family Papers,
    Minnesota Historical Society, St. Paul.
```

8.18 For more examples of unpublished materials in parenthetical references and reference lists, see 11.52–56.

8.19 A parenthetical reference should be placed just before a mark of punctuation:

```
Before discussing our methods of analysis, it is

necessary to describe the system of scaling

quantitative scores (Guilford 1950).
```

If this placement is impractical, the reference should be inserted at a logical place in the sentence:

```
One investigator (Carter 1980) has reported findings

at variance with the foregoing.
```

PARENTHETICAL REFERENCES WITH NOTES

8.20 Sometimes a content note (see 9.143) or a notice of permission granted may be called for in a paper using parenthetical references. Such notes may appear as footnotes or endnotes (but be consistent), based on the specific requirements of a particular paper, though it is usually better to include such information in the text.

```
    [1]This notion seems to have something in common
with Piaget's (1977) concept of nonbalance and
equilibrium in the area of knowledge.
```

Or in text, use the following style:

```
Jones's theory, which seems to have something in

common with Piaget's (1977) concept of nonbalance and

equilibrium in knowledge, was actually developed at

the local clinic.
```

REFERENCE-LIST STYLE

8.21 When parenthetical references are used, the reader is best served by references arranged in one alphabetical list (see sample

14.46). Alphabetization of reference lists should follow the guidelines set forth in 10.14–32.

8.22 Where many works by the same author(s) are cited, authors' names may stand alone, their works listed by year below (see sample 14.47). Several works by a single author or group of authors that are published in the same year should be alphabetized by title, as shown in the sample.

CROSS-REFERENCES

8.23 When a parenthetical reference in the text does not correspond exactly to the alphabetical listing of the source, a cross-reference may be necessary in the reference list (see 8.11, 11.2, and 12.2). Cross-references may also be used to shorten repeated listings of the same book, such as a multiauthor book from which several authors' contributions are cited. In the below example, "PR." stands for parenthetical reference and "RL." for the corresponding reference-list entry; "PR/CR." stands for the parenthetical reference that should be used when referring to a work given in the reference list as a cross-reference, indicated by the initials "RL/CR.":

PR.   (Hay et al. 1975)

RL.   Hay, Douglas, Peter Linebaugh, John G. Rule,
          E. P. Thompson, and Cal Winslow. 1975.
          <u>Albion's fatal tree: Crime and society in
          eighteenth-century England</u>. New York:
          Pantheon.

PR/CR.   (Hay 1975)

RL/CR.   Hay, Douglas. 1975. Poaching and the game laws
          on Canning Chase. <u>See</u> Hay et al. 1975.

PR/CR.   (Linebaugh 1975)

RL/CR.   Linebaugh, Peter. 1975. The Tyburn riot
          against the surgeons. <u>See</u> Hay et al.
          1975.

ARRANGEMENT OF ELEMENTS IN A REFERENCE-LIST ENTRY

8.24 In reference-list entries, use a period after each main segment (explained below) of an entry.

8.25 Reference-list entries begin with *authors' names,* treated exactly as they would be in bibliographical entries (see 10.9–10).

8.26   In reference-list entries, the *year of publication* follows the name of the author. In addition, for periodicals, the month or season of publication in parentheses follows the volume or series number, and for newspapers, the month and day of publication follow the newspaper title:

> Hallinan, Maureen T., and Aage B. Sørensen. 1985. Class size, ability group size, and student achievement. <u>American Journal of Education</u> 94 (November): 71–89.
>
> Santmyer, Helen Hooven. 1982. <u>"--And the ladies of the club"</u>. New York: Putnam's.
>
> Showtime--The Movie Channel said to pay $500 million for Paramount's film rights. 1983. <u>Wall Street Journal</u>, 19 December, 14(W).

8.27   In this parenthetical reference system, the full titles and subtitles of books are capitalized sentence style (see 4.9) and underlined as titles are in notes.

> Slavin, Morris. 1984. <u>The French revolution in miniature: "Section Droits-de-l'Homme," 1789–1795</u>. Princeton, N.J.: Princeton University Press.
>
> Strier, Richard. 1983. <u>Love known: Theology and experience in George Herbert's poetry</u>. Chicago and London: University of Chicago Press.

8.28   The titles of series are capitalized headline style and set in roman in reference-list entries:

> Charpentrat, Pierre. 1967. <u>L'Art baroque</u>. Les Neuf Muses. Paris: Presses Universitaires de France.
>
> Creeley, Robert. 1970. <u>Quick graph: Collected notes and essays</u>. Edited by Donald Allen. Writing Series, no. 22. San Francisco: Four Seasons Foundation.
>
> Pollak, Ellen. 1985. <u>The poetics of sexual myth: Gender and ideology in the verse of Swift and Pope</u>. Women in Culture and Society Series. Chicago and London: University of Chicago Press.

8.29   The titles of chapters are capitalized sentence style with no quotation marks around them in reference-list entries:

> McNeill, William H. 1976. The ecological impact of medical science and organization since 1700. Chapter 6 of <u>Plagues and peoples</u>. Garden City, N.Y.: Anchor Press/Doubleday.

8.30 The titles of articles are capitalized sentence style with no quotation marks around them in reference-list entries:

```
Lindgren, G. L. 1985. Facing up to
    internationalization. UNIX™ Review: The
    Publication for the UNIX Community 3 (December):
    50-56.
```

The trademark sign in the above example is a part of the title of the journal and must be included.

```
Longstreth, Richard. 1985. From farm to campus:
    Planning, politics, and the agricultural college
    idea in Kansas. Winterthur Portfolio 20 (Summer/
    Autumn): 149-79.
```

8.31 The titles of journals are capitalized headline style and underlined as they are in notes. The names of professional journals may be abbreviated in reference lists, using abbreviations accepted within the field in which research for the paper was conducted:

```
Chien Yu-chin and Barbara Lust. 1985. The concepts of
    topic and subject in first language acquisition
    of Mandarin Chinese. Child Development 56
    (December): 1359-75.

Demsetz, Harold, and Kenneth Lehn. 1985. The structure
    of corporate ownership: Causes and consequences.
    JPE 93 (December): 1155-77.

Fleugelman, Andrew. 1984. Word processing's new look.
    MACWORLD: The Macintosh Magazine 1 (February,
    Premiere Issue): 62-71.

Miller, Joanne, Kazimierz M. Slomczynski, and Melvin
    L. Kohn. 1985. Continuity of learning-
    generalization: The effect of job on men's
    intellective process in the United States and
    Poland. AJS 91 (November): 593-615.
```

8.32 Abbreviations are used for "edited by" (ed.), "translated by" (trans.), and "compiled by" (comp.), unless they might be misunderstood or unless they appear at the beginning of a segment in a reference-list entry, when they are spelled out (see the last two examples below):

```
Currie, David P. 1985. Sovereign immunity and suits
    against government officers. In 1984 Supreme
    Court Review, ed. Philip W. Kurland, Gerhard
    Casper, and Dennis J. Hutchinson, 149-68. Chicago
    and London: University of Chicago Press.
```

Pollitt, Ernesto, Cutberto Garza, and Rudolph L. Leibel. 1984. Nutrition and public policy. In <u>Child development research and social policy</u>, ed. Harold W. Stevenson and Alberta E. Siegel, 1:421–70. Chicago and London: University of Chicago Press.

Derrida, Jacques. 1985. Racism's last word. Translated by Peggy Kamuf. <u>Critical Inquiry</u> 12 (Autumn, Special Issue on "Race," Writing, and Difference): 290–99.

Ortega y Gasset, José. 1984. <u>Historical reason</u>. Translated by Philip W. Silver. New York: W. W. Norton & Co.

8.33 With the exception of the placement of year of publication after the name of the author, facts of publication in a reference-list entry are given exactly as they would be given in a bibliographical entry (see 10.11; and see also 9.55–90). For examples comparing parenthetical references and corresponding reference-list entries with notes and bibliographical entries for the same works, see chapters 11 and 12.

PARENTHETICAL REFERENCES USING NUMBERS

8.34 A related method of text reference gives only a number in the text: (9) or [9] or [9], as in some medical publications. This number refers not to a note but to an entry in a numbered list of works cited, at the end of the paper. This list may be arranged either alphabetically by authors' names or in order of appearance of each source in the text, as specified within the discipline governing the research. For guidelines recommended by particular fields in the physical and biological sciences, see the bibliography at the end of this manual.

8.35 In certain fields, principally the sciences, reference lists may follow a severely abbreviated style in which article titles are omitted and journal titles abbreviated. Consult the dissertation secretary or thesis adviser to determine whether the references in a paper should follow such a style, and use an authoritative manual recommended within the field.

9   Citation II: Footnotes and Endnotes

METHOD OF CITATION

9.1 The rules for the method of citation set forth in this chapter apply to papers that use notes placed at the bottom of the page, called footnotes, or notes placed at the end of a paper, called endnotes. Papers written using parenthetical references and reference lists may also include footnotes or endnotes (see 8.20). The use of footnotes rather than endnotes or parenthetical references allows a paper to be read from beginning to end on microfilm, without the reader's having to search for a reference in the back matter of the paper. For theses and dissertations that are held and distributed on microfilm, particularly those in fields of the humanities, where footnotes have traditionally been used, the use of footnotes and a bibliography is preferred. For the rules governing bibliographical style, see chapter 10; for examples of notes and corresponding bibliographical entries, see chapter 11. Guidelines for the layout of footnotes, bibliographies, and endnotes are also included in chapter 14.

USES OF NOTES

9.2 Notes have four main uses: *(a)* to cite the authority for statements in text—specific facts or opinions as well as exact quotations; *(b)* to make cross-references; *(c)* to make incidental comments upon, to amplify, or to qualify textual discussion—in short, to provide a place for material which the writer deems worthwhile to include but which would in the writer's judgment interrupt the flow of thought if introduced into the text; and *(d)* to make acknowledgments. Notes, then, are of two kinds: *reference* (*a* and *b* above) and *content* (*c* and *d* above). A content note may also include one or more references. Interpretations and examples of note form are given in the following pages.

9.3 Tables, outlines, lists, letters, and the like, that are not immediately relevant to the text are best placed in an appendix and referred to in the text by a simple content footnote:

> [5]The member banks and their contributors are listed in appendix 3.

In a paper using endnotes or parenthetical references, references to the above materials should be placed in parentheses in the text, so that the reader does not have to consult two parts of the back matter to find a source:

> Auditors traced this error to the member banks and
>
> their contributors (see appendix 3).

9.4 If a block quotation (see 5.4) contains note references from the original source, the corresponding notes should be placed beneath the quotation, not among the notes belonging to the paper itself. An eight-space rule (made by underscoring) should separate the note or notes from the quotation. The reference index—whether number or symbol—and the form of the note should follow exactly the style found in the original material:

Given the course of events, they might all have said,
along with Bataille himself:

> My tension, in a sense, resembles a great
> welling up of laughter, it is not unlike the
> burning passions of Sade's heroes, and yet, it is
> close to that of the martyrs, or of the saints.[23]

---

[23]"Ma tension ressemble, en un sens, à une
folle envie de rire, elle diffère peu des passions
dont brûlent les héros de Sade, et pourtant, elle
est proche de celle des martyrs ou des saints" Sur
Nietzsche, 12.[8]

If the writer of the paper adds note references in a block quotation—to identify persons mentioned, for example, or to translate
words or passages in a foreign language—these superscript numbers are inserted in square brackets, and the references are numbered in sequence with the other notes in the paper. The corresponding notes themselves are placed at the bottom of the page
in the footnote system or at the end of the paper in the endnote
system.

9.5 Unless short and uncomplicated, tables, outlines, lists, letters,
or the like, should not be placed in a note.

NOTE NUMBERS

9.6 The place in the text at which a note is introduced, whether a
footnote or endnote, reference or content, should be marked with
an arabic numeral typed slightly above the line (superscript).

9.7 Note numbers preceding footnotes themselves are also typed
slightly above the line. In endnotes, however, which appear in
the back matter, note numbers may be either superscript, as in
footnotes, or typed on the line, followed by a period and two
spaces (see sample 14.45).

9.8 Many typewriters and computer systems can elevate characters a
uniform half-space above the line of text. Never elevate note
numbers a full space above the line. If the computer system used
to prepare a paper with notes is not able to produce superscript
numbers, these numbers may be typed into the text using a typewriter with a typeface compatible with that used to produce the
rest of the manuscript on the computer system.

9.9 Do not put a period after a superscript note number or embellish it with parentheses, brackets, or slash marks. The superscript numeral follows a punctuation mark, if any, except the dash, which it precedes.

9.10 The note number should always follow the passage to which it refers. If the passage is an exact quotation, the note number comes at the end of the quotation, not after the author's name or at the end of the textual matter introducing the quotation.

9.11 Note numbers must follow one another in numerical order, beginning with the number one. Numbering should start at the beginning of each chapter. In papers that are not divided into chapters, the numbering will run continuously throughout. Care must be taken to ensure that the final sequence is correct. If it is found, on checking the manuscript, that a note has been omitted or that one should be deleted, the notes must be renumbered from the point of the desired change to the end of the chapter or paper. The insertion of a note numbered, for example, *2a* is not permissible, and the omission of a number likewise is not permissible.

9.12 Some computer systems will allow automatic numbering and renumbering if a new note is added to a chapter, or if a note is deleted (see 13.24).

9.13 Double numbering (such as [1,2]) may not be used except in scientific fields where this practice is acceptable (see 8.34). Consult an authoritative manual recommended within the discipline before using double numbering in a paper (see the bibliography at the end of this manual).

POSITION OF NOTES

9.14 Notes should be arranged in numerical order either at the foot of the page (footnotes) or at the end of the paper (endnotes). A footnote must begin at the bottom of the page on which it is referenced, though it may extend to the bottom of the next page if the note is long (see sample 14.43).

9.15 In preparing the manuscript, time and space can be saved and the appearance of the page improved by reducing the number of note references in the text. In a single paragraph containing several quotations, for example, a reference number following the last quotation will permit all the quotations to be cited in one note. If instead of the four reference numbers used in the first version of the example below, one number is placed after the last name, as in the second version, all four citations may be made in one note:

```
The means by which the traditional Western composers
have attempted to communicate with their audience has
been discussed at length by Eduard Hanslick,² Heinrich
Schenker,³ Suzanne Langer,⁴ and Leonard Meyer,⁵ to
name but a few.
```

Or:

```
The means by which the traditional Western composers
have attempted to communicate with their audience has
been discussed at length by Eduard Hanslick, Heinrich
Schenker, Suzanne Langer, and Leonard Meyer, to name
but a few.²
```

The single footnote would then read:

```
    ²Eduard Hanslick, The Beautiful in Music, trans.
G. Cohen (New York: Novello, Ewer, 1891); Heinrich
Schenker, Der freie Satz, trans. and ed. T. H. Kreuger
(Ann Arbor: University Microfilms, 1960), pub. no. 60-
1558; Suzanne Langer, Philosophy in a New Key (New
York: Mentor, 1959); Leonard B. Meyer, Emotion and
Meaning in Music (Chicago: University of Chicago
Press, 1956), and Music, the Arts, and Ideas (Chicago:
University of Chicago Press, 1967).
```

ABBREVIATIONS IN NOTES

9.16 Except in scientific and technical writing, few abbreviations are permissible in text (see 2.1), but in notes, bibliographies, reference lists, tabular matter, and in some kinds of illustrative matter, abbreviations are normally preferred to complete words. Abbreviations commonly found in these parts of a paper are listed in 2.18 and 2.23–26.

9.17 An abbreviation designating a part of a written work (*vol., pt., chap.,* etc.) should never be used unless it is followed or preceded by a number (*vol. 2, 4 vols., pt. 1, chap. 10,* etc.). When used without numbers, these words should be spelled out.

9.18 Titles of journals, dictionaries, and other sources used frequently in a paper may be abbreviated by the initials of the words of their names, without spaces or periods between the letters. Such abbreviations are permissible in notes but not in bibliographical entries and some kinds of reference lists (see also 8.31 and 8.35).

American Historical Review	AHR
Nouvelle Revue Française	NRF
Dictionary of National Biography	DNB
Oxford English Dictionary	OED

Journals that have initials as actual titles should be so cited in bibliographies and reference lists as well as in notes:

PMLA   MLN   ELN

9.19 It is permissible for a writer who must refer frequently to the same work to devise an abbreviated, or shortened, form to be used after the first full reference, but full words from the work's title rather than an acronym or initials only of the title should be used:

Pagan Mysteries of the Renaissance   Pagan Mysteries

See also 9.140–42.

REFERENCE NOTES

First, or Full, Reference

9.20 Sample reference notes with corresponding bibliographical entries and parenthetical references with corresponding reference-list entries are set forth in chapters 11 and 12. For the layout of notes on the page, see 14.13–24 for directions and 14.42, 14.43, and 14.51 for samples.

9.21 The first time a work is mentioned in a note, the entry should be in complete form; that is, it should include not only the author's full name, the title of the work, and the specific reference (i.e., volume, if any, and page number), but the facts of publication as well. For a book, the source of information, except the page number(s), should be the title page and copyright page; for a periodical, it should be the cover and the article itself. Once a work has been cited in full, subsequent references to it should be in shortened form. These forms are fully discussed and illustrated in paragraphs 9.130–42.

9.22 With some exceptions, such as references to legal, classical, and biblical works, and to certain classes of public documents (see chapter 12), information in notes citing a published work the first time is given in the sequence indicated in 9.23–24.

9.23   For a book, the first, full reference should include the following information in the order shown:

Name of author(s)
Title and, if any, subtitle
Name of editor, compiler, or translator, if any
Name of author of preface, introduction, or foreword
Number or name of edition, if other than the first
Name of series in which book appears, if any, with volume or
> number in the series
Facts of publication, consisting of
> Place of publication
> Name of publishing agency
> Date of publication
Page number(s) of the specific citation

9.24   The first, or full, reference to a chapter in a book should be given as follows:

Name of author(s)
Title of chapter
Title of book, preceded by the word *in*
Facts of publication
Page number(s) of the specific citation

NAME OF AUTHOR

9.25   Whether or not it appears in the text close to the citation, the author's name must be given in the reference. Present the name in normal order—given name followed by family name (Robert John Blank, for example)—and follow with a comma. The name should appear as it does on the title page or in a byline. Except for well-known authors who habitually use only the initials of their given names (e.g., T. S. Eliot, D. H. Lawrence, J. B. S. Haldane, W. B. Yeats), initials only should not be used if the author's given names are known. For an author whose given names appear in full on the title pages of some works, and as initials only on others, notes referring to the latter should complete the names in brackets: H[enry] R[obert] Anderson. Otherwise some of the works by an author may be separated from others in a bibliography or alphabetical reference list.

9.26   If the title page, or the byline at the head of a chapter (or article), gives a pseudonym known to be that of a certain author, give the pseudonym only. The pseudonym followed by the author's real name enclosed in brackets appears in bibliographies and reference lists (see 11.9). Such familiar pseudonyms as Anatole France, George Eliot, and Mark Twain may, however, be used throughout a paper in place of the real name.

9.27   If a pseudonym is printed as such on the title page or in the byline, the abbreviation "pseud." is enclosed in parentheses and placed after the pseudonym: Helen Delay (pseud.).

9.28   If pseudonymity is not indicated on the title page or in the byline but is nevertheless an established fact, the abbreviation "pseud." may be placed in brackets after the pseudonym, or the author's real name, if known, may be placed in brackets after it.

9.29   If the title page or byline gives no author's name, or if it designates the work as anonymous, and if in either case the authorship has been definitely established, the author's name, enclosed in brackets, may be placed before the title:

> [1][James Stetson], review of Secret Service, by William Hooker Gillette, Life, 22 October 1896, 306–7.

The use of "Anonymous" in place of the name of an author is not recommended. If the authorship is not reliably established, the note reference should begin with the title of the work.

9.30   For a work by two or by three authors, give the full names in normal order, separating the names of two authors with "and"; and of three authors with commas, the last comma followed by "and":

> [1]Mary Lyon, Bryce Lyon, and Henry S. Lucas, The Wardrobe Book of William de Norwell, 12 July 1338 to 27 May 1340, with the collaboration of Jean de Sturler (Brussels: Commission Royale d'Histoire de Belgique, 1983), 175.

> [2]Dana Carleton Munro and Raymond James Sontag, The Middle Ages, 395–1500, rev. ed., The Century Historical Series (New York and London: The Century Co., 1928), 69.

9.31   If a work has more than three authors, it is usual to cite in the note (but not in the bibliography or reference list) only the name of the author given first on the title page and to follow it with "et al." or its English equivalent, "and others." Whether you choose to follow it with "et al." or with "and others," the same style should be used throughout the paper. No comma comes between the author's name and "et al." A period always follows "al." (see also 11.6):

[2]Martin Greenberger et al., eds., <u>Networks for Research and Education: Sharing of Computer Information Resources Nationwide</u> (Cambridge: MIT Press, 1974), 54.

9.32 For coauthors with the same family name, cite each name in full in the first reference—Sidney Webb and Beatrice Webb, not Sidney and Beatrice Webb. In later references, write "Webb and Webb," not "the Webbs" (see 11.5).

9.33 Even though a title page or byline may include after an author's name a title such as doctor, professor, or president, or indicate a scholastic degree or official position, all such designations should be omitted except in rare instances where one or more of them would have significance for the subject of the paper:

[1]Leon R. Kass, M.D., <u>Toward a More Natural Science: Biology and Human Affairs</u> (New York: Free Press, a division of Macmillan, 1985), 252.

9.34 The "author" may be a corporate body—a country, state, city, legislative body, institution, society, business firm, committee, or the like (see example 11.10).

9.35 Some works—compilations, anthologies—are produced by compilers or editors, whose names are given in place of authors' names and are followed by the abbreviation "ed." (or "eds.") or "comp." (or "comps."):

[1]Russell Hardin, John J. Mearsheimer, Gerald Dworkin, and Robert E. Goodin, eds., <u>Nuclear Deterrence: Ethics and Strategy</u> (Chicago: University of Chicago Press, 1985), 23.

See also example 11.11.

TITLE OF THE WORK

9.36 Enter the full title (and subtitle, if any) of a book as it appears on the title page. See 9.38 for instructions on punctuating titles and subtitles that are distinguished on the title page by size and style of type rather than by punctuation. Enter the title of an article or chapter as it appears in the work. In the case of an article, follow with a comma and the name of the periodical underlined. In the case of a chapter, follow the comma with the title of the book preceded by "in." Adhere to the peculiarities, if any, of spelling and punctuation within titles, but in notes capitalize the titles of all works headline style, whether they are published or unpublished (see 4.6–8).

9.37   Underline the title of a whole published work, that is, the title of a book and the title of a periodical. Enclose in quotation marks the title of a chapter in a book or an article in a periodical. Place a comma after the title of a book unless it is followed immediately by parentheses enclosing the facts of publication, in which case the comma follows the final parenthesis (see 11.3).

[2]W. Edmund Farrar, "Antibiotic Resistance in Developing Countries," Journal of Infectious Diseases 152 (December 1985): 1103.

[3]E. J. Clegg and J. P. Garlick, eds., Disease and Urbanization, Symposia of the Society for the Study of Human Biology, vol. 20 (Atlantic Highlands, N.J.: Humanities Press International, 1980), 16.

[4]Virgil Thomson, "Cage and the Collage of Noises," in American Music since 1910 (New York: Holt, Rinehart, and Winston, 1971), 25.

9.38   Since display headings, both on title pages and at the heads of articles, frequently set a title in two or more lines, and since punctuation is normally omitted at the ends of lines of display headings, it is often necessary to add marks of punctuation to a title as it will appear when written out in text, note, reference list, or bibliography. This need occurs most often in titles composed of a main title and a subtitle. Consider the following example of a title and its subtitle:

The Early Growth of Logic in the Child

Classification and Seriation

Here, as the title is shown on the title page, no punctuation follows *Child*. When the title and subtitle are referred to, they should appear as follows:

The Early Growth of Logic in the Child: Classification and Seriation

NAME OF EDITOR, TRANSLATOR, OR COMPILER

9.39   If the title page contains in addition to the name of an author that of an editor, translator, or compiler, that name follows the title, being preceded by a comma and the appropriate abbreviation: "ed." or "trans." or "comp." In this case the abbreviation stands for "edited by" or "translated by" or "compiled by" and thus is never given in the plural form:

[1]Edward Chiera, They Wrote on Clay, ed. George G. Cameron (Chicago: University of Chicago Press, 1938), 42.

[2]John Stuart Mill, Autobiography and Literary Essays, ed. John M. Robson and Jack Stillinger (Toronto: University of Toronto Press, 1980), 15.

9.40 A work may have both an editor and a translator as well as an author, and the same person may be both editor and translator:

[1]August von Haxthausen, Studies on the Interior of Russia, ed. S. Frederick Starr, trans. Eleanore L. M. Schmidt (Chicago: University of Chicago Press, 1972), 47.

[2]Helmut Thielicke, Man in God's World, trans. and ed. John W. Doberstein (New York and Evanston, Ill.: Harper & Row, 1963), 43.

9.41 Similar in style is the entry of an edited or translated work in which the author's name is included in the title. Here the author's name as the first item of information is omitted, although it might properly be inserted even though it is omitted on the title page:

[1]The Works of Shakespear, ed. Alexander Pope (London: printed for Jacob Tonson in the Strand, 1725), 6:20.

Or:

[1]Shakespear, The Works of Shakespear, ed. Alexander Pope (London: printed for Jacob Tonson in the Strand, 1725), 6:20.

Although the foregoing arrangement, which gives the editor's name following the title of the work, is the form of reference most commonly used for this kind of work, it would be permissible in a paper dealing primarily with the work of Pope to give his name first, followed by "ed.":

[1]Alexander Pope, ed., The Works of Shakespear (London: printed for Jacob Tonson in the Strand, 1725), 6:20.

A bibliographical entry begins with the author's name even if the name is also in the title (see 11.13).

NAME OF AUTHOR OF PREFACE, FOREWORD, OR INTRODUCTION

9.42   If the title page of a book includes the name of the author of a preface, foreword, or introduction, that name is included in the reference. Note the style of the first of the following references, which is to Hammarskjöld's text:

> [1]Dag Hammarskjöld, <u>Markings</u>, with a foreword by
> W. H. Auden (New York: Alfred A. Knopf, 1964), 38.

The following reference, however, refers to the foreword by Auden:

> [1]W. H. Auden, foreword to <u>Markings</u> by Dag
> Hammarskjöld (New York: Alfred A. Knopf, 1964), ix.

EDITION

9.43   Information concerning the edition is required if the work cited is other than the first edition. The information is frequently printed on the title page, but it is often found on the copyright page (the reverse of the title page). Besides numbered editions, there are reprint editions, paperback editions, and named editions.

9.44   *Numbered edition.* Although new editions are usually numbered, they may be designated on the title page merely as New Edition or New Revised Edition (abbreviated in notes, bibliographies, and reference lists as "rev. ed.," "new rev. ed.," etc.) and so on. Also found are Second Edition, Revised (2d ed., rev.); Revised Second Edition (rev. 2d ed.); Third Edition, Revised and Enlarged (3d ed., rev. and enl.); Revised Edition in One Volume (rev. ed. in 1 vol.); Fourth Edition, Revised by John Doe (4th ed., rev. John Doe); and so forth:

> [5]William Garzke, Jr., and Robert O. Dulin, Jr.,
> <u>Battleships: Axis Battleships in World War II</u>, 3d ed.,
> Battleship Series, vol. 3 (Annapolis, Md.: Naval
> Institute Press, 1985), 379.

> [6]Richard Ellmann, <u>James Joyce</u>, new and rev. ed.
> (New York: Oxford University Press, 1982), 705.

9.45   *Reprint edition.* Works that are out of print are frequently reissued in special reprint editions. Notes, reference lists, and bibliographies should include the reprint information and give also the date of the original publication and if possible the original publisher:

[1]Gunnar Myrdal, <u>Population: A Problem for Democracy</u> (Cambridge: Harvard University Press, 1940; repr., Gloucester, Mass.: Peter Smith, 1956), 9.

It is not necessary to note a new printing—e.g., fourth impression—by the original publisher.

9.46 *Paperback edition.* Not all paperback editions are reprints, but when they are, they should be treated as reprints, giving original publication data as well as reprint data. A book published originally as a paperback should be listed as any other book, except that the name of the press or series may identify it as a paperback:

[4]Mary Wollstonecraft Shelley, <u>Frankenstein: Or, The Modern Prometheus (the 1818 Text)</u>, ed. James Reiger (Indianapolis: Bobbs-Merrill, 1974; Chicago: University of Chicago Press, Phoenix Books, 1982), 37.

[5]Leon F. Litwack, <u>North of Slavery: The Negro in the Free States, 1790–1860</u> (Chicago: University of Chicago Press, 1961; Phoenix Books, 1965), 65.

[6]Howard P. Segal, <u>Technological Utopianism in American Culture</u> (Chicago: University of Chicago Press, Chicago Original Paperback, 1985), 31.

9.47 *Named edition.* Many classics are found in named editions. When they are used in references, they should be specified:

[9]Blaise Pascal, <u>Pensées and the Provincial Letters</u>, The Modern Library (New York: Random House, 1941), 418.

The title pages of some named editions do not give the names of the publisher. If only city and date can be given, they are separated by a comma.

NAME OF SERIES

9.48 Books and pamphlets are sometimes published as parts of named series (e.g., Oxford English Monographs, Yale Studies in Political Science, Monographs of the Society for Research in Child Development), which are sponsored by publishers, institutions—especially universities and graduate schools—governmental agencies, learned societies, commercial and industrial firms, and so on. Although a series bears some resemblance to a periodical publication and to a multivolume work, there are important differences stemming from individual plans of publication—differences that are reflected in the particular style of reference appropriate to each.

9.49   The publication of a series is an ongoing project of its sponsors, whose purpose is the issuance from time to time of books or pamphlets by different writers on topics which may range rather widely over a specific field or discipline or area of interest. Many series are numbered; the citation of a particular work in a numbered series should include the volume number (or issue number) after the name of the series. Note that the volume number here applies to the series and the page number to the book; therefore, the citation differs from that for a multivolume work (see 9.73). Note also that although the title of the work is underlined, the name of the series is not, nor does it appear in quotation marks:

[1]Luli Callinicos, <u>Workers on the Rand: Factories, Townships, and Popular Culture, 1886–1942</u>, A People's History of South Africa, vol. 2 (Athens, Ohio: Ohio University Press, 1985), 48.

[2]Kenneth M. Setton, <u>The Papacy and the Levant 1204–1571</u>, vol. 1, <u>The Thirteenth and Fourteenth Centuries</u>, Memoirs of the American Philosophical Society, no. 114 (Philadelphia: The Society, 1976), 398–400.

[1]Leonard L. Watkins, <u>Commercial Banking Reform in the United States</u>, Michigan Business Studies, vol. 6, no. 5 (Ann Arbor: University of Michigan, 1938), 464.

FACTS OF PUBLICATION

9.50   As listed in paragraph 9.23, the facts of publication include place (city), publisher, and date. They appear in notes as follows:

(London: Hogarth Press, 1964)

These facts are given for printed books, monographs, and pamphlets, and for published works that are mimeographed, photocopied, microfilmed, or otherwise reproduced. But note the following exceptions:

1. Biblical, classical, and medieval works omit all facts of publication (see 9.103–13).

2. Legal works and some public documents usually omit all but the date (see 9.116–18 and chapter 12).

3. Dictionaries, general encyclopedias, and atlases omit all but edition and date (see 9.96).

4. In certain disciplines and in certain fields, citations omit name of publisher (see 9.65 and 8.35).

5. Periodicals, in general, omit all but the date (see 9.85).

9.51 *Place of publication.* If the names of two or more cities appear under the publisher's imprint, the first name gives the location of the editorial offices, and that is normally all that need be given in the reference. All the names mentioned may be included, however; for example, "Oxford, London, and New York." Do not assume, however, that London and New York may properly be added when Oxford alone appears on the title page.

9.52 If the city is not generally well known, give the state as well, using the standard abbreviation for the state, as "Glenview, Ill." For abbreviations of the names of states, see 2.13. Use of two-letter postal abbreviations for the names of states is discouraged by some thesis advisers, dissertation secretaries, and degree-granting institutions. Identify Cambridge by writing either "Cambridge, England" (never "Engl.") or "Cambridge, Mass.," unless the first is followed by "Cambridge University Press" and the second by "Harvard University Press" or "MIT Press."

9.53 For foreign cities, use the English name if there is one: Cologne, not Köln; Munich, not München; Florence, not Firenze; Padua, not Padova; Milan, not Milano; Rome, not Roma; Vienna, not Wien; Prague, not Praha; and so forth.

9.54 Follow the place of publication with a colon if a publisher is given, with a comma if only the date follows. If neither the title page nor the copyright page gives the place of publication, write "n.p." (for "no place") as the first item of information on facts of publication.

9.55 The abbreviation "n.p." may also stand for "no publisher." If both place and publisher are missing, "n.p." with the date is sufficient.

9.56 *Name of publishing agency.* The broader term *publishing agency*, rather than *publisher*, is used here because some of the works are published by societies, institutions of learning or commerce or banking, and the like, which are not publishers per se.

The terms are used interchangeably in the text of this section. After place of publication and a colon followed by one space, the name of the publisher may be given either in the style used by the company itself or in the accepted abbreviated form as it is given for American publishers in *Books in Print,* issued annually by R. R. Bowker Company, and for British publishers in *British Books in Print,* published by J. Whitaker & Sons and R. R. Bowker Company.

9.57 Note carefully the spelling and punctuation of publishers' names. There is no comma in Houghton Mifflin Co., for example; but there is a comma in the name of Little, Brown & Co., and in that of Harcourt, Brace & Co., as the firm was formerly known. Hyphens separate the names in McGraw-Hill Book Co. and in Appleton-Century-Crofts. There is a small *m,* not a capital *M,* in the middle of Macmillan. The name of the New York firm is Macmillan Co., and that of the London firm is Macmillan & Co.

9.58 Even though publishers' names may be written in full, in notes it is customary to omit an initial "The" and the abbreviations "Inc." or "Ltd." or "S.A."; to use the ampersand (&) in place of "and"; and to abbreviate "Company" as "Co." and "Brother" or "Brothers" as "Bro." or "Bros." The name of a publisher, such as "Knopf" (Alfred A. Knopf, Inc.), "Norton" (W. W. Norton and Company), and "Scribner" (Charles Scribner's Sons), may also be given in shortened form. Whatever style is chosen, it must be used consistently throughout the paper.

9.59 If the title page indicates that a work was copublished, the reference should give both publishers:

(New York: Alfred A. Knopf and Viking Press, 1966)

(Boston: Ginn & Co., 1964; Montreal: Round Press, 1964)

9.60 The title page of a book issued by a subsidiary of a publisher gives both names, and references to such a book should include both:

(Cambridge: Harvard University Press, Belknap Press, 1965)

9.61 If a work has been published for an institution or association whose name appears on the title page together with the publisher's name, the references should include both names:

(New York: Columbia University Press for the American
Geographical Society, 1947)

9.62   If a work has been reissued at a date later than that of the original publication, the fact will usually be noted on the entry card
for the work in the library catalog. Such information is especially useful for locating some hard-to-find old works. See 9.45
for the style of reference used in citing a reprint edition.

9.63   Do not substitute the present name of a publishing firm for that
shown on the title page of the work being cited.

9.64   Do not translate parts of the names of foreign publishers, even
when you have anglicized the name of the city (see 9.53). Do
not, for example, change "Compagnie" or "Cie." to "Company" or "Co."; or "et Frère" to "and Brother" or "and
Bro."

9.65   In accordance with long-established practice within some scientific fields, the names of publishers are routinely omitted from
citations. Thus, only place and date of publication appear, as,
for example, "New York, 1970." Note that when only two facts
of publication are given, they are separated by a comma.

9.66   *Date of publication.* The date of copyright is the one to use in a
reference, unless a different date appears with the publisher's
imprint on the title page or on the copyright page itself; the latter
would then be the one to use. There may be more than one
copyright date; if so, the last is the one under which the work in
hand was issued. There may also be one or more dates shown
in addition to the date of copyright. Since those refer to reprint-
ings, or new impressions, not new editions, they should not be
given for the date of publication. If no date is shown any place,
write "n.d." (for "no date"):

(New York: Grosset & Dunlap, n.d.)

9.67   If, however, the date has been established by means other than
the title page or copyright date, place the date in brackets. The
entry for the work in the card catalog of the library often carries
the date of publication when the title page omits it. When the
date has been discovered through the efforts of the library, it
will be shown on the entry card in brackets. In a note, it is given
thus:

(New York: Grosset & Dunlap, [1831])

9.68   If a writer finds it desirable to cite a work that has been accepted for publication but is not yet published, he may do so in the following style for a book:

> [6]John G. Cawelti and Bruce A. Rosenberg, <u>The Spy Story</u> (Chicago: University of Chicago Press, forthcoming).

PAGE REFERENCE

9.69   Refer to page(s) by number alone, whether in arabic or lower-case roman (for preliminaries). The abbreviations "p." and "pp." should precede page numbers only where the absence of such abbreviations might cause confusion. Refer to inclusive page numbers in accordance with the scheme set forth in 2.67. For use of a colon before the page number(s) in references to multivolume works, see 9.79, and in references to articles, see 9.86.

9.70   The first reference to an article in a periodical may be to a specific page or pages, as with a quotation. Inclusive page numbers for the whole article need only be given when the whole article is being cited, rather than merely a part of it. Use exact inclusive page numbers in preference to such designations as "80f." (80 and following page) or "82, 83ff." (82, 83, and following pages). Since "f." refers to only a single page immediately following the number given, the exact pages should be cited: "80–81." Similarly, avoid using "82, 83ff." by giving inclusive pages, "82, 83–85," for example.

9.71   Although inclusive page numbers are desirable in referring to an article as a whole, they should not be given when an article begins in the front of a magazine and skips to the back. In this case, inclusive page numbers are meaningless, and the first page number alone should be cited (see 11.41).

9.72   The word "passim" (here and there) should be used with discretion. Employ it only in referring to information scattered over a considerable stretch of text, or throughout a chapter or other long section. Give the inclusive page numbers or the chapter number and place "passim" at the end of the reference:

> [1]Jean Comaroff, <u>Body of Power, Spirit of Resistance: The Culture and History of a South African People</u> (Chicago: University of Chicago Press, 1985), chap. 1 passim.

²Jacqueline Desbarats and Karl D. Jackson, "Vietnam 1975–1982: The Cruel Peace," <u>Washington Quarterly</u> 8 (Fall 1985): 170–80 passim.

Note that "passim" is a whole word and not an abbreviation and is not, therefore, followed by a period unless it comes at the end of a citation. Do not underline it.

SPECIAL FORMS

MULTIVOLUME WORKS

9.73 The publication of a multivolume work falls within limits that are more or less clearly defined in advance. The work consists, or will consist, of a limited number of volumes related to the same subject. All the volumes may be the work of one author and bear the same title (note 1); or they may be by one author and have different titles (note 2); or they may be by different authors and bear different titles, with the entire work carrying an overall title and having a general editor (note 3):

¹Muriel St. Clare Byrne, ed., <u>The Lisle Letters</u> (Chicago: University of Chicago Press, 1981), 6:38.

²William Makepeace Thackeray, <u>The Complete Works</u> (Boston, 1899), vol. 13, <u>The English Humorists of the Eighteenth Century</u>, 121–330.

³Eric Cochrane and Julius Kirshner, eds., <u>The Renaissance</u>, vol. 5 of <u>University of Chicago Readings in Western Civilization</u>, ed. John W. Boyer and Julius Kirshner (Chicago: University of Chicago Press, 1986), 402.

9.74 A reference to a multivolume work as a whole should include the total number of volumes.

¹Paul Tillich, <u>Systematic Theology</u>, 3 vols. (Chicago: University of Chicago Press, 1951–63).

A reference to one of the volumes of a multivolume work may be in one of the styles discussed in paragraphs 9.77–81. See also 9.75–76.

9.75 If the individual volumes have been issued in different years, the reference to the work as a whole must indicate that fact in the following form:

²John Dryden, <u>The Works of John Dryden</u>, ed. H. T. Swedenberg, 8 vols. (Berkeley and Los Angeles: University of California Press, 1956–62).

9.76   When the publication of a multivolume work is not complete, give the date when publication began and follow with a hyphen:

1968–

9.77   The following style should be used when referring to the whole of a specific volume in a multivolume work:

[2]Paul Tillich, Systematic Theology, vol. 2 (Chicago: University of Chicago Press, 1957).

9.78   When all of the volumes in a multivolume work were published in the same year, only one publication date is required:

[3]Gordon N. Ray, ed., An Introduction to Literature, vol. 2, The Nature of Drama, by Hubert Hefner (Boston: Houghton Mifflin Co., 1959).

9.79   When all of the volumes in a multivolume work have the same title, a reference to pages within a single volume is given in the following manner:

[5]Pierre de Ronsard, Les Oeuvres de Pierre de Ronsard: Texte de 1587, ed. Isidore Silver (Chicago: University of Chicago Press, 1970), 8:55.

Note that the page reference follows the volume number, and that the two are separated by a colon. Note also that the volume number is given in arabic numerals, even when expressed in roman numerals in the work cited, and that the abbreviation "vol." is omitted.

9.80   When each volume in a multivolume work has a different title, a reference to pages within a single volume is given as follows:

[1]Gabriel Marcel, The Mystery of Being, vol. 2, Faith and Reality (Chicago: Henry Regnery Co., 1960), 19–20.

9.81   When in addition to volume and page, another division of a work must be given to indicate the location of a reference, that division must be appropriately designated even though the abbreviations "vol." and "p." are omitted:

[1]Donald Lach, Asia in the Making of Europe (Chicago: University of Chicago Press, 1965), 2, bk. 1:165.

9.82   The use of arabic rather than roman numerals to indicate volume numbers is noted in 9.79. Arabic numerals are also used, with some few exceptions, for all the divisions of a written work: parts, volumes, books, chapters, pages; acts and scenes of a play; lines and stanzas of a poem; columns of a tabulation; figures, tables, and maps; and so on. There are three exceptions: (1) References to a book's preliminary pages that are numbered with small roman numerals should use the same style of numeral (see 9.69). (2) References to divisions of unpublished public documents or to manuscript materials should follow the numbering style of the source (see 9.114–15 and 12.25). (3) References to a collection of inscriptions, papyri, or ostraca that is divided into volumes should use roman numerals for the volume numbers (see 9.110).

JOURNALS AND PERIODICALS

9.83 The first, full reference to an article in a journal or periodical includes the following, in the order shown:

Name of author(s)
Title of article
Name of periodical
Volume number or issue
Publication date, if any, in parentheses
Page number(s)

9.84 A periodical is published at stated intervals—daily, weekly, monthly, quarterly, and so on—the issues being numbered in succession. In general, each issue of a magazine or journal is composed of articles by different authors. References to such articles follow the pattern set forth in 9.83. The proper style for citing articles is not likely to raise any question except when an entire issue of a publication is devoted to one long paper, usually by one author. Sometimes such an issue replaces the more usual multiarticle issue, bearing the number of that issue in the succession of numbers; sometimes it bears a supplementary number. In either case, its citation raises a question: Should the citation conform to the style used for a whole publication, or to that used for an article in a whole publication? The answer lies in the view taken by the publishers of the periodicals and by the libraries, that a paper occupying a whole issue is published *in* the periodical. Thus it is cited as an article, except that the special designation shown on the cover of the particular issue is included in the reference (e.g., supplement, special issue, etc.):

[1]Elias Folker, "Report on Research in the Capital Markets," Journal of Finance 39, supplement (May 1964): 15.

9.85 References to periodicals normally omit place and publisher (newspaper names do, however, include place; see 9.90–95), except that for foreign periodicals of limited circulation and titles that are identical or similar to periodicals published elsewhere, the place of publication should be included:

> [1]Jack Fishman, "Un grand homme dans son intimité: Churchill," Historia (Paris), no. 220 (November 1964): 684–94.

9.86 References to magazines and journals that are issued weekly, monthly, bimonthly, quarterly, and so on, should give the volume number in arabic numerals immediately after the title of the publication. Ordinarily, the date—month and/or year—is enclosed in parentheses and placed immediately after the volume number. Note that there is no mark of punctuation between the title of the publication and the volume number, and none between month and year. A colon follows the date in parentheses, and the page reference follows the colon.

> [1]Don Swanson, "Dialogue with a Catalogue," Library Quarterly 34 (December 1963): 113–25.
>
> [2]John W. Verty, "The Shifting Shape of SNA," Datamation 31 (15 November 1985): 94.

9.87 The month or season or issue number may also be given, but all citations to the same journal must be consistent. Identification of the issue number is required only if each issue is paginated separately, rather than in sequence throughout the volume. If the issue is identified by season or month, that is given in parentheses after the volume number:

> [1]Patricia A. Cooper, "What Ever Happened to Adolph Strasser?" Labor History 20 (Summer 1979): 17–30.
>
> [2]J. F. Eisenberg, "A Splendid Predator Does Its Own Thing Untroubled by Man," Smithsonian 1 (June 1970): 48–53.

If the issues are numbered, the issue number is given after the volume number, following a comma, and is preceded by the abbreviation "no.":

> [3]Lisa Steinman, "Moore, Emerson, and Kreymborg: The Use of Lists in 'The Monkey,'" Marianne Moore Newsletter 4, no. 1 (1980): 9.

Some journals have only issue numbers and no volume numbers. These are cited as follows:

[1]Konrad Lorenz, "The Wisdom of Darwin," <u>Midway</u>, no. 22 (1965): 43.

Note that when issue number alone is given, a comma separates it from the title of the periodical.

9.88 Some periodicals publish volumes in successive series, each beginning with volume 1. In some cases the successive series are numbered; in some they are lettered; and in some they are designated as "Old Series" or "New Series," abbreviated as "o.s." and "n.s." This information must be noted in the reference.

[1]"Letters of Jonathan Sewall," <u>Proceedings of the Massachusetts Historical Society</u>, 2d ser., 10 (January 1896): 414.

[2]G. M. Moraes, "St. Francis Xavier, Apostolic Nuncio, 1542–52," <u>Journal of the Bombay Branch of the Royal Asiatic Society</u>, n.s., 26 (1950): 279–313.

MAGAZINES AND NEWSPAPERS

9.89 Magazines of general interest, even though they may carry volume numbers, are best identified by date alone. The date then takes the place of the volume number and is not enclosed in parentheses:

[4]Anne B. Fisher, "Ford Is Back on the Track," <u>Fortune</u>, 23 December 1985, 18.

[2]Michael Rogers, "Software for War, or Peace: All the World's a Game," <u>Newsweek</u>, 9 December 1985, 82.

9.90 For reference to a newspaper, the name of the paper and the date are sufficient; but many large metropolitan papers—especially Sunday editions—are made up in sections that are separately paginated. For these, section number (or letter), page number, and edition letter (often in uppercase) must be given. It is convenient for the reader if the title of the article and the name of the author, if given, are included in the reference:

[7]Tyler Marshall, "200th Birthday of Grimms Celebrated," <u>Los Angeles Times</u>, 15 March 1985, sec. 1A, p. 3.

[2]Michael Norman, "The Once-Simple Folk Tale Analyzed by Academe," <u>New York Times</u>, 5 March 1984, p. 15(N).

9.91   If the name of an American newspaper does not include the name of the city, add the city before the newspaper title and underline both. If the city is not well known, give the name of the state in parentheses:

Houlton (Maine) Pioneer Times
Hiawatha (Kans.) Daily World

9.92   If the name of the city is the same as that of a well-known city, add the name of the state in parentheses:

Ottawa (Ill.) Times
St. Paul (Alberta) Journal

9.93   For foreign newspapers in which the city of publication does not form a part of the title, the name of the city should be given in parentheses after the title:

Times (London)
Le Monde (Paris)

But:

Frankfurter Zeitung
Manchester Guardian

9.94   The city of publication need not be given for such well-known newspapers as the *Christian Science Monitor,* the *Wall Street Journal,* and the *National Observer.*

9.95   An initial "The" in English-language newspaper titles is omitted, but its equivalent in a foreign language is retained: thus, *Times* (London) but *Le Monde* (Paris). This practice holds for notes, bibliographies, and reference lists. When a newspaper (or journal or magazine) title appears in the text, "the" may precede if the syntax requires it, but it is not treated as part of the title:

The Sunday edition of the San Francisco Examiner
includes an excellent section on entertainment.

The New York Times gives superior coverage to foreign
news.

He prefers New York Times editorials to those of any
other newspaper.

ARTICLES IN ENCYCLOPEDIAS AND DICTIONARIES

9.96 In citing alphabetically arranged reference works such as encyclopedias and dictionaries, it is best to give the title of the article
preceded by "s.v." (*sub verbo,* "under the word") rather than
volume and page numbers. Place of publication and publisher's
name are omitted from citations of most reference works. The
edition, unless it is the first, is normally mentioned. But here
just a word is in order concerning the policy of "continuous
revision" under which some major encyclopedias have operated
for many years. In such encyclopedias, the number of the edition
is not mentioned on the title page, and the date of publication
shown on the copyright page thus becomes the means of identification. When the title page does give the number of the edition, the reference should include that (as in note 1 below); when
the title page does not mention the edition, identify the particular
work by date of publication (note 2). In referring to a signed
article, the name of the author may be included. If only the
author's initials appear beneath the article, the list of authors in
the front matter of the work may provide the name:

[1]*Encyclopaedia Britannica*, 11th ed., s.v.
"Blake, William," by J. W. Cosyns–Carr.

[2]*Encyclopedia Americana*, 1963 ed., s.v. "Sitting
Bull."

[3]*Columbia Encyclopedia*, 3d ed., s.v. "Cano, Juan
Sebastian del."

[4]*Webster's Geographical Dictionary*, rev. ed.
(1964), s.v. "Dominican Republic."

An alternate form is to cite the author, if known, and the name
of the article first, followed by the title of the encyclopedia or
dictionary and information about the edition and the date of publication:

[1]J. W. Cosyns–Carr, "Blake, William," in
Encyclopaedia Britannica, 11th ed.

NOVELS, PLAYS, AND POEMS

9.97 *Novels.* References to novels are treated exactly as references to
nonfiction books. The particular edition referred to must be specified in the first reference, with a comment to tell the reader
when subsequent citations will be to that edition:

[3]James Joyce, <u>Ulysses</u>, a critical and synoptic edition prepared by Hans Walter Gabler with Wolfhard Steppe and Claus Melchior, 3 vols. (New York: Garland Publishing, 1984), 1:177 (all subsequent references are to this edition).

A subsequent reference to this would be as follows:

[9]Joyce, <u>Ulysses</u>, 2:34–35.

See also 9.130–42.

9.98 *Plays and long poems.* References to modern plays follow the style for books, except that act, scene, and line numbers are given instead of pages when the page number alone is not adequate.

[1]David Mamet, <u>The Poet and the Rent: A Play for Kids from Seven to 8:15</u> (New York: S. French, 1981), 35.

[2]Jean Anouilh, <u>Antigone</u>, ed. Raymond Laubreaux, Les Classiques de la civilisation française, ed. Yves Brunswick and Paul Givestier (Paris: Éditions de la Table Ronde, 1946; Didier, 1964), lines 1678–79, p. 87.

9.99 For English classics, the style of reference may be that used for Greek and Latin classical works (see 9.103–11). If the work is recognized as that of a widely known author, the author's name is frequently omitted; the title is underlined, whether the work is published as a separate volume or as part of a collection, and the facts of publication are given with the first reference but may be omitted thereafter with a suitable note to the reader. Among the works so treated are the plays of Shakespeare and Jonson and such long poems as *The Faerie Queene, Paradise Lost,* and *The Ring and the Book:*

<u>Romeo and Juliet</u> 3.2.1–30

for

<u>Romeo and Juliet</u>, act 3, scene 2, lines 1–30

<u>Paradise Lost</u> 1.83–86

for

<u>Paradise Lost</u>, book 1, lines 83–86

9.100 *Short poems.* To cite short poems, which most often are published in collections, the title is placed between quotation marks and the name of the collection underlined. Stanzas, lines, and pages may be included. When quoting poems in their entirety in a thesis or dissertation, it may be necessary to seek or obtain permissions (see 5.1).

REVIEWS

9.101   In a first reference to a review, give the name of the reviewer first; the title of the review (if any); the phrase "review of" followed by an identification of the work reviewed, as illustrated in the examples below; and finally the book, periodical, or newspaper in which the review appears.

Book reviews:

[1]Steven Spitzer, review of The Limits of Law Enforcement, by Hans Zeisel, in American Journal of Sociology 91 (November 1985): 726–29.

[2]David Scott Kastan, review of Johnson's Gypsies Unmasked: Background and Theme of "The Gypsies Metamorphos'd," by Dale B. J. Randall, Modern Philology 76 (May 1979): 391–94.

[3]Susan Lardner, "Third Eye Open," review of The Salt Eaters, by Toni Cade Bambara, New Yorker, 5 May 1980, 169.

Play reviews:

[4]Review of Fool for Love, by Sam Shepard, as performed by the Circle Repertory Company, New York, New York Times, 27 May 1983, p. 18(N).

Reviews of televised plays:

[5]Review of a televised version of True West, by Sam Shepard, in the New York Times, 31 January 1984, p. 22(N).

INTERVIEWS

9.102   References to interviews include the name of the person or the group interviewed; the title, if any, of the interview in quotation marks; the words "interview by" followed by the interviewer's name; the medium in which the interview appeared, whether a book, journal, radio program, or whatever, underlined or in quotation marks, as it would be in the first reference to any such medium; reference to an editor, translator, etc., if any, as in a first reference to a book (9.39–41); and facts of publication or other information required for references to printed and nonprinted sources:

[1]Raymond Bellour, "Alternation, Segmentation, Hypnosis: Interview with Raymond Bellour," interview by Janet Bergstrom, <u>Camera Obscura</u>, no. 3/4 (Summer 1979): 93.

[2]Isaac Bashevis Singer, interview by Harold Flender, in <u>Writers at Work: The "Paris Review" Interviews</u>, ed. George Plimpton, Fifth Series (New York: Viking Press, 1981), 85.

[3]Horace Hunt [pseud.], interview by Ronald Schatz, 16 May 1976, Tape recording, Pennsylvania Historical and Museum Commission, Harrisburg.

References to interviews conducted by the author of a paper should include the name of the person interviewed; a description of the type of interview conducted, capitalized sentence style; and the place and date of the interview:

[1]Mrs. Merle A. Roemer, interview by author, Tape recording, Millington, Maryland, 26 July 1973.

GREEK AND LATIN CLASSICAL WORKS

9.103 References to classical works use abbreviations extensively for author's name; title of the work; collections of inscriptions, papyri, ostraca, and so on; and for the titles of well-known periodical publications and other reference tools. For a list of accepted abbreviations, the *Oxford Classical Dictionary* should be consulted (see also 2.22). It is recommended, however, that such abbreviations not be used except in papers on predominantly classical topics. Sample notes appear in 9.111 below.

9.104 Titles of individual works, collections, and periodicals are underlined, whether they are given in full or abbreviated. In Greek and Latin titles, only the first word, proper nouns, and proper adjectives are capitalized.

9.105 The different levels of division of a work (book, part, section, chapter, lines, etc.) are indicated with arabic numerals. When designated by number only, the different levels are separated with periods (no spaces follow the internal periods):

[1]Stat. <u>Silv</u>. 1.3.32.

In a succession of references to the same level, commas separate the several references:

[2]Ovid <u>Met</u>. 1.240, 242.

A hyphen separates continued numbers (see 9.111, notes 1, 2, 8, and 9). If for the sake of clarity, identifying abbreviations are used before the numbers, the several divisions are separated with commas, not periods (bk. 2, sec. 4).

9.106 There is no punctuation between the author's name and the title of the work, and none between the title of the work and the first reference, unless the reference is preceded by an identifying word or abbreviation, in which case a comma intervenes (see 9.111, notes 3 and 4).

9.107 In general, the facts of publication are omitted, but the name of the edition may be given after the title (9.111, note 4), and it *must be given* if the reference is made to page numbers rather than to book, chapter, and so on.

9.108 The number of an edition, other than the first, is indicated by a superior number placed either after the title (9.111, note 8) or, if the reference includes a volume number, after that (9.111, note 7).

9.109 A superior letter or figure placed immediately after a number referring to a division of a work (other than a volume) indicates a subdivision (9.111, note 9). If preferred, the letters may be placed on the line, and either capital or small letters may be used, the choice depending upon usage in the source cited.

9.110 Despite the preference indicated in this manual for arabic numerals rather than roman numerals for volume numbers (see 2.44), references to collections of inscriptions, papyri, ostraca, and so forth, should continue to express volume numbers in capital roman numerals. After the volume number comes the document number, followed by numbers indicating the remaining divisions to which reference is made. Note that a comma separates title from volume number, and that the volume number and document number are also set off by commas, but that therafter periods separate the remaining divisions (see 9.111, note 6).

9.111 The following examples illustrate points discussed in 9.103–10:

[1]Homer <u>Odyssey</u> 9.266–71.

Or:

[2]Hom. <u>Od.</u> 9.266–71.

[3]Cicero <u>De officiis</u> 2.133, 140.

[4]Horace <u>Satires, Epistles and Ars poetica</u>, Loeb Classical Library, p. 12.

[5]H. Musurillo <u>TAPA</u> 93 (1926): 231.

⁶IG Rom., III, 739, 9.10, 17.

Note 6 refers to *Inscriptiones Graecae ad res Romanas pertinentes,* vol. 3, document 739, section 9, lines 10 and 17.

⁷E. Meyer Kleine Schriften 1² (Halle, 1924):
382.

⁸Stolz–Schmaiz Lat. Gram.⁵ (rev. Lausann–Hoffmann: Munich, 1928), 490–91.

⁹Aristotle Poetica 20.1456² 20.34–35.

¹⁰POxy. 1485.

In note 10, *POxy.* refers to *Oxyrhynchus Papyri.* The number cited is the document number; there is no volume number.

MEDIEVAL WORKS

9.112   References to medieval works may be in the same style as that used for Greek and Latin classical works:

¹Irenaeus Against Heresies 1.8.3.

²John of the Cross Ascent of Mount Carmel (trans. E. Allison Peers in The Complete Works of Saint John of the Cross [London: Burns, Oates, & Washbourne, Ltd., 1934–35]) 2.20.5.

³Beowulf, lines 2401–7.

When the specific part is named, as in note 3, a comma separates title from reference.

SCRIPTURAL REFERENCES

9.113   Exact references to the Bible and the Apocrypha use abbreviations for the books both in text and in notes. Chapter and verse, separated with either a colon or a period (be consistent), are both indicated with arabic numerals. The King James version is assumed unless another is cited (see 2.20–21):

¹Psalm 103:6–14.

²1 Cor. 13.1–13 NEB (New English Bible).

Non-Christian sacred scriptures are referred to in the same manner as Christian.

UNPUBLISHED MATERIAL

9.114   When a specific unpublished document is first discussed in the paper, include the pertinent facts within the text and in summary form within the note. In the note, list the author's name first, or if using a letter, list it in conjunction with a correspondent (notes 2 and 6). For uncertain authorship or titles, use brackets (see note 2 below). If no authorship can be established, begin the note entry with the document's title, if any, in quotation marks. If the document has both an author and a title, the title in quotation marks should follow the author's name (notes 3 and 4). The description of the document should follow the title if there is one, otherwise the author's name (see note 1). Capitalize the description of the document sentence style (see 4.9) in notes or abbreviate it according to guidelines set forth in 2.19. If the document is dated, that date should follow. Next give the full name of the collection to which the manuscript belongs, capitalized headline style (4.6–8). The full name of the depository follows (e.g., "Beinecke Rare Book and Manuscript Library, Yale University," not "Yale University Library"), and next its location by city and, if the city's name alone is insufficient, state. Last comes the page number, if any.

[1]Thomas Jefferson, Blank pass for a ship, 1801–1809, DS by Jefferson as president, Special Collections, Joseph Regenstein Library, University of Chicago, Chicago.

[2]Garnett Duncan, Louisville, Kentucky, to [Joel Tanner Hart, Florence, Italy], ALS, 12 June 1961, Durrett Collection, Special Collections, Joseph Regenstein Library, University of Chicago, Chicago.

[3]Abraham Lincoln, "Gettysburg Address" [final draft], AD [Photostat], 19 November 1863, Special Collections, Joseph Regenstein Library, University of Chicago, Chicago; original in the Library of Congress, Washington, D.C.

[4]Sandra Landis Gogel, "A Grammar of Old Hebrew" (Ph.D. diss., University of Chicago, 1985), 46–50.

[5]Eulogy of Charles V in Latin, apparently written at the monastery of St. Just, Spain, [ca. 1500], Special Collections, Joseph Regenstein Library, University of Chicago, Chicago.

[6]Hiram Johnson to John Callan O'Laughlin, 13, 16 July, 28 November 1916, O'Laughlin Papers, Roosevelt Memorial Collection, Harvard College Library, Cambridge.

9.115   References to formal speeches should include all of the above information in addition to the meeting and the sponsoring organization (if any), the location, and the date, all spelled out, capitalized sentence style, and placed after the name of the speaker and the title of the speech or the name of the type of speech (e.g., eulogy, sermon, lecture). The title of the speech is capitalized headline style and enclosed in quotation marks. The name and location of the depository in which the unpublished speech is located should follow information about the meeting at which the speech was delivered (or was to be delivered):

[1]David J. Bredehoft, "Self-Esteem: A Family Affair, an Evaluation Study," Paper presented at the annual meeting of the National Council on Family Relations, St. Paul, Minnesota, 11-15 October 1983, ERIC, ED 240461.

[2]Thomas Foxcroft, "A Seasonal Memento for New Year's Day," Sermon preached at the Old Church lecture in Boston on 1 January 1746-47 (Boston: S. Kneeland and T. Green, 1747).

LEGAL CITATIONS

9.116   Research papers on topics that are predominantly legal should employ the style of reference discussed in *A Uniform System of Citation*, thirteenth edition, 1981, a detailed guide published by the Harvard Law Review Association. When papers in other fields refer to books and periodicals in the field of law, as, for example, is frequently done in the social sciences, the references to legal works should be adapted to that of the research field in order to preserve a uniform style throughout the paper.

9.117   A paper may cite government documents other than those mentioned above. In such cases, the discussion and examples in chapter 12 may be useful. For reference works and style manuals relevant to government documents, see the bibliography.

9.118   Though names of cases are underlined in prose, they are not underlined if included in reference notes, bibliographies, and reference lists:

[1]Thompson v. Smith, 270 F. Supp. 331 (D. Conn. 1987).

The names of the first plaintiff and the first defendant are capitalized. Volume name (capitalized and abbreviated) and page of the law report follow. Next come the name of the court that decided the case and the year in which it was decided. Note that "v." not "vs." for "versus" is used in such references:

[1]United States v. Dennis, 183 F.2d 201 (2d Cir. 1950).

[2]Bridges v. California, 314 U.S. 252 (1941).

MICROFORM EDITIONS

9.119 Works issued commercially in microfilm, microfiche, or text-fiche (printed text and microfiche illustrations issued together) are treated much like books, except that the form of publication is given at the end of the entry (if it is not given in the name of the publisher), and a sponsoring organization may be listed as well as the publisher:

[1]Abraham Tauber, <u>Spelling Reform in the United States</u> (Ann Arbor, Mich.: University Microfilms, 1958), 50.

[2]Charles Wilson Peale, <u>The Collected Papers of Charles Wilson Peale and His Family</u>, ed. Lillian B. Miller, National Portrait Gallery, Smithsonian Institution, Washington, D.C. (Millwood, N.Y.: Kraus–Thomson Organization, 1980), 37, microfiche.

[3]Harold Joachim, <u>French Drawings and Sketchbooks of the Nineteenth Century</u>, Art Institute of Chicago (Chicago: University of Chicago Press, 1978), 1:59, text–fiche.

9.120 Microfilm or other photographic processes used only to preserve printed material, such as newspaper files, in a library are not mentioned as such in a citation. The source is treated as it would be in its original published version. Such is not the case, how-ever, with materials obtained through computer or information services.

MATERIAL OBTAINED THROUGH LOOSE-LEAF, COMPUTER, OR INFORMATION SERVICES

9.121 References to material obtained through loose-leaf services such as the Federal Tax Service, computer services such as Dialog or Orbit, and information services such as ERIC (Educational Resources Information Center) or NTIS (National Technical Information Service) are exactly like first references to the original printed material, except the pertinent facts within an entry are followed at the end of the entry by the name of the service, the name of the vendor providing the service, and the accession or identifying numbers within the service. If the service is revised annually, the year must be included. For some loose-leaf services, paragraphs rather than pages are given:

[1]2 P-H 1966 Fed. Tax Serv. par. 10182.

[3]Rosabel Flax et al., <u>Guidelines for Teaching Mathematics K-12</u> (Kansas: Kansas State Department of Education, Topeka Division of Education Services, June 1979), 85, Dialog, ERIC, ED 178312.

[4]D. Beevis, "Ergonomist's Role in the Weapon System Development Process in Canada" (Downsview, Ontario: Defence and Civil Institute of Environmental Medicine, 1983), 8, NTIS, AD-A145 5713/2, microfiche.

Some material available through computer and information services is not previously published. Treat such documents as any unpublished material (see 9.114–15), giving the name of the service, the name of the vendor providing the service, and the accession or identifying numbers within the service at the end of the entry:

[1]Linda B. Rudolf, "The Impact of the Divorce Process on the Family," Paper presented at the 29th annual meeting of the Southeastern Psychological Association, 23–26 March 1983, 12, EDRS, ED 233277, microfiche.

COMPUTER PROGRAMS

9.122 A reference to a computer program, package, language, system, and so forth, all collectively known as software, should include, in general, the fully spelled-out title, except for such common ones as BASIC, FORTRAN, COBOL, which are not spelled out; the identifying detail, such as version, level, release number, or date; in parentheses, the short name or acronym, where applicable, and any other information necessary for specific identification; and the location and name of the person, company, or organization having the proprietary rights to the software. If important for identification of the software, the author's name may also be mentioned. The following examples suggest how to make the names of computer programs into first references in notes:

[1]FORTRAN H-extended Version [or "Ver."] 2.3 (White Plains, N.Y.: IBM).

[2]Houston Automatic Spooling Priority II Ver. 4.0 (White Plains, N.Y.: IBM).

[3]International Mathematical Subroutine Library
Edition 8 (IMSL 8) (Houston, Tex.: International
Mathematical Subroutine Library, Inc.).

[4]Operating System/Virtual Storage Rel. 1.7 (OS/
VS 1.7) (White Plains, N.Y.: IBM).

[5]Statistical Package for the Social Sciences
Level M Ver. 8 (SPSS Lev. M 8.1) (Chicago: SPSS).

MUSICAL SCORES

9.123 References to musical scores follow rules similar to those for
books:

[1]Giuseppe Verdi, <u>Rigoletto</u>, melodrama in three
acts by Francesco Maria Piave, ed. Martin Chusid, in
<u>The Works of Giuseppe Verdi</u>, ser. 1, <u>Operas</u> (Chicago:
University of Chicago Press; Milan: G. Ricordi, 1982).

[2]Wolfgang Amadeus Mozart, <u>Sonatas and Fantasies
for the Piano</u>, prepared from the autographs and
earliest printed sources by Nathan Broder, rev. ed.
(Bryn Mawr, Pa.: Theodore Presser, 1960), 42.

MUSICAL COMPOSITIONS

9.124 In references to musical compositions, first list the composer's
name, then the title of the work underlined and capitalized headline style (see 4.6–8). An instrumental composition identified
only by form, number, and key should not be underlined or in
quotation marks. A published score with such a title, however,
is treated as is a book and underlined:

[1]Francis Poulenc, <u>Gloria</u>.

[2]Ludwig van Beethoven, Symphony no. 5 in C
Minor.

[3]Charles Gounod, <u>Faust</u>, libretto by J. Barbier
and M. Carré (New York: G. Schirmer, Inc., 1930), 113.

SOUND RECORDINGS

9.125 Records, tapes, and other forms of recorded sound are generally
listed under the name of the composer, writer, or other person(s)
responsible for the content. Collections or anonymous works are
listed by title. The title of a record or album is underlined. If
included, the name of the performer follows the title. The re-

cording company and the number of the record are sufficient to identify it. Facts added when desirable are date of copyright, kind of recording (stereo, quadraphonic, four-track cassette, etc.), the number of records in an album, and so on. This information may be found on the label of a recording or on its container (sleeve, box, etc.) or in printed material accompanying it. If the fact that it is a recording is not implicit in the designation from the label, a description may be added to the listing. In notes, it is sometimes necessary to identify audio recordings, since disks, cassettes, and tapes may be used for video, as well as sound recordings, and for computer programs.

[1]Johann Sebastian Bach, The Brandenburg Concertos, Paillard Chamber Orchestra, RCA CRL2-5801.

[2]Peg Leg Howell, "Blood Red River," The Legendary Peg Leg Howell, Testament T-2204.

[3]Archie Green, Introduction to brochure notes for Glenn Ohrlin, The Hell-Bound Train, University of Illinois Campus Folksong Club CFC 301, reissued as Puritan 5009.

[4]Genesis of a Novel: A Documentary on the Writing Regimen of Georges Simenon (Tucson, Ariz.: Motivational Programming Corp., 1969), sound cassette.

[5]M. J. E. Senn, Masters and Pupils, Audiotapes of lectures by Lawrence S. Kubie, Jane Loevinger, and M. J. E. Senn, presented at meeting of the Society for Research in Child Development, Philadelphia, March 1973 (Chicago: University of Chicago Press, 1974).

VIDEORECORDINGS

9.126 References to the many varieties of visual and audiovisual materials now available follow basically the same format. Give name of producer, director, and so forth, first whenever relevant; otherwise first list the title, capitalized headline style and underlined. Next should follow any facts pertinent to the purpose of the entry (e.g., the names of actors and actresses in a film, etc.) and the facts necessary to find the reference:

[1]Louis J. Mihaly, Landscapes of Zambia, Central Africa (Santa Barbara, Calif.: Visual Education, 1975), slides.

[2]The Greek and Roman World (Chicago: Society for Visual Education, 1977), filmstrip.

[3]China: An End to Isolation? 16mm, 25 min.,
1970, distributed by ACI Films, New York.

[4]L. K. Wolff, prod. Rock-a-bye Baby (New York:
Time-Life Films, 1971).

[5]Jean-Paul Sartre, Sartre, full text from a film
produced by Alexandre Astruc and Michel Contat with
the participation of Simone de Beauvoir, Jacques-
Laurent Bost, André Gortz, and Jean Pouillon (Paris:
Gallimard, 1977).

PERFORMANCES

9.127 References to performances begin with the most relevant name, whether it be that of the author, director, conductor, or whatever. Next comes the name of the performance, underlined, though in studies of a certain play, opera, or operetta, the name of the composition might come before relevant name(s). See 9.124 for treatment of musical compositions. For the location of the performance, give the name of the theater and the city, with the abbreviation of the name of the state in which the city is located if the latter might be unfamiliar to the reader. The date of the performance is given last:

[1]Sir Georg Solti, conductor, Brandenburg
Concerto, no. 1, by Bach, BWV 1046, Chicago Symphony
Orchestra concert, Chicago, 2 June 1985.

[2]Placido Domingo as Don José, in Carmen, by
Bizet, New York Metropolitan Opera, New York, 13 March
1987.

[4]Anton Chekhov, The Sea Gull, Court Theatre,
Chicago, 5 November 1981.

[5]Orson Welles and the Mercury Theatre, "Invasion
from Mars," radio performance, CBS, 30 October 1938,
8:00-9:00 P.M.

[6]Sesame Street, television performance, PBS, 22
November 1985.

WORKS OF ART

9.128 Works of art reproduced in a book are given in the style of book references. When referring to a work of art not found in an illustration in a published source, give the artist's name first, then the title of the work of art underlined, followed by the medium and the support (e.g., ''oil on canvas''), the date, the name of the institution holding the work of art, and the location of the institution (the city and, if the city might be unfamiliar to the reader, the state or country). If the location of a work of art is unknown, use the phrase "whereabouts unknown" in parentheses. If a work of art is in a private collection and the holder prefers that its location not be given, use the phrase "private collection."

[1]Pablo Picasso, Crouching Woman, oil drawing on plywood, 1946, Musée Picasso, Antibes.

[2]Lorado Taft, Fountain of Time, steel-reinforced hollow-cast concrete, 1922, Washington Park, west end of Midway Plaisance, Chicago.

[3]Lake Price, An Interior, print of collodon negative from 1855–56 Photographic Exchange Club album, ca. 1855, International Museum of Photography at George Eastman House, Rochester.

CITATION TAKEN FROM A SECONDARY SOURCE

9.129 In citing the work of one author as found in that of another, both the work in which the reference was found (secondary source) and the title of the work mentioned therein must be given in the reference. The style for such references is illustrated in note 1 below, but if it is more significant for the purposes of the paper to emphasize the secondary author's citing of the original work, the style of the second note should be used:

[1]Louis Zukofsky, "Sincerity and Objectification," Poetry 37 (February 1931): 269, quoted in Bonnie Costello, Marianne Moore: Imaginary Possessions (Cambridge and London: Harvard University Press, 1981), 78.

[2]Bonnie Costello, Marianne Moore: Imaginary Possessions (Cambridge and London: Harvard University Press, 1981), 78, citing Louis Zukofsky, "Sincerity and Objectification," Poetry 37 (February 1931): 269.

SECOND, OR SUBSEQUENT, REFERENCES

9.130 When a work has once been cited in complete form, later references to it are made in shortened form. For this, shortened titles or, where appropriate, the Latin abbreviation "ibid." should be used. The use of "op. cit." and "loc. cit.," formerly common in scholarly references, is now discouraged.

IBID.

9.131   When references to the same work follow one another without any intervening reference, even though the references are separated by several pages, the abbreviation "ibid." (for the Latin *ibidem*, "in the same place") is used to repeat as much of the preceding reference as is appropriate for the new entry. The following is a first, and therefore complete, reference to a work:

> [1]Max Plowman, <u>An Introduction to the Study of Blake</u> (London: Gollancz, 1952), 32.

With no intervening reference, a second mention of the same page of Plowman's work requires only "Ibid." Notice that "Ibid." is not underlined.

> [2]Ibid.

With no intervening reference since the last to Plowman's work, "Ibid." is still correct, but in the following the reference is to a different page.

> [3]Ibid., 68.

9.132   Since "ibid." means "in the same place," it must not be used to repeat an author's name when references to two works by the same author follow each other without an intervening reference. Although repetition of the author's name in the second reference is the style preferred by many scholars, in several references *within one note* to works by the same author, "idem" may be used. This Latin word, meaning "the same," is commonly used only in place of a person's name. It may be abbreviated to "id." if the abbreviation is consistently used. Do not confuse "ibid." and "idem." In note 2 below, "ibid." stands for all the items of the preceding reference except the page number, whereas in note 5 "idem" stands for only the author:

> [1]Arthur Waley, <u>The Analects of Confucius</u> (London: George Allen & Unwin, 1938), 33.
>
> [2]Ibid., 37.
>
> [3]Arthur Waley, <u>Chinese Poems</u> (London: George Allen & Unwin, 1946), 51.
>
> [4]Ibid., 17.
>
> [5]Ibid., 19; idem, <u>The Analects of Confucius</u>, 25.

Note that "idem" is a complete word, not an abbreviation, and is therefore not followed by a period.

9.133   References following legal style, however, employ "idem" (abbreviated as "id.") where this manual stipulates "ibid." Legal style reserves "ibid." for references where there is no change in page or other part from the preceding reference. This special application of "ibid." and "idem" as set forth in *A Uniform System of Citations,* thirteenth edition, should be used only for scholarly papers in the field of law.

SHORTENED REFERENCES

9.134   Reference to a work that has already been cited in full form, but not in a reference immediately preceding, is made in one of two styles, which shall be called method A and method B. Method A uses the first author's family name, title of book or article (sometimes in shortened form), and specific page reference. Method B uses the first author's family name and specific page reference, and lists the title of the book or article only when two or more works by the same author are cited. For examples of method A and method B, see 9.136 and 9.137.

9.135   The author's name must be given in the reference whether or not it appears in the text close to the citation. This avoids textual ambiguities, difficult constructions in the text, and needless double-checking for the reader.

METHOD A

9.136   The first three notes below contain first, and therefore full, references. Notes 4 through 5 show second, or subsequent, references given in the style of method A.

> [1]Max Plowman, <u>Introduction to the Study of Blake</u> (London: Gollancz, 1952), 58–59.
>
> [2]Max Plowman, <u>William Blake's Design for "The Marriage of Heaven and Hell"</u> (London: Faber and Faber, 1960), ix–xii.
>
> [3]Elspeth Longacre, "Blake's Conception of the Devil," <u>Studies in English</u> 90 (June 1937): 384.

Note 4 refers to the first mentioned work of Plowman, given in full in note 1, and uses the shortened title:

> [4]Plowman, <u>Study of Blake</u>, 125.

Note 5 gives a second, or subsequent, reference to Longacre's journal article, first cited in note 3, and here uses a shortened title, as required by method A, even though the article is the only work by the author previously cited:

[5]Longacre, "Blake's Devil," 381.

METHOD B

9.137   The following notes present later references to the same sources cited in full in the first three notes in 9.136. Here the subsequent references are given in the style of method B. Note 4 makes a second reference to the work by Plowman cited first in note 2. Since two works by this author have been cited, the shortened reference must contain a shortened version of the title:

[4]Plowman, <u>Blake's Design</u>, 25.

Note 5 contains a second reference to Longacre's article. Since only one work by this author has been previously mentioned, the name and page number are sufficient under method B:

[5]Longacre, 382.

9.138   A second, or subsequent, reference to a multivolume work already cited in full form, but not in the reference immediately preceding, omits the subtitle, if any; the facts of publication; series title, if any; edition (unless more than one edition of the same work has been cited); and total number of volumes. Note the full reference in note 1 and a later reference to the work as shown in (arbitrarily numbered) note 9 (method A) and note 10 (method B):

[1]Gabriel Marcel, <u>The Mystery of Being</u> (Chicago: Henry Regnery Co., 1960), 1:42.

[9]Marcel, <u>Mystery of Being</u>, 2:98–99.

Or:

[10]Marcel, 2:98–99.

Now consider another multivolume work, which has an overall title and different titles for the individual volumes, only one of which is referred to in the notes:

[2]Tucker Brooke, <u>The Renaissance (1500–1600)</u>, vol. 2 in <u>A Literary History of England</u>, ed. Albert C. Baugh (New York: Appleton–Century–Crofts, 1948), 104.

[3]Brooke, <u>Renaissance</u>, 130.

Or in the style of method B:

[3]Brooke, 130.

9.139 For a subsequent reference to an article in a magazine or journal, a chapter in a book, or an essay, poem, or the like in an anthology, omit the name of the periodical or book and omit also the volume number, if any, and the date. The reference should consist of the author's last name (methods A and B), the title of the work in shortened form (method A only), and the page number. Examples of a full note to an article in a scholarly journal and its corresponding shortened forms are shown in notes 3 and 5 in 9.136 (method A) and in note 5 in 9.137 (method B).

SHORTENED TITLES

9.140 Titles of five or fewer words need not be shortened, unless the words are very long. Such a title as the following may be shortened as indicated:

The Essential Tension: Selected Studies in Scientific
Tradition and Change

shortened to

Essential Tension

9.141 A shortened title uses the key words of the main title, omitting an initial article when the title is in English. Titles beginning with such words as "A Dictionary of," "Readings in," and "An Index to" would normally omit those words, using the topic as the short title:

A Guide to Rehabilitation of the Handicapped

shortened to

Handicapped

Bibliography of North American Folklore and Folksong

shortened to

Folklore and Folksong

There are, however, dictionaries and bibliographies that cover a variety of topics: *An Index to General Literature, Biographical, Historical, and Literary Essays and Sketches, Reports and Publications of Boards and Societies Dealing with Education.* It would not do to include only one category in a short title; the only reasonable short title is simply *Education Index.*

9.142 When a shortened title might cause confusion, it is a convenience for the reader if the first full citation of the work notes that shortened title.

CONTENT NOTES

9.143   Content (or substantive) notes consist of explanations or ampli-
fications of the textual discussion and therefore resemble the text
more than reference notes. When it is desirable to give the
source of material included in a content note, the reference may
be placed in one of several ways. It may be worked into a sentence, much as sources are sometimes worked into the text (as
shown in notes 1 and 2 below), or it may follow as a separate
item (note 3). In either case, whether the title is cited in full and
whether the facts of publication are given depend upon whether
the source has been referred to in a previous note:

[1]Detailed evidence of the great increase in the
array of goods and services bought as income increases
is shown in S. J. Prais and H. S. Houthaker, The
Analysis of Family Budgets (Cambridge: Cambridge
University Press, 1955), table 5, 52.

[2]Ernst Cassirer takes important notice of this
in Language and Myth (59–62), and offers a searching
analysis of man's regard for things on which his power
of inspirited action may crucially depend.

Since the work referred to in note 2 has already been cited in
full form, page reference only is required here.

[3]In 1962 the premium income received by all
voluntary health insurance organizations in the United
States was $6.3 billion, while the benefits paid out
were $7.1 billion.   Health Insurance Institute, Source
Book of Health Insurance Data (New York: Health
Insurance Institute, 1963), 36, 46.

CROSS-REFERENCES

9.144   Occasionally a writer finds it necessary to refer to material in
another part of the paper. Such references often consist simply
of page or note numbers, or both, inserted in parentheses in the
text. Cross-references may also appear in notes. Whether in
notes or text, however, cross-references with page numbers pose
a difficulty because these can only be added after all pagination
is final.

9.145   The words "above" (earlier in the paper) and "below" (later in
the paper) are frequently used with cross-references because they
make it clear that the reference is to the paper in hand, not to
another source mentioned. "Supra" and "infra" are sometimes
used, chiefly in law references, in place of "above" and "be-

low.'' See 13.24 and 13.26 for discussions of the use of computer systems to prepare papers with numbered sections that may be cross-referenced.

9.146 The word ''see'' is often used with cross-references; ''cf.'' should be used only in the sense of ''compare'' and is not an alternate for ''see'':

[1]For a detailed discussion of this matter see pp. 31–35 below.

9.147 A cross-reference such as ''See n. 3 above'' intended simply to refer to the title of a source is not permissible. The regular style for the second reference (whether following method A or method B) should be used consistently throughout the paper (see 9.130–42).

10 Citation III: Bibliographies

10.1 The rules for bibliographical style in this chapter and the examples of bibliographical entries in chapter 11 apply mainly to papers in nonscientific fields, especially in the humanities. The style for reference lists accompanying papers using parenthetical references is explained in chapter 8. Samples 14.48–49 show the correct layout on the page of a bibliography.

GENERIC HEADING

10.2 The bibliography lists the sources used in writing the paper. Since a bibliography rarely includes all that has been written on a given topic, a more accurate heading for this section of the paper would be, for example, SELECTED BIBLIOGRAPHY, WORKS CITED, or SOURCES CONSULTED. The last is especially suitable if the list includes such sources as personal interviews, lectures, tape recordings, radio or television broadcasts, or information available through computer services, which for the sake of convenience are by common usage included in a bibliography.

CLASSIFICATION

10.3   Unless the bibliography is very short, it may be classified, divided into sections. For example, in a paper using manuscript sources as well as printed works, the two kinds of sources may be put in separate sections, the manuscripts arranged either by depository or by name of collection. In a work with many references to newspapers, the newspapers may be separated from the rest of the bibliography and listed together, each with its run of relevant dates (see 11.45). In a lengthy bibliography listing many printed sources, books are sometimes separated from articles. In a study of the work of one person, it is usually best to list works *by* that person separately from works *about* him or her. A list of works by one author may be arranged in chronological order (i.e., by date of publication) rather than alphabetical order. In a paper about one person, such a list may constitute the entire bibliography. Whatever the arrangement of a bibliography, it is recommended that no source be listed more than once. If the same work is listed more than once, the arrangement should be examined. When a bibliography is divided into sections, a headnote sometimes states the fact and indicates the titles of the sections.

10.4   The topic of the paper, its order of presentation, and its thesis will determine how the bibliography should be classified, or divided into sections. Do not, however, divide a long bibliography into sections by themes or concepts, e.g., "love," "hate," "war," "peace," etc.

10.5   Sometimes the variety of source materials calls for further subdivision of the main classes, under second-level subheadings. For example, a list entitled PRIMARY SOURCES may be divided into two parts: "Published Works" and "Unpublished Works."

10.6   Within the divisions and subdivisions, the entries should be arranged in a definite order. Although alphabetical order by family name of author is the most common, for some papers another order—for example, chronological—is more helpful. If a scheme other than alphabetical is used, it should be explained at the beginning of the bibliography or in a footnote on the first page of the bibliography.

BIBLIOGRAPHICAL ENTRIES COMPARED WITH NOTES

10.7   A bibliographical entry is similar to a full note in that it includes much of the same material arranged in much the same order. Differences between the two in the way of presenting this material stem from the differences in purpose and placement. The purpose of a bibliographical entry is to list a work in full bibliographical detail: name(s) of author(s); full title of work; place, publisher, and date of publication. The purpose of a note is primarily to inform the reader of the particular location—page, section, or other segment—from which the writer of the paper has taken certain material cited in the text. The secondary purpose of the note—to enable the reader to find the source—dictates the inclusion of full bibliographical details in the first reference to a work (see 9.2). The differences in style of presentation between notes and bibliography are described below (10.8–13) and illustrated by parallel examples in chapters 11 and 12.

10.8   The bibliography of a paper is single-spaced with one blank space between entries. The first line of each entry is flush left, and all subsequent lines, if any, are indented five spaces (see 14.48–49).

10.9   In a note, the author's full name is given in the natural order, given name first, because there is no reason to reverse the order. In the bibliographical entry, the family name is given first because bibliographies are usually arranged in alphabetical order by family names of authors:

```
McDougall, Walter A. . . . The Heavens and the Earth:
    A Political History of the Space Age. New York:
    Basic Books, 1985.
```

10.10   Where there are two or more authors' names, only the first is reversed in the bibliography, in order to alphabetize the item. The following names are given in normal order, given name first and then family name last:

```
Stockwell, R. P., P. Schachter, and B. H. Partee. The
    Major Syntactic Structures of English. New York:
    Holt, Rinehart and Winston, 1973.
```

10.11   Whereas commas and parentheses are used in a note, periods are used in a bibliographical entry at the end of each main part—author's name, title of work, and facts of publication. Bibliographical references to periodicals, however, retain the parenthe-

167

ses around the dates of publication when these follow volume number (see 11.39–40).

10.12   Page numbers are listed in bibliographical entries only when the item is part of a whole work—a chapter in a book or an article in a periodical. When given, page numbers must be inclusive—first and last page of the relevant section (see 11.40). When an article is continued in the back of a journal or magazine, however, only its first page need be given (see 11.41).

10.13   If the institution or discipline for which the paper is written requires a notation of the total number of pages for each book and pamphlet, the information is noted at the end of the entry: "Pp. xiv + 450."

ALPHABETIZING AUTHORS' NAMES

10.14   Bibliographies are arranged alphabetically by authors' family names, letter-by-letter (ignoring word spaces); in the case of identical family names, by given name.

10.15   Family names containing particles vary widely both in capitalization and in form of alphabetization when arranged with family name first, as in bibliographies, reference lists, and indexes. The preference of the bearer of the name—or tradition concerning this preference—as reflected in the biographical list at the end of *Webster's Ninth New Collegiate Dictionary* or of *Webster's New Biographical Dictionary*, should be followed when alphabetizing family names with particles. Lists should be arranged in letter-by-letter alphabetical order, regardless of upper- and lowercase spellings and intervening punctuation. Such common abbreviations as "Mc" and "M'" for "Mac," and "St." and "Ste" for "Saint" and "Sainte" are alphabetized as they appear when abbreviated, rather than as if they were spelled out:

```
Augustine, Saint
Becket, Thomas à (or Thomas Becket, Saint alphabetized
    under the T's)
Braun, Wernher von
D'Annunzio, Gabriel
de Gaulle, Charles
de Kooning, Willem
De la Rey, Jacobus Hercules
Della Robbia, Luca
De Mille, Agnes George
De Valera, Eamon
Deventer, Jacob Louis van
```

```
De Vere, Aubrey Thomas
De Vries, Hugo
DiMaggio, Joseph Paul
Gogh, Vincent van
Guardia, Ricardo Adolfo de la
Hindenburg, Paul von
Lafontaine, Henri-Marie
La Fontaine, Jean de
La Guardia, Fiorello Henry
Linde, Otto zur
Mabie, Hamilton Wright
Macalister, Donald
MacArthur, Douglas
Macaulay, Emilie Rose
MacMillan, Donald Baxter
Macmillan, Harold
McAdoo, William Gibbs
McAllister, Alister
M'Carthy, Justin
McAuley, Catherine Elizabeth
Ramée, Marie Louise de la
Sainte-Beuve, Charles-Augustin
Saint-Gaudens, Augustus
Saint-Saëns, Charles-Camille
St. Denis, Ruth
St. Laurent, Louis Stephen
Thomas à Kempis
Van Devanter, Willis
Van Rensselaer, Stephen
```

10.16   In an optional style of alphabetization, names beginning with abbreviated forms such as "Mc" or "M'" for "Mac" and "St." for "Saint," for example, would be alphabetized letter-by-letter in an arrangement determined by the spelled-out form and *not* by the abbreviation. If spelled with the abbreviation, such names are nevertheless alphabetized as if spelled out. For examples, see *The Chicago Manual of Style*, thirteenth edition, 18.103 and 18.105.

10.17   Compound family names are alphabetized by the first name in the compound. For hyphenation and inversion, follow the preferences of the bearers of such names or established usage:

```
Ap Ellis, Augustine
Campbell-Bannerman, Henry
Castelnuovo-Tedesco, Mario
Fénelon, François de Salignac de La Mothe-
Gatti-Casazza, Giulio
Ippolitov-Ivanov, Mikhail Michaylovich
La Révellière-Lépeaux, Louis-Marie de
Lloyd George, David
```

```
Mendes, Frederic de Sola
Mendès-France, Pierre
Merle d'Aubigné, Jean-Henri
Merry del Val, Rafael
Pinto, Fernao Mendes
Teilhard de Chardin, Pierre
Vaughan Williams, Ralph
Watts-Dunton, Walter Theodore
Wilson Lang, John
```

10.18 Spanish names which consist of given name (or names) and paternal family name and maternal family name joined with the conjunction *y* are alphabetized under the paternal name. Many names omit the conjunction, however, and in such a name as *Manuel Ramón Albeniz*, it is not clear whether the father's family name is *Ramón* or whether *Ramón* is a second given name. If the facts cannot be determined, the library catalog may often serve as a guide.

10.19 Arabic, Chinese, and Japanese names should be alphabetized with particular care. In *Arabic*, family names beginning with *Abd, abu-,* or *ibn* are usually alphabetized under these elements. Those beginning with *al-* ("the") are alphabetized by the element following this particle. The particle itself may be placed after the whole inverted name (*Hakim, Tawfiq al-*) or retained before it (*al-Hakim, Tawfiq*), which is the modern practice. Elided forms of the article (e.g., *ad-, an-, ar-,* etc.) are treated the same way, though the practice of spelling in the elided form is discouraged by most orientalists.

```
Hmisi, Ahmad Hamid
Husayn, Taha
al-Jamal, Muhammad Hamid
```

Or:

```
Jamal, Muhammad Hamid al-
```

10.20 *Chinese* names usually consist of three syllables, the one-syllable family name coming first, the two-syllable given name following. In romanized form, both names are capitalized. In the Wade-Giles system, the given name is hyphenated; and in pinyin, closed up:

WADE-GILES	PINYIN
Chao Wu-chi	Zhoa Wuji
Ch'eng Shih-fa	Cheng Shifa
Li K'o-jan	Li Keran
Tseng Yu-ho	Zeng Youhe

Alphabetization of Chinese names will vary depending upon whether the Wade-Giles or pinyin system is used. When alphabetizing Chinese names that are written in traditional form, even those of two instead of three syllables, the family name precedes the given name, and so the name is not reversed in alphabetizing a bibliography or reference list.

10.21   *Japanese* names normally consist of two elements, a family name and a given name—in that order. If the name is Westernized, as it often is by authors writing in English, the order is reversed. In recent years, however, there has been a tendency among authors writing in English on Japanese subjects to use the traditional order for personal names. When alphabetizing Japanese names in a bibliography, decide how to list each entry on a case-by-case basis, depending upon the preference of the author(s):

JAPANESE ORDER	WESTERN ORDER
Kurosawa Noriaki	Kurosawa, Noriaki
Tojo Hideki	Tojo, Hideki
Yoshida Shigeru	Yoshida, Shigeru

10.22   For treatment of Hungarian names and such other non-Western names as Vietnamese, Thai, Indian, Burmese, Javanese, and Indonesian names, see *The Chicago Manual of Style,* thirteenth edition, 18.109 and 18.116–22.

10.23   Authors with the same family name and the same first initial, one identified by initials alone, one by a single given name, and one by the same name plus a middle name (or initial), are alphabetized as follows:

```
Adams, J. B.
Adams, John
Adams, John Q.
Adams, John Quincy
```

10.24   When reversed, names with *Sr.* or *Jr.* or a roman numeral are punctuated as follows and arranged in letter-by-letter order:

```
Brownell, Arthur P., Jr.
Brownell, Arthur P., Sr.
Brownell, Arthur P. III
Brownell, Arthur Patrick, Jr.
```

10.25   A writer who has adopted a religious name sometimes writes under that name alone, preceded by the appropriate title. Sometimes the family name is added to the religious name. Alphabetize the name rather than the title:

```
Thérèse, Sister
Hayden, Father Cuthbert
```

10.26   Works published under a pseudonym should be listed under the author's pseudonym. The author's name may be enclosed in brackets and placed after the pseudonym if desired, and the bibliography or reference list may include a cross-reference (see 11.2 and 11.9):

```
Stendahl [Marie Henri Beyle]
Bell, Currer [Charlotte Brontë]
```

SUCCESSION OF WORKS BY THE SAME AUTHOR

10.27   In a succession of works by the same author, the name is given for the first entry, and an eight-space line (the underscore key struck eight times) ending with a period takes its place in subsequent entries. The entries are arranged alphabetically by title or chronologically by date. When alphabetizing titles, disregard introductory articles, prepositions, and conjunctions.

```
Eliot, T. S. The Sacred Wood: Essays on Poetry and
     Criticism. London: Methuen, 1920.

_____. The Waste Land. New York: Boni & Liveright,
     1922.

_____. Murder in the Cathedral. New York: Harcourt,
     Brace, 1935.
```
Or:
```
Eliot, T. S. Murder in the Cathedral. New York:
     Harcourt, Brace, 1935.

_____. The Sacred Wood: Essays on Poetry and
     Criticism. London: Methuen, 1920.

_____. The Waste Land. New York: Boni & Liveright,
     1922.
```

10.28   Titles of works edited by the author or written by the author in collaboration with others should not be alphabetized along with works written by the author alone. In a list including all three categories, put the edited titles after the works written by the author in question, using an eight-space line of underscores for the author's name, followed by a comma, a space, and "ed." Unless there are coauthored works (see 10.29), translations (use "Translated by") would follow and then compilations (use "Compiled by").

10.29 Coauthored works follow edited works, but the author's name must be repeated in them. Do not use an eight-space line of underscores to take the place of a coauthor's name or the names of two or more coauthors.

10.30 A long bibliography of works by one author may carry a heading including the author's name, which would then *not* appear with each item. Works edited by the author would either be under a subheading or begin with the abbreviation "Ed." Works written in collaboration with others would begin, for example, "With Joseph P. Jones and John Q. Adams."

10.31 A work for which no author (editor, compiler, or other) is known appears in a bibliography under the title of the work, alphabetized by the first word, or the first word following an initial article, preposition, or conjunction, if the title is in English.

10.32 When the names of a person, a place, and a thing are spelled the same way and are set at the beginnings of bibliographical entries, they are arranged person first, place second, and thing third, whether or not the next words in the bibliographical entries are in strict alphabetical order. This rule applies in lists where works by an author are followed by those works listed by titles in which the author's family name is the first word of a title.

10.33 Underlining titles of whole publications—books, periodicals, and all other works whose titles are underlined in notes and text—is optional in a bibliography, but the same style must be followed throughout.

10.34 In a bibliography, quotation marks must be used around titles of articles and other component parts of whole publications, as discussed in 4.15 and 4.17.

FOREIGN-LANGUAGE TITLES IN A BIBLIOGRAPHY

10.35 Treat underlining in foreign-language titles just as it would be treated in titles in English, even when the full titles in a bibliography are not underlined. If an English title contains a foreign word or phrase, however, it should be underlined unless the entire title is already underlined. In that case, put the foreign word or phrase in quotation marks. Titles of works within underlined titles are treated the same way (see 11.22–23).

Autobiographical Aspects of Melville's "Moby Dick"
Aspects autobiographiques de "Moby Dick" de Melville

Or:

Autobiographical Aspects of Melville's Moby Dick
Aspects autobiographiques de Moby Dick de Melville

ANNOTATING BIBLIOGRAPHIES

10.36   A bibliography may be annotated either in whole or in part. The annotation need not be a grammatically complete sentence, but it should begin with a capital and end with a period. The first line begins on the line following the entry proper and must be indented at least five spaces or more for a paragraph indention.

Thompson, Oscar, ed. International Cyclopaedia of
     Music and Musicians. New York: Dodd, Mead & Co.,
     1936.

          It is an admirable work that brings Grove up
     to date and deals adequately with contemporary
     music and American composers.

11   Citation IV: Samples

Works of Art 11.63
Works of Art Reproduced in Books 11.64
Multiple References Contained in a Single Note 11.65

11.1 The following sets of examples illustrate note (N.) and parenthetical-reference (PR.) forms and corresponding bibliographical (B.) and reference-list (RL.) entries exclusive of those used in citations of public documents (see chapter 12).

11.2 When documenting a paper using parenthetical references keyed to a reference list, and even in some papers using notes and a bibliography, it is often desirable to use cross-references. It might be desirable to use a cross-reference for a work by a person who uses a pseudonym or for a work in which both author and writer of the foreword should be listed. The choice of which name to cross-reference depends on the context in which the work is discussed within the paper. A usage once selected must be retained consistently throughout the paper. If citation to one of the works referenced below should require a cross-reference, an example is included to illustrate the cross-reference in the reference-list (RL/CR.) and the parenthetical reference that would be appropriate for use with each such cross-reference (PR/CR.). Cross-references in bibliographies resemble those in reference lists, exclusive of the dates. See also 8.11, 8.23, and 12.2.

BOOKS

SINGLE AUTHOR

11.3 N.   [1]John Hope Franklin, <u>George Washington Williams: A Biography</u> (Chicago: University of Chicago Press, 1985), 54.

B.   Franklin, John Hope. <u>George Washington Williams: A Biography</u>. Chicago: University of Chicago Press, 1985.

PR.   (Franklin 1985, 54)

RL.   Franklin, John Hope. 1985. <u>George Washington Williams: A biography</u>. Chicago: University of Chicago Press.

Two Authors

11.4 N.   [2]Brian W. Kernighan and Dennis M. Ritchie, <u>The C Programming Language</u> (Englewood Cliffs, N.J.: Prentice-Hall, 1978), 185.

B.   Kernighan, Brian W., and Dennis M. Ritchie. <u>The C Programming Language</u>. Englewood Cliffs, N.J.: Prentice-Hall, 1978.

PR.   (Kernighan and Ritchie 1978, 185)

RL.   Kernighan, Brian W., and Dennis M. Ritchie. 1978. <u>The C programming language</u>. Englewood Cliffs, N.J.: Prentice-Hall.

Three Authors

11.5 N.   [3]Mary Lyon, Bryce Lyon, and Henry S. Lucas, <u>The Wardrobe Book of William de Norwell, 12 July 1338 to 27 May 1340</u>, with the collaboration of Jean de Sturler (Brussels: Commission Royale d'Histoire de Belgique, 1983), 42.

B.   Lyon, Mary, Bryce Lyon, and Henry S. Lucas. <u>The Wardrobe Book of William de Norwell, 12 July 1338 to 27 May 1340</u>. With the collaboration of Jean de Sturler. Brussels: Commission Royale d'Histoire de Belgique, 1983.

PR.   (Lyon, Lyon, and Lucas 1983, 42)

RL.   Lyon, Mary, Bryce Lyon, and Henry S. Lucas. 1983. <u>The wardrobe book of William de Norwell, 12 July 1338 to 27 May 1340</u>. With the collaboration of Jean de Sturler. Brussels: Commission Royale d'Histoire de Belgique.

More than Three Authors

11.6 N.   [4]Martin Greenberger and others, eds., <u>Networks for Research and Education: Sharing of Computer and Information Resources Nationwide</u> (Cambridge: MIT Press, 1974), 50.

B.   Greenberger, Martin, Julius Aronofsky, James L. McKenney, and William F. Massy, eds. <u>Networks for Research and Education: Sharing of Computer and Information Resources Nationwide</u>. Cambridge: MIT Press, 1974.

PR.   (Greenberger and others 1974, 50)

RL.   Greenberger, Martin, Julius Aronofsky, James
        L. McKenney, and William F. Massy, eds.
        1974. <u>Networks for research and
        education: Sharing of computer and
        information resources nationwide</u>.
        Cambridge: MIT Press.

No Author Given

11.7 N.   [5]<u>The Lottery</u> (London: J. Watts [1732]),
        20–25.

B.   <u>The Lottery</u>. London: J. Watts [1732].

PR.   (<u>The lottery</u> [1732], 20–25)

RL.   <u>The lottery</u>. [1732]. London: J. Watts.

No Author Given; Name Supplied

11.8 N.   [6][Henry K. Blank], <u>Art for Its Own Sake</u>
        (Chicago: Nonpareil Press, 1910), 8.

B.   [Blank, Henry K.]. <u>Art for Its Own Sake</u>.
        Chicago: Nonpareil Press, 1910.

PR.   ([Blank] 1910, 8)

RL.   [Blank, Henry K.]. 1910. <u>Art for its own sake</u>.
        Chicago: Nonpareil Press.

Pseudonymous Author; Real Name Supplied

11.9 See 9.26–29.

N.   [7]Mrs. Markham, <u>A History of France</u>
        (London: John Murray, 1872), 9.

B.   Markham, Mrs. [Elizabeth Cartright Penrose]. <u>A
        History of France</u>. London: John Murray,
        1872.

PR.   (Markham 1872, 9)

Or:

PR/CR. (Penrose 1872, 9)

RL.   Markham, Mrs. [Elizabeth Cartright Penrose].
        1872. <u>A history of France</u>. London: John
        Murray.

RL/CR. Penrose, Elizabeth Cartright. 1872. <u>See</u>
        Markham, Mrs. [Elizabeth Cartright
        Penrose]. 1872.

INSTITUTION, ASSOCIATION, OR THE LIKE, AS "AUTHOR"

11.10 N.   [8]American Library Association, Young
Adult Services Division, Services Statement
Development Committee, <u>Directions for Library
Service to Young Adults</u> (Chicago: American
Library Association, 1978), 25.

B.   American Library Association, Young Adult
Services Division, Services Statement
Development Committee. <u>Directions for
Library Service to Young Adults</u>. Chicago:
American Library Association, 1978.

PR.   (American Library Association 1978, 25)

RL.   American Library Association, Young Adult
Services Division, Services Statement
Development Committee. 1978. <u>Directions
for library service to young adults</u>.
Chicago: American Library Association.

EDITOR OR COMPILER AS "AUTHOR"

11.11 N.   [9]Robert von Hallberg, ed., <u>Canons</u>
(Chicago: University of Chicago Press, 1984),
225.

B.   von Hallberg, Robert, ed. <u>Canons</u>. Chicago:
University of Chicago Press, 1984.

PR.   (von Hallberg 1984, 225)

RL.   von Hallberg, Robert, ed. 1984. <u>Canons</u>.
Chicago: University of Chicago Press.

AUTHOR'S WORK TRANSLATED OR EDITED BY ANOTHER

11.12 N.   [10]Jean Anouilh, <u>The Lark</u>, trans.
Christopher Fry (London: Methuen, 1955), 86.

B.   Anouilh, Jean. <u>The Lark</u>. Translated by
Christopher Fry. London: Methuen, 1955.

PR.   (Anouilh 1955, 86)

RL.   Anouilh, Jean. 1955. <u>The lark</u>. Translated by
Christopher Fry. London: Methuen.

AUTHOR'S WORK CONTAINED IN COLLECTED WORKS

11.13 N.   [11]<u>The Complete Works of Samuel Taylor
Coleridge</u>, ed. W. G. T. Shedd, vol. 1, <u>Aids to</u>

> Reflection (New York: Harper & Bros., 1884),
> 18.

B.   Coleridge, Samuel Taylor. The Complete Works
of Samuel Taylor Coleridge. Edited by W.
G. T. Shedd. Vol. 1, Aids to Reflection.
New York: Harper & Bros., 1884.

PR.   (Coleridge 1884, 1:18)

RL.   Coleridge, Samuel Taylor. 1884. The complete
works of Samuel Taylor Coleridge. Edited
by W. G. T. Shedd. Vol. 1, Aids to
reflection. New York: Harper & Bros.

SEPARATELY TITLED VOLUME IN A MULTIVOLUME WORK WITH A GENERAL TITLE AND EDITOR(S)

11.14 N.   [12]Gordon N. Ray, ed., An Introduction to
Literature (Boston: Houghton Mifflin Co.,
1959), vol. 2, The Nature of Drama, by Hubert
Hefner, 47–49.

B.   Ray, Gordon N., ed. An Introduction to
Literature. Vol. 2, The Nature of Drama,
by Hubert Hefner. Boston: Houghton
Mifflin Co., 1959.

PR.   (Ray 1959, 2:47–49)

Or:

PR/CR.   (Hefner 1959, 47–49)

RL.   Ray, Gordon N., ed. 1959. An introduction to
literature. Vol. 2, The nature of drama,
by Hubert Hefner. Boston: Houghton
Mifflin Co.

RL/CR.   Hefner, Hubert. 1959. See Ray, Gordon N., ed.
1959.

See also 9.73.

SEPARATELY TITLED VOLUME IN A MULTIVOLUME WORK WITH A GENERAL TITLE AND ONE AUTHOR

11.15 N.   [13]Sewall Wright, Evolution and the
Genetics of Populations, vol. 4, Variability
within and among Natural Populations (Chicago:
University of Chicago Press, 1978), 67.

B.   Wright, Sewall. Evolution and the Genetics of
Populations. Vol. 4, Variability within
and among Natural Populations. Chicago:
University of Chicago Press, 1978.

PR.   (Wright 1978, 4:67)

RL.   Wright, Sewall. 1978. <u>Evolution and the genetics of populations</u>. Vol. 4, <u>Variability within and among natural populations</u>. Chicago: University of Chicago Press.

BOOK IN A SERIES

11.16 N.   [14]Ellen Pollak, <u>The Poetics of Sexual Myth: Gender and Ideology in the Verse of Swift and Pope</u>, Women in Culture and Society Series (Chicago: University of Chicago Press, 1985), 124.

B.   Pollak, Ellen. <u>The Poetics of Sexual Myth: Gender and Ideology in the Verse of Swift and Pope</u>. Women in Culture and Society Series. Chicago: University of Chicago Press, 1985.

PR.   (Pollak 1985, 124)

RL.   Pollak, Ellen. 1985. <u>The poetics of sexual myth: Gender and ideology in the verse of Swift and Pope</u>. Women in Culture and Society Series. Chicago: University of Chicago Press.

BOOK IN A SERIES WHEN THE SERIES EDITOR'S NAME IS INCLUDED

11.17 N.   [15]Charles Issawi, <u>The Economic History of Turkey, 1800–1914</u>, Publication of the Center for Middle Eastern Studies, ed. Richard L. Chambers, no. 13 (Chicago: University of Chicago Press, 1980), 48.

B.   Issawi, Charles. <u>The Economic History of Turkey, 1800–1914</u>. Publication of the Center for Middle Eastern Studies, ed. Richard L. Chambers, no. 13. Chicago: University of Chicago Press, 1980.

PR.   (Issawi 1980, 48)

RL.   Issawi, Charles. 1980. <u>The economic history of Turkey, 1800–1914</u>. Publication of the Center for Middle Eastern Studies, ed. Richard L. Chambers, no. 13. Chicago: University of Chicago Press.

PAPERBACK SERIES

11.18 N.   [16]George F. Kennan, <u>American Diplomacy,</u>
<u>1900–1950</u> (Chicago: University of Chicago
Press, 1951; Phoenix Books, 1970), 50.

B.   Kennan, George F. <u>American Diplomacy, 1900–</u>
<u>1950</u>. Chicago: University of Chicago
Press, 1951; Phoenix Books, 1970.

PR.   (Kennan 1970, 50)

RL.   Kennan, George F. 1970. <u>American diplomacy,</u>
<u>1900–1950</u>. Chicago: University of Chicago
Press, Phoenix Books; first published
University of Chicago Press, 1951.

In reference-list entries for paperback series or reprint editions
when there are two dates in the facts of publication, after the
author's name give the date of the source from which the citation
was taken, and include the other date as shown above.

EDITION OTHER THAN FIRST

11.19 N.   [17]M. M. Bober, <u>Karl Marx's Inter-</u>
<u>pretation of History</u>, 2d ed., Harvard Economic
Studies (Cambridge: Harvard University Press,
1948), 89.

B.   Bober, M. M. <u>Karl Marx's Interpretation of</u>
<u>History</u>. 2d ed. Harvard Economic Studies.
Cambridge: Harvard University Press,
1948.

PR.   (Bober 1948, 89)

RL.   Bober, M. M. 1948. <u>Karl Marx's interpretation</u>
<u>of history</u>. 2d ed. Harvard Economic
Studies. Cambridge: Harvard University
Press.

REPRINT EDITION

11.20 For a work that has been reprinted, it is important to give publisher and date of the reprint following the usual information
about the book as originally issued:

N.   [18]Neil Harris, <u>The Artist in American</u>
<u>Society: The Formative Years, 1790–1860</u> (New
York: George Braziller, 1966; reprint,
Chicago: University of Chicago Press, Phoenix

Books, 1982), 43–44 (page references are to
reprint edition).

B.   Harris, Neil. <u>The Artist in American Society:
The Formative Years, 1790–1860</u>. New York:
George Braziller, 1966; reprint, Chicago:
University of Chicago Press, Phoenix
Books, 1982.

PR.   (Harris 1982, 43–44)

RL.   Harris, Neil. 1982. <u>The artist in American
society: The formative years, 1790–1860</u>.
New York: George Braziller, 1966;
reprint, Chicago: University of Chicago
Press, Phoenix Books (page references are
to reprint edition).

TITLE WITHIN A TITLE

11.21   A title of another work that would ordinarily be underlined itself
is enclosed in double quotation marks when it appears as part of
an underlined title:

N.   [19]Allen Forte, <u>The Harmonic Organization
of "The Rite of Spring</u>," (New Haven: Yale
University Press, 1978), 50.

B.   Forte, Allen. <u>The Harmonic Organization of
"The Rite of Spring</u>." New Haven: Yale
University Press, 1978.

PR.   (Forte 1978, 50)

RL.   Forte, Allen. 1978. <u>The harmonic organization
of "The rite of spring</u>." New Haven: Yale
University Press.

11.22   When the title of a book occurs within the title of a journal
article, poem, or short story, whether the latter are in quotation
marks or in roman (as in a reference list), the book title is underlined:

N.   [21]Carl Avren Levenson, "Distance and
Presence in Augustine's <u>Confessions</u>," <u>Journal
of Religion</u> 65 (October 1985): 508, n. 4.

B.   Levenson, Carl Avren. "Distance and Presence
in Augustine's <u>Confessions</u>." <u>Journal of
Religion</u> 65 (October 1985): 500–12.

PR.   (Levenson 1985, 508, n. 4)

RL.   Levenson, Carl Avren. 1985. Distance and
presence in Augustine's <u>Confessions</u>.
<u>Journal of Religion</u> 65 (October): 500–12.

11.23   When the title of an article appears within the title of another article, single quotation marks are used:

```
"Comment on 'How to Make a Burden of the Public
Debt'"
```

BOOK WITH NAMED AUTHOR OF INTRODUCTION, PREFACE, OR FOREWORD

11.24   N.   [23]Dag Hammarskjöld, <u>Markings</u>, with a
Foreword by W. H. Auden (New York: Alfred A.
Knopf, 1964), 10.

B.   Hammarskjöld, Dag. <u>Markings</u>. With a Foreword
by W. H. Auden. New York: Alfred A.
Knopf, 1964.

PR.   (Hammarskjöld 1964, 10)

RL.   Hammarskjöld, Dag. 1964. <u>Markings</u>. With a
Foreword by W. H. Auden. New York: Alfred
A. Knopf.

If Auden's authorship of the foreword were more significant than Hammarskjöld's book in respect to a paper citing this work, the following would be the correct form:

N.   [24]W. H. Auden, foreword to <u>Markings</u>, by
Dag Hammarskjöld (New York: Alfred A. Knopf,
1964), ix.

B.   Auden, W. H. Foreword to <u>Markings</u>, by Dag
Hammarskjöld. New York: Alfred A. Knopf,
1964.

PR.   (Auden 1964, ix)

RL.   Auden, W. H. 1964. Foreword to <u>Markings</u>, by
Dag Hammarskjöld. New York: Alfred A.
Knopf.

BOOK IN FOREIGN LANGUAGE; ENGLISH TITLE SUPPLIED

11.25   N.   [25]Martin Buber, <u>Das Problem des Menschen</u>
[The problem of man] (Heidelberg: Lambert
Scheider Verlag, 1948), 35.

B.   Buber, Martin. <u>Das Problem des Menschen</u>. [The
problem of man]. Heidelberg: Lambert
Scheider Verlag, 1948.

PR.   (Buber 1948, 35)

RL.   Buber, Martin. 1948. <u>Das Problem des Menschen</u>.
[The problem of man]. Heidelberg: Lambert
Scheider Verlag.

Note that the English translation of the title and its subtitle, if any, is neither underlined nor enclosed in quotation marks, but is enclosed in brackets and capitalized sentence style.

COMPONENT PART BY ONE AUTHOR IN A WORK BY ANOTHER

11.26   N.   [26]Mary Higdon Beech, "The Domestic Realm in the Lives of Hindu Women in Calcutta," in <u>Separate Worlds: Studies of Purdah in South Asia</u>, ed. Hanna Papanek and Gail Minault (Delhi: Chanakya, 1982), 115.

   B.   Beech, Mary Higdon. "The Domestic Realm in the Lives of Hindu Women in Calcutta." In <u>Separate Worlds: Studies of Purdah in South Asia</u>, ed. Hanna Papnanek and Gail Minault, 110–38. Delhi: Chanakya, 1982.

   PR.   (Beech 1982, 115)

   RL.   Beech, Mary Higdon. 1982. The domestic realm in the lives of Hindu women in Calcutta. In <u>Separate worlds: Studies of Purdah in South Asia</u>, ed. Hanna Papanek and Gail Minault, 110–38. Delhi: Chanakya.

COMPONENT PART WITHIN A WORK BY ONE AUTHOR

11.27   N.   [27]Bruno Bettelheim, "The Frame Story of <u>Thousand and One Nights</u>," chap. in <u>The Uses of Enchantment: The Meaning and Importance of Fairy Tales</u> (New York: Vintage Books, a Division of Random House, 1976), 87.

   B.   Bettelheim, Bruno. "The Frame Story of <u>Thousand and One Nights</u>." Chap. in <u>The Uses of Enchantment: The Meaning and Importance of Fairy Tales</u>. New York: Vintage Books, a Division of Random House, 1976.

   PR.   (Bettelheim 1976, 87)

   RL.   Bettelheim, Bruno. 1976. The frame story of <u>Thousand and one nights</u>. Chap. in <u>The uses of enchantment: The meaning and importance of fairy tales</u>. New York: Vintage Books, a Division of Random House.

COMPONENT PART THAT IS AN ENTITY IN ITSELF IN A
WORK BY A SINGLE AUTHOR

11.28   Titles of short poems and short stories should be enclosed in
double quotation marks, but underline the titles of longer works.

N.   [28]John Milton, <u>Paradise Lost</u>, in <u>The
            Complete Poetical Works of John Milton</u>, ed.
            William Vaughn Moody, Student's Cambridge
            Edition (Boston: Houghton Mifflin, 1899), 102.

B.   Milton, John. <u>Paradise Lost</u>. In <u>The Complete
            Poetical Works of John Milton</u>, ed.
            William Vaughn Moody. Student's Cambridge
            Edition. Boston: Houghton Mifflin, 1899.

PR.   (Milton 1899, 102)

RL.   Milton, John. 1899. <u>Paradise lost</u>. In <u>The
            complete poetical works of John Milton</u>,
            ed. William Vaughn Moody. Student's
            Cambridge Edition. Boston: Houghton
            Mifflin.

BOOK PRIVATELY PRINTED

11.29 N.   [29]John G. Barrow, <u>A Bibliography of
            Bibliographies in Religion</u> (Austin, Tex.: By
            the author, 716 Brown Bldg., 1955), 25.

B.   Barrow, John G. <u>A Bibliography of
            Bibliographies in Religion</u>. Austin, Tex.:
            By the author, 716 Brown Bldg., 1955.

PR.   (Barrow 1955, 25)

RL.   Barrow, John G. 1955. <u>A bibliography of
            bibliographies in religion</u>. Austin, Tex.:
            By the author, 716 Brown Bldg.

The street address is not always given in such references.

BOOK PRIVATELY PRINTED, PUBLISHER NOT KNOWN

11.30 N.   [30]Frank Budgen, <u>Further Recollections of
            James Joyce</u> (London: Privately printed, 1955),
            10.

B.   Budgen, Frank. <u>Further Recollections of James
            Joyce</u>. London: Privately printed, 1955.

PR.   (Budgen 1955, 10)

RL.   Budgen, Frank. 1955. <u>Further recollections of James Joyce</u>. London: Privately printed.

SECONDARY SOURCE OF QUOTATION

11.31 N.   [31]Roland Barthes, "La mort de l'auteur" [The death of the author], <u>Manteia</u> vol. 5 (1968); trans. Stephen Heath in <u>Image/Music/Text</u> (New York: Hill & Wang, 1977), 147; quoted in Wayne C. Booth, <u>Critical Understanding: The Powers and Limits of Pluralism</u> (Chicago: University of Chicago Press, 1979), 372–73, n. 9.

B.   Barthes, Roland. "La mort de l'auteur" [The death of the author]. <u>Manteia</u> vol. 5 (1968). Translated by Stephen Heath in <u>Image/Music/Text</u>. New York: Hill & Wang, 1977, 147. Quoted in Wayne C. Booth. <u>Critical Understanding: The Powers and Limits of Pluralism</u>, 372–73, n. 9. Chicago: University of Chicago Press, 1979.

PR.   (Barthes 1968)

RL.   Barthes, Roland. 1968. "La mort de l'auteur" [The death of the author]. <u>Manteia</u> vol. 5. Translated by Stephen Heath in <u>Image/music/text</u>. New York: Hill & Wang, 1977, 147. Quoted in Wayne C. Booth. <u>Critical understanding: The powers and limits of pluralism</u>, 372–73, n. 9. Chicago: University of Chicago Press, 1979.

PUBLISHED REPORTS AND PROCEEDINGS

PUBLISHED REPORTS

11.32 *Author named*

N.   [32]B. G. F. Cohen, <u>Human Aspects in Office Automation</u> (Cincinnati: National Institute for Occupational Safety and Health, Division of Biomedical and Behavioral Science, 1984), 150, NTIS, PB84–240738.

B.   Cohen, B. G. F. <u>Human Aspects in Office Automation</u>. Cincinnati: National Institute for Occupational Safety and Health, Division of Biomedical and Behavioral Science, 1984. NTIS, PB84–240738.

PR.   (Cohen 1984, 150)

RL.   Cohen, B. G. F. 1984. <u>Human aspects in office automation</u>. Cincinnati: National Institute for Occupational Safety and Health, Division of Biomedical and Behavioral Science. NTIS, PB84–240738.

11.33 *Chairman of committee named*

N.   [33]<u>Report of the Committee on Financial Institutions to the President of the United States</u>, by Walter W. Heller, Chairman (Washington, D.C.: Government Printing Office, 1963), 12.

B.   <u>Report of the Committee on Financial Institutions to the President of the United States</u>. By Walter W. Heller, Chairman. Washington, D.C.: Government Printing Office, 1963.

PR.   (<u>Report of the Committee on Financial Institutions</u> 1963, 12)

Or:

PR/CR.   (Heller 1963, 12)

RL.   <u>Report of the Committee on Financial Institutions to the President of the United States</u>. 1963. By Walter W. Heller, Chairman. Washington, D.C.: Government Printing Office.

RL/CR.   Heller, Walter W. 1963. <u>See</u> <u>Report of the Committee on Financial Institutions</u>. 1963.

PUBLISHED PROCEEDINGS

11.34 *Author and editor named*

N.   [35]S. Akazawa, "The Scope of the Japanese Information Industry in the 1980s," in <u>The Challenge of Information Technology: Proceedings of the Forty–First FID (Fédération Internationale de Documentation) Congress Held in Hong Kong 13–16 September 1982</u>, ed. K. R. Brown (Amsterdam, New York, and Oxford: North-Holland Publishing Company, 1983), 20.

B.   Akazawa, S. "The Scope of the Japanese Information Industry in the 1980s." In

The Challenge of Information Technology: Proceedings of the Forty-First FID (Fédération Internationale de Documentation) Congress Held in Hong Kong 13-16 September 1982, edited by K. R. Brown, 19-22. Amsterdam, New York, and Oxford: North-Holland Publishing Company, 1983.

PR.   (Akazawa 1983, 20)

RL.   Akazawa, S. 1983. The scope of the Japanese information industry in the 1980s. In The challenge of information technology: Proceedings of the forty-first FID (Fédération Internationale de Documentation) congress held in Hong Kong 13-16 September 1982, edited by K. R. Brown, 19-22. Amsterdam, New York, and Oxford: North-Holland Publishing Company.

11.35 *Authored article within proceedings published by an institution, association, etc.*

N.   [36]Pere Martin Oelberg, "Norway and Latin American Development," in Latin American-European Business Cooperation: Proceedings of the Symposium in Montreaux, Switzerland, November 20-22, 1979, by the Inter-American Development Bank (Switzerland: Inter-American Development Bank, 1979), 81.

B.   Oelberg, Pere Martin. "Norway and Latin American Development." In Latin American-European Business Cooperation: Proceedings of the Symposium in Montreaux, Switzerland, November 20-22, 1979, by the Inter-American Development Bank. Switzerland: Inter-American Development Bank, 1979, 80-83.

PR.   (Oelberg 1979, 81)

RL.   Oelberg, Pere Martin. 1979. Norway and Latin American development. In Latin American-European business cooperation: Proceedings of the symposium in Montreaux, Switzerland, November 20-22, 1979, by the Inter-American Development Bank. Switzerland: Inter-American Development Bank, 80-83.

UNPUBLISHED REPORTS AND PROCEEDINGS

11.36 Titles of unpublished reports and proceedings are enclosed in
quotation marks. When not given in the title, place and date
follow the title. There may also be the notation "Typewritten"
or "Photocopied."

N.   [1]George Psacharopoulos and Keith
          Hincliffe, "Tracer Study Guidelines"
          (Washington, D.C.: World Bank, Education
          Department, 1983), 5, photocopied.

B.   Psacharopoulos, George, and Keith Hincliffe.
          "Tracer Study Guidelines." Washington,
          D.C.: World Bank, Education Department,
          1983. Photocopied.

PR.   (Psacharopoulos and Hincliffe 1983, 5)

RL.   Psacharopoulos, George, and Keith Hincliffe.
          1983. Tracer study guidelines.
          Washington, D.C.: World Bank, Education
          Department. Photocopied.

YEARBOOKS

DEPARTMENT OF GOVERNMENT

11.37 N.   [37]Department of Agriculture, <u>Will There
          Be Enough Food? The 1981 Yearbook of
          Agriculture</u>, (Washington, D.C.: Government
          Printing Office, 1981), 250.

B.   U.S. Department of Agriculture. <u>Will There Be
          Enough Food? The 1981 Yearbook of
          Agriculture</u>. Washington, D.C.: Government
          Printing Office, 1981.

PR.   (U.S. Department of Agriculture 1981, 250)

RL.   U.S. Department of Agriculture. 1981. <u>Will
          there be enough food? The 1981 yearbook
          of agriculture</u>. Washington, D.C.:
          Government Printing Office.

ARTICLE IN A YEARBOOK

11.38 N.   [2]G. M. Wilson, "A Survey of the Social
          Business Use of Arithmetic," in <u>Sixteenth
          Yearbook of the National Society for the Study
          of Education</u> (Bloomington, Ill.: Public School
          Publishing Co., 1917), 21.

B.   Wilson, G. M. "A Survey of the Social Business Use of Arithmetic." In <u>Sixteenth Yearbook of the National Society for the Study of Education</u>, 20–22. Bloomington, Ill.: Public School Publishing Co., 1917.

PR.   (Wilson 1917, 21)

RL.   Wilson, G. M. 1917. A survey of the social business use of arithmetic. In <u>Sixteenth yearbook of the National Society for the Study of Education</u>, 20–22. Bloomington, Ill.: Public School Publishing Co.

ARTICLES IN JOURNALS AND MAGAZINES

ARTICLE IN A JOURNAL

11.39 N.   [38]Richard Jackson, "Running Down the Up-Escalator: Regional Inequality in Papua New Guinea," <u>Australian Geographer</u> 14 (May 1979): 180.

B.   Jackson, Richard. "Running Down the Up-Escalator: Regional Inequality in Papua New Guinea." <u>Australian Geographer</u> 14 (May 1979): 175–84.

PR.   (Jackson 1979, 180)

RL.   Jackson, Richard. 1979. Running down the up-escalator: Regional inequality in Papua New Guinea. <u>Australian Geographer</u> 14 (May): 175–84.

11.40 In citing journals that are numbered only by issue, not volume, note the style set forth in 9.85. In citing journals that publish volumes in successive series, numbered or lettered, see 9.88.

N.   [39]R. Broom and J. T. Robinson, "Man Contemporaneous with the Swartkrans Ape-Man," <u>American Journal of Physical Anthropology</u>, n.s. 8 (1950): 154.

B.   Broom, R., and J. T. Robinson. "Man Contemporaneous with the Swartkrans Ape-Man." <u>American Journal of Physical Anthropology</u>, n.s. 8 (1950): 151–56.

PR.   (Broom and Robinson 1950, 154)

RL.   Broom, R., and J. T. Robinson. 1950. Man contemporaneous with the Swartkrans Ape-Man. <u>American Journal of Physical Anthropology</u>, n.s. 8: 151–56.

ARTICLE IN A MAGAZINE

11.41   N.   [40]Bruce Weber, "The Myth Maker: The
Creative Mind of Novelist E. L. Doctorow," <u>New
York Times Magazine</u>, 20 October 1985, 42.

B.   Weber, Bruce. "The Myth Maker: The Creative
Mind of Novelist E. L. Doctorow." <u>New
York Times Magazine</u>, 20 October 1985, 42.

PR.   (Weber 1985, 42)

RL.   Weber, Bruce. 1985. The myth maker: The
creative mind of novelist E. L. Doctorow.
<u>New York Times Magazine</u>, 20 October, 42.

See also 9.70.

ARTICLES IN ENCYCLOPEDIAS

SIGNED ARTICLE

11.42   N.   [41]Dagobert D. Runes and Harry G.
Schrickel, eds. <u>Encyclopedia of the Arts</u> (New
York: Philosophical Library, 1946), s.v.
"African Negro Art," by James A. Porter.

B.   Runes, Dagobert D., and Harry G. Schrickel,
eds. <u>Encyclopedia of the Arts</u>. New York:
Philosophical Library, 1946. S.v.
"African Negro Art," by James A. Porter.

PR.   (Runes and Schrickel 1946)

RL.   Runes, Dagobert D., and Harry G. Schrickel,
eds. 1946. <u>Encyclopedia of the arts</u>. New
York: Philosophical Library. S.v.
"African Negro art," by James A. Porter.

See 9.96.

UNSIGNED ARTICLE

11.43   N.   [42]<u>Encyclopedia Americana</u>, 1975 ed., s.v.
"Sumatra."

B.   <u>Encyclopedia Americana</u>, 1975 ed. S.v.
"Sumatra."

PR.   (<u>Encyclopedia Americana</u> 1975)

RL.   <u>Encyclopedia Americana</u>, 1975 ed. S.v.
"Sumatra."

NEWSPAPERS

11.44 If a newspaper is cited only once in a research paper, a note is sufficient documentation:

N.   [43]*Irish Daily Independent* (Dublin), 16
        June 1904.

In research papers using parenthetical references, the name and date of a newspaper being cited only once or twice should be included in the text, and the newspaper need not be included among the list of works cited:

This event is also recorded in the *Irish Daily Independent* dated 16 June 1904.

In the example below, the bibliographical and reference-list entries are similar, and they contain the same information as the note. Though each contains the same information, the items differ slightly in terms of order of authors' names and treatment of capitalization and punctuation in the entries:

N.   [44]André Camille, "Deciding Who Gets Dibs
        on Health—Care Dollars," *Wall Street Journal*,
        27 March 1984, 30(W) and 34(E).

B.   Camille, André. "Deciding Who Gets Dibs on
            Health—Care Dollars." *Wall Street
            Journal*, 27 March 1984, 30(W) and 34(E).

PR.   (Camille 1984, 34[E])

RL.   Camille, André. 1984. Deciding who gets dibs
            on health—care dollars. *Wall Street
            Journal*, 27 March, 30(W) and 34(E).

Several matters to be considered in referring to newspapers are discussed in 9.90–95.

COMBINED REFERENCES TO PERIODICALS OR NEWSPAPERS

11.45 If the writer has used the issues of a newspaper or periodical covering a considerable period of time, this fact may be indicated by giving the title of the work with the dates as in the bibliographical and reference-list entries below:

B.   *Saturday Review*. 2, 16, 30 July; 2, 20, 27
            August 1966.

RL.   *Saturday Review*. 1966. 2, 16, 30 July; 2, 20,
            27 August.

B.   *Times* (London). 4 January–6 June 1964.

RL.   <u>Times</u> (London). 1964. 4 January–6 June.

Two or more articles in an encyclopedia or similar reference work may be contained in one bibliographical or reference-list entry:

B.   Leiter, Samuel L. <u>Kabuki Encyclopedia: An English–Language Adaptation of "Kabuki Jiten</u>." Westport, Conn., and London: Greenwood Press, 1979. S.v. "Kaneru yakusha," "Sosori."

RL.   Leiter, Samuel L. 1979. <u>Kabuki encyclopedia: An English–language adaptation of "Kabuki Jiten</u>." Westport, Conn., and London: Greenwood Press. S.v. "Kaneru yakusha," "Sosori."

REVIEWS

BOOK REVIEW IN A JOURNAL

11.46   N.   [45]Dwight Frankfather, review of <u>The Disabled State</u>, by Deborah A. Stone, In <u>Social Service Review</u> 59 (September 1985): 524.

B.   Dwight Frankfather. Review of <u>The Disabled State</u>, by Deborah A. Stone. In <u>Social Service Review</u> 59 (September 1985): 523–25.

PR.   (Frankfather 1985, 524)

RL.   Frankfather, Dwight. 1985. Review of <u>The disabled state</u>, by Deborah A. Stone. In <u>Social Service Review</u> 59 (September): 523–25.

Citations of reviews of films and performances in a journal should follow the same style.

UNSIGNED PERFORMANCE REVIEW IN A NEWSPAPER

11.47   Citations of reviews of plays, films, and musical performances published in newspapers or weekly magazines should follow the same style, though reference to a location is customary only in a play review.

N.   [46]Review of <u>Fool for Love</u>, by Sam Shepard (Circle Repertory Company, New York), <u>New York Times</u>, 27 May 1983, 18(N) and C3(L).

B.   Review of <u>Fool for Love</u>, by Sam Shepard.
Circle Repertory Company, New York. <u>New York Times</u>, 27 May 1983, 18(N) and C3(L).

PR.   (Review of <u>Fool for love</u> 1983, 18[N])

RL.   Review of <u>Fool for love</u>, by Sam Shepard. 1983.
Circle Repertory Company, New York. <u>New York Times</u>, 27 May, 18(N) and C3(L).

INTERVIEWS

PUBLISHED INTERVIEW

11.48 N.   [47]John Fowles, "A Conversation with John Fowles," interview by Robert Foulke (Lyme Regis, 3 April 1984), <u>Salmagundi</u>, no. 68–69 (Fall 1985–Winter 1986): 370.

B.   Fowles, John. "A Conversation with John Fowles." Interview by Robert Foulke (Lyme Regis, 3 April 1984). <u>Salmagundi</u>, no. 68–69 (Fall 1985–Winter 1986): 367–84.

PR.   (Fowles 1985–86: 370)

RL.   Fowles, John. 1985–86. A conversation with John Fowles. Interview by Robert Foulke (Lyme Regis, 3 April 1984). <u>Salmagundi</u>, no. 68–69 (Fall–Winter): 367–84.

UNPUBLISHED INTERVIEW

11.49 N.   [48]Benjamin Spock, Interview by Milton J. E. Senn, 20 November 1974, interview 67A, transcript, Senn Oral History Collection, National Library of Medicine, Bethesda, Md.

B.   Spock, Benjamin. Interview by Milton J. E. Senn, 20 November 1974. Interview 67A, transcript. Senn Oral History Collection, National Library of Medicine, Bethesda, Md.

PR.   (Spock 1974)

RL.   Spock, Benjamin. 1974. Interview by Milton J. E. Senn, 20 November. Interview 67A, transcript. Senn Oral History Collection, National Library of Medicine, Bethesda, Md.

UNPUBLISHED INTERVIEW BY WRITER OF RESEARCH PAPER

11.50 N. [49]Mayor Harold Washington of Chicago, interview by author, 23 September 1985, Chicago, tape recording, Chicago Historical Society, Chicago.

   B. Washington, Harold, mayor of Chicago. Interview by author, 23 September 1985, Chicago. Tape recording. Chicago Historical Society, Chicago.

   PR. (Washington 1985)

   RL. Washington, Harold, mayor of Chicago. 1985. Interview by author, 23 September, Chicago. Tape recording. Chicago Historical Society, Chicago.

MICROFORM EDITIONS

11.51 N. [50]William Voelke, ed., <u>Masterpieces of Medieval Painting: The Art of Illumination</u> (Pierpont Morgan Library; Chicago: University of Chicago Press, 1980, text–fiche), p. 56, 4F6–4F10.

   B. Voelke, William, ed. <u>Masterpieces of Medieval Painting: The Art of Illumination</u>. Pierpont Morgan Library; Chicago: University of Chicago Press, 1980. Text–fiche.

   PR. (Voelke 1980, 56, 4F6–4F10)

   RL. Voelke, William, ed. 1980. <u>Masterpieces of medieval painting: The art of illumination</u>. Pierpont Morgan Library; Chicago: University of Chicago Press. Text–fiche.

UNPUBLISHED MATERIALS

LETTER

11.52 N. [51]Percy Bysshe Shelley, Padua, to Mary Wollstonecraft Shelley, Este, 22 September 1818, Transcript in the hand of Mary Wollstonecraft Shelley, Special Collections, Joseph Regenstein Library, University of Chicago, Chicago.

B. Shelley, Percy Bysshe, Padua, to Mary Wollstonecraft Shelley, Este, 22 September 1818. Transcript in the hand of Mary Wollstonecraft Shelley. Special Collections, Joseph Regenstein Library, University of Chicago, Chicago.

PR. (Shelley 1818)

RL. Shelley, Percy Bysshe. 1818. Letter from Padua, to Mary Wollstonecraft Shelley, Este, 22 September. Transcript in the hand of Mary Wollstonecraft Shelley. Special Collections, Joseph Regenstein Library, University of Chicago, Chicago.

See also 2.19 for abbreviations to be used to describe manuscripts and 9.114–15.

SPEECH

11.53 N. [52]Eulogy of Charles V in Latin, apparently written at the monastery of St. Just, Spain, [ca. 1500], Special Collections, Joseph Regenstein Library, University of Chicago, Chicago.

B. Eulogy of Charles V. In Latin, apparently written at the monastery of St. Just, Spain, [ca. 1500]. Special Collections, Joseph Regenstein Library, University of Chicago, Chicago.

PR. (Eulogy of Charles V [ca. 1500])

RL. Eulogy of Charles V. [ca. 1500]. In Latin, apparently written at the monastery of St. Just, Spain. Special Collections, Joseph Regenstein Library, University of Chicago, Chicago.

MANUSCRIPT

11.54 N. [53]Robert Craft, "A Catalog of Manuscripts and Documents [of] the Original Works of Igor Stravinsky, 1970(?)" TMs [photocopy], p. 136, Special Collections, Joseph Regenstein Library, University of Chicago, Chicago.

B. Craft, Robert. "A Catalog of Manuscripts and Documents [of] the Original Works of Igor Stravinsky, 1970(?)" TMs [photocopy].

>   Special Collections, Joseph Regenstein
>   Library, University of Chicago, Chicago.

PR.   (Craft 1970(?) 136)

RL.   Craft, Robert. 1970(?) A catalog of
        manuscripts and documents [of] the
        original works of Igor Stravinsky. TMs
        [photocopy]. Special Collections, Joseph
        Regenstein Library, University of
        Chicago, Chicago.

The use of the question mark in parentheses after the date means
that its accuracy is uncertain, even though parts of the manuscript may have been dated with some certainty. Note that if an
unpublished manuscript is undated but a reliable date has been
supplied, this date appears in brackets (see 9.67).

THESIS OR DISSERTATION

11.55 N.   [54]Gilberto Artioli, "Structural Studies
                of the Water Molecules and Hydrogen Bonding in
                Zeolites" (Ph.D. diss., University of Chicago,
                1985), 10.

B.   Artioli, Gilberto. "Structural Studies of the
        Water Molecules and Hydrogen Bonding in
        Zeolites." Ph.D. diss., University of
        Chicago, 1985.

PR.   (Artioli 1985, 10)

RL.   Artioli, Gilberto. 1985. Structural studies of
        the water molecules and hydrogen bonding
        in zeolites. Ph.D. diss., University of
        Chicago.

MATERIAL OBTAINED THROUGH AN INFORMATION SERVICE

11.56 N.   [1]Susan J. Kupisch, Stepping In, Paper
                presented as part of the symposium "Disrupted
                and Reorganized Families" at the Annual
                Meeting of the Southeastern Psychological
                Association, Atlanta, Ga., 23–26 March 1983,
                Dialog, ERIC, ED 233 276.

B.   Kupisch, Susan J. Stepping In. Paper presented
        as part of the symposium "Disrupted and
        Reorganized Families" at the Annual
        Meeting of the Southeastern Psychological
        Association, Atlanta, Ga., 23–26 March
        1983. Dialog, ERIC, ED 233 276.

PR.   (Kupisch 1983)

RL.   Kupisch, Susan J. 1983. <u>Stepping in</u>. Paper presented as part of the symposium "Disrupted and reorganized families" at the Annual Meeting of the Southeastern Psychological Association, Atlanta, Ga., 23–26 March. Dialog, ERIC, ED 233 276.

See also 9.121 and 12.20.

Computer Program

11.57 N.   [55]Lotus 1-2-3 Rel. 2, Lotus Development Corporation, Cambridge, Mass.

B.   Lotus 1-2-3 Rel. 2. Lotus Development Corporation, Cambridge, Mass.

PR.   (Lotus 1-2-3 Rel. 2)

RL.   Lotus 1-2-3 Rel. 2. Lotus Development Corporation, Cambridge, Mass.

MUSIC

Unpublished Musical Score

11.58 N.   [56]Ralph Shapey, "Partita for Violin and 13 Players," Score, 1966, Special Collections, Joseph Regenstein Library, University of Chicago, Chicago.

B.   Shapey, Ralph. "Partita for Violin and 13 Players." Score. 1966. Special Collections, Joseph Regenstein Library, University of Chicago, Chicago.

PR.   (Shapey 1966)

RL.   Shapey, Ralph. 1966. Partita for violin and 13 players. Score. Special Collections, Joseph Regenstein Library, University of Chicago, Chicago.

Published Musical Score

11.59 N.   [57]Wolfgang Amadeus Mozart, <u>Don Giovanni</u>, libretto by Lorenzo da Ponte, English version by W. H. Auden and Chester Kallman (New York and London: G. Schirmer, 1961), 55.

B.   Mozart, Wolfgang Amadeus. <u>Don Giovanni</u>. Libretto by Lorenzo da Ponte, English

version by W. H. Auden and Chester
Kallman. New York and London: G.
Schirmer, 1961.

PR.   (Mozart 1961, 55)

RL.   Mozart, Wolfgang Amadeus. 1961. <u>Don Giovanni</u>.
        Libretto by Lorenzo da Ponte, English
        version by W. H. Auden and Chester
        Kallman. New York and London: G.
        Schirmer.

SOUND RECORDINGS

11.60 N.   [58]Norman Mailer, <u>The Naked and the Dead</u>,
        excerpts read by the author, cassette CP1619,
        Caedmon, 1983.

B.   Mailer, Norman. <u>The Naked and the Dead</u>.
        Excerpts read by the author. Cassette
        CP1619. Caedmon, 1983.

PR.   (Mailer 1983)

RL.   Mailer, Norman. 1983. <u>The naked and the dead</u>.
        Excerpts read by the author. Cassette
        CP1619. Caedmon.

VIDEORECORDINGS

11.61 N.   [59]Itzak Perlman, <u>Itzak Perlman: In My
        Case Music</u>, produced and directed by Tony
        DeNonno, 10 min., DeNonno Pix, 1985,
        videocassette.

B.   Perlman, Itzak. <u>Itzak Perlman: In My Case
        Music</u>. Produced and directed by Tony
        DeNonno. 10 min. DeNonno Pix, 1985.
        Videocassette.

PR.   (Perlman 1985)

RL.   Perlman, Itzak. 1985. <u>Itzak Perlman: In my
        case music</u>. Produced and directed by Tony
        DeNonno. 10 min. DeNonno Pix.
        Videocassette.

PERFORMANCES

11.62 N.   [60]William Shakespeare, <u>The Winter's
        Tale</u>, Festival Theatre, Stratford, Ontario, 24
        September 1986.

B.   Shakespeare, William. The Winter's Tale.
Festival Theatre, Stratford, Ontario, 24
September 1986.

PR.   (Shakespeare 1986)

RL.   Shakespeare, William. 1986. The winter's tale.
Festival Theatre, Stratford, Ontario, 24
September.

WORKS OF ART

11.63 N.   [61]Jackson Pollock, Reflection of the Big
Dipper, oil on canvas, 1946, Stedelijk Museum,
Amsterdam.

B.   Pollock, Jackson. Reflection of the Big
Dipper. Oil on canvas. 1946. Stedelijk
Museum, Amsterdam.

PR.   (Pollock 1946)

RL.   Pollock, Jackson. 1946. Reflection of the big
dipper. Oil on canvas. Stedelijk Museum,
Amsterdam.

WORKS OF ART REPRODUCED IN BOOKS

11.64 N.   [62]Thomas Nast, "The Tammany Tiger Loose:
'What Are You Going to Do about It,'"
Cartoon, Harper's Weekly, 11 November 1871, as
reproduced in J. Chal Vinson, Thomas Nast:
Political Cartoonist (Athens, Ga.: University
of Georgia Press, 1967), plate 52.

B.   Nast, Thomas. "The Tammany Tiger Loose: 'What
Are You Going to Do about it.'" Cartoon.
Harper's Weekly, 11 November 1871. As
reproduced in J. Chal Vinson, Thomas
Nast: Political Cartoonist. Athens, Ga.:
University of Georgia Press, 1967. Plate
52.

PR.   (Nast 1967, plate 52)

RL.   Nast, Thomas. 1967. The Tammany Tiger loose:
"What are you going to do about it."
Cartoon. Harper's Weekly, 11 November
1871. As reproduced in J. Chal Vinson,
Thomas Nast: Political cartoonist.
Athens, Ga.: University of Georgia Press.
Plate 52.

MULTIPLE REFERENCES CONTAINED IN A SINGLE NOTE

11.65 The individual references in a note citing several works are separated with semicolons and listed in the order in which they were cited:

> [62]See Samuel P. Langley, <u>James Smithson</u> (Washington, D.C.: Smithsonian Institution, 1904), 18–19; Paul Oehser, <u>Sons of Science</u> (New York: Henry Schuman, 1949), 1, 9–11; and Webster True, <u>The First Hundred Years of the Smithsonian Institution, 1846–1946</u> (Washington, D.C.: Smithsonian Institution, 1946), 2–106.

11.66 The bibliographical entries for multiple references in a single note should, of course, be alphabetized separately:

> Langley, Samuel P. <u>James Smithson</u>. Washington, D.C.: Smithsonian Institution, 1904.
>
> Oehser, Paul. <u>Sons of Science</u>. New York: Henry Schuman, 1949.
>
> True, Webster. <u>The First Hundred Years of the Smithsonian Institution, 1846–1946</u>. Washington, D.C.: Smithsonian Institution, 1946.

11.67 In papers using parenthetical references, the multiple citations appear as follows:

> (Langley 1904, 18–19; Oehser 1949, 1, 9–11; True 1946, 2–106)

11.68 A reference-list entry should be included for each author:

> Langley, Samuel P. 1904. <u>James Smithson</u>. Washington, D.C.: Smithsonian Institution.
>
> Oehser, Paul. 1949. <u>Sons of science</u>. New York: Henry Schuman.
>
> True, Webster. 1946. <u>The first hundred years of the Smithsonian Institution, 1846–1946</u>. Washington, D.C.: Smithsonian Institution.

12 Citation V: Public Documents

12.1   Consider the form that citations to public documents should take in a paper before beginning research, so that full bibliographical data can be gathered from printed, microfilmed, televised, or on-line materials at the time they are being examined. For example, all citations to on-line materials must include identifying numbers within the information services. All dates of publication must be recorded in order to include them in reference-list entries. While conducting research for a paper that includes a reference list, it is also a good idea to keep a list of any abbreviations and authors' names that will have to be cross-referenced in the list.

12.2 In papers using parenthetical references, it is often useful to cite the agency issuing a work rather than the government responsible for the work, which should be the first item in a reference-list entry. For this reason, the reference list may need a number of cross-references. For example, the parenthetical reference "(U.S. Congress 1941)" is adequate if a reference list includes only one such entry. If there are both Senate and House entries for 1941, however, the parenthetical reference should read "(U.S. Congress, House 1941)." Sometimes a document is known by its title or by the name of the committee of the Senate or House that drafted it. In that case, a parenthetical reference keyed to the first item in the reference-list entry, "(U.S. Congress 1941)," for example, would not be as useful as a parenthetical reference keyed to a cross-reference in the reference list. For example, the parenthetical reference "(*Declarations of a state of war with Japan, Germany, and Italy*. 1941)" must be keyed to a cross-reference in the reference list that reads "*Declarations of a state of war with Japan, Germany, and Italy*. 1941. *See* U.S. Congress. 1941." In referring to the source within the text, use either a parenthetical reference (PR.) keyed to the full citation in the reference list (RL.) or a parenthetical cross-reference (PR/CR.) keyed to a cross-reference in the reference list (RL/CR.), and do one or the other consistently for a particular item. The full citation in the reference list is the same whether a parenthetical reference or a parenthetical cross-reference is used. The examples in this chapter also include samples of notes (N.) and corresponding bibliographical entries (B.).

FORM OF CITATIONS

12.3 The form used for citing public documents should be one that makes them readily accessible to anyone wishing to locate them in standard indexes, information services, and libraries. The arrangement of information on the title pages of the documents themselves, its amount, and its complexity raise puzzling questions of how much of the information it is necessary to include and in what order within a note, bibliographical entry, or reference-list entry. Here reference to the card catalog of the library can be of great assistance, although it is not a safe guide in such matters as capitalization and punctuation of titles, which for public documents as well as for other references must follow the scheme of the paper. When in doubt about how much to include in a reference, it is better to err on the side of giving too much rather than too little information.

12.4 The name of the country, state, city, town, or other governmental district (e.g., U.S., U.K. [United Kingdom], Illinois, Baltimore) is given first in the citation of an official publication issued by one of these or issued under one of their auspices. Unlike bibliographical or reference-list entries, note references to public documents need not begin with the name of the country because this is usually obvious from the text. Next comes the name of the legislative body, court, executive department, bureau, board, commission, or committee. The name of the office rather than the title of the officer should be given except where the title of the officer is the only name of the office, as, for example, "Illinois, State Entomologist." The name of the division, regional office, etc., if any, follows the name of the department, bureau, or commission. Thus the "author" of a document might read: "U.S., Department of Labor, Manpower Administration, Office of Manpower Policy and Research." Following the name of the author, the title of the document, if any, should be given and underlined, capitalized headline style in note and bibliographical entries, and capitalized sentence style in reference lists. From this point, the information noted is dependent largely upon the nature of the material.

UNITED STATES GOVERNMENT DOCUMENTS

12.5 The United States government publishes its official documents in two main categories, those originating in the Congress and those originating in the executive departments. Publications are issued by both houses (Senate and House of Representatives), by the executive departments (State, Justice, Labor, etc.), and by agencies (Federal Trade Commission, General Services Administration, etc.). In addition to these, the *Monthly Catalog of United States Government Publications* also lists an array of technical report literature: government-sponsored research, development, and engineering reports and foreign technical reports and other analyses prepared by national and local government agencies, and by their contractors or grantees. The proliferation of these materials, many of them available through such information services as the National Technical Information Service (NTIS) and the Educational Resources Information Center (ERIC) (see 12.20), requires that the information in citations to public documents include all available facts of publication (dates, serial and print numbers, etc.) as well as information-service identifying and accession numbers, when available.

12.6 For citations to government publications, use consistently throughout a paper one of the following styles:

```
Washington, D.C.: U.S. Government Printing Office,
    1980.
Washington, D.C.: Government Printing Office, 1980.
Washington, D.C.: GPO, 1980.
Washington, 1980.
```

12.7 The *Congressional Information Service Index (CIS/Index)* provides current comprehensive coverage of committee hearings, House and Senate reports and documents, Senate executive reports, and Senate treaty documents. This information may be accessed through printed serial volumes and microfiches available at depository libraries or through several large computer services. The proceedings of each house of Congress, together with the presidential messages to it, are published at the close of each legislative day. Citations to all such hearings, reports, and documents must include—in addition to the authorizing body— the number, session, and date of the Congress; title and number (if any) of the document; and in some instances, the title of the work in which the document can be found, with relevant volume and page number(s).

PUBLISHED DOCUMENTS

LEGISLATIVE PUBLICATIONS

12.8 N. [2]Congress, House, Committee on Interior and Insular Affairs, Subcommittee on Energy and the Environment, International Proliferation of Nuclear Technology, report prepared by Warren H. Donnelley and Barbara Rather, 94th Cong., 2d sess., 1976, Committee Print 15, p. 5.

B. U.S. Congress. House. Committee on Interior and Insular Affairs. Subcommittee on Energy and the Environment. International Proliferation of Nuclear Technology.

	Report prepared by Warren H. Donnelley and Barbara Rather. 94th Cong., 2d sess., 1976. Committee Print 15.
PR.	(U.S. Congress, House 1976, 5)
	Or:
PR/CR.	(Donnelley and Rather 1976, 5)
	Or:
PR/CR.	(<u>International proliferation of nuclear technology</u> 1976, 5)
RL.	U.S. Congress. House. Committee on Interior and Insular Affairs. Subcommittee on Energy and the Environment. 1976. <u>International proliferation of nuclear technology</u>. Report prepared by Warren H. Donnelley and Barbara Rather. 94th Cong., 2d sess. Committee Print 15.
RL/CR.	Donnelley and Rather. 1976. <u>See</u> U.S. Congress. House. 1976.
	Or:
RL/CR.	<u>International proliferation of nuclear technology</u>. 1976. <u>See</u> U.S. Congress. House. 1976.
N.	[2]House, <u>A Bill to Require Passenger-Carrying Motor Vehicles Purchased for Use by the Federal Government to Meet Certain Safety Standards</u>, 86th Cong., 1st sess., 1959, H.R. 1341, 8.
B.	U.S. Congress. House. <u>A Bill to Require Passenger-Carrying Motor Vehicles Purchased for Use by the Federal Government to Meet Certain Safety Standards</u>. 86th Cong., 1st sess., 1959. H.R. 1341.
PR.	(U.S. Congress, House 1959, 8)
RL.	U.S. Congress. House. 1959. <u>A bill to require passenger-carrying motor vehicles purchased for use by the federal government to meet certain safety standards</u>. 86th Cong., 1st sess. H.R. 1341.
N.	[3]Congress, <u>Declarations of a State of War with Japan, Germany, and Italy</u>, 77th

```
                Cong., 1st sess., 1941, S. Doc. 148, Serial
                10575.
```

B.   U.S. Congress. <u>Declarations of a State of War
            with Japan, Germany, and Italy</u>. 77th
            Cong., 1st sess., 1941. S. Doc. 148.
            Serial 10575.

PR.   (U.S. Congress 1941)

Or:

PR/CR.   (<u>Declarations of a state of war</u> 1941)

RL.   U.S. Congress. 1941. <u>Declarations of a state
            of war with Japan, Germany, and Italy</u>.
            77th Cong., 1st sess. S. Doc. 148. Serial
            10575.

RL/CR.   <u>Declarations of a state of war</u>. 1941. <u>See</u> U.S.
            Congress. 1941.

N.   ³Congress, Senate, Committee on Foreign
            Relations, <u>U.S. Scholarship Program for
            Developing Countries</u> (Washington, D.C.: GPO,
            1984), 7.

B.   U.S. Congress. Senate. Committee on Foreign
            Relations. <u>U.S. Scholarship Program for
            Developing Countries</u>. Washington, D.C.:
            GPO, 1984.

PR.   (U.S. Congress, Senate 1984, 7)

RL.   U.S. Congress. Senate. Committee on Foreign
            Relations. 1984. <u>U.S. scholarship program
            for developing countries</u>. Washington,
            D.C.: GPO.

12.9 *Hearings.* Hearings should be cited by title. Even if the "author" listed on the publication does not indicate the committee before whom the hearings were held, the committee should be named as the "author" in the reference:

N.   ¹Congress, Senate, Committee on Foreign
            Relations, <u>Famine in Africa: Hearing before
            the Committee on Foreign Relations</u>, 99th
            Cong., 1st sess., 17 January 1985, 57.

B.   U.S. Congress. Senate. Committee on Foreign
            Relations. <u>Famine in Africa: Hearing
            before the Committee on Foreign
            Relations</u>. 99th Cong., 1st Sess., 17
            January 1985.

PR.   (U.S. Congress, Senate 1985, 57)

RL. U.S. Congress. Senate. Committee on Foreign
    Relations. 1985. <u>Famine in Africa:
    Hearing before the Committee on Foreign
    Relations</u>. 99th Cong., 1st Sess., 17
    January.

12.10 *Bills and resolutions.* Congressional bills and resolutions are published in pamphlet form and are available at many libraries on microfiche. When a bill is enacted into law, it becomes a part of the *Statutes at Large*. In the interim between its having been introduced into one of the houses and its passage and publication as a law in the *Statutes* (see 12.11), a bill is cited to a slip bill or to the *Congressional Record* if it is contained therein:

N.   [2]Congress, House, <u>Food Security Act of
    1985</u>, 99th Cong., 1st sess., H.R. 2100,
    <u>Congressional Record</u>, vol. 131, no. 132, daily
    ed. (8 October 1985), H8485.

B. U.S. Congress. House. <u>Food Security Act of
    1985</u>. 99th Cong., 1st sess., H.R. 2100.
    <u>Congressional Record</u>. Vol. 131, no. 132.
    Daily ed. (8 October 1985), H8353–H8486.

PR. (U.S. Congress, House 1985, H8485)

Or:

PR/CR. (<u>Food Security Act of 1985</u>, H8485)

RL. U.S. Congress. House. 1985. <u>Food Security Act
    of 1985</u>. 99th Cong., 1st sess., H.R.
    2100. <u>Congressional Record</u>. Vol. 131, no.
    132. Daily ed. (8 October), H8353–H8486.

RL/CR. <u>Food Security Act of 1985</u>. <u>See</u> U.S. Congress.
    House. 1985.

12.11 After their passage, bills and joint resolutions are cited as statutes. Statutes are published in the *Statutes at Large* issued for the year during which they have gone into effect (note 13). Later, the statutes are incorporated into the *United States Code* (note 14).

N.   [13]<u>Administrative Procedure Act</u>, <u>Statutes
    at Large</u>, 60, sec. 10, 243 (1946).

B. <u>Administrative Procedure Act</u>. <u>Statutes at
    Large</u>. Vol. 60 (1946).

PR. (<u>Administrative Procedure Act</u> 1946)

RL. <u>Administrative Procedure Act</u>. <u>Statutes at
    large</u>. 1946. Vol. 60, sec. 10, 243.

N.   [14]Declaratory Judgment Act, U.S. Code,
            vol. 28, secs. 2201-2 (1952).

B.   Declaratory Judgment Act. U.S. Code. Vol. 28,
            secs. 2201-2 (1952).

PR.   (Declaratory Judgment Act 1952)

RL.   Declaratory Judgment Act. U.S. code. 1952.
            Vol. 28, secs. 2201-2.

Citations to the *Code* are always to section number, not page.

12.12 *Debates.* Congressional debates are printed in the *Congressional Record.* Unless the subject of the speech or remarks is mentioned in the text, it is proper to include it in the citation. This example refers to the bound volume, which often contains material revised since its appearance in the *Daily Digest* and paged differently.

N.   [3]Congress, Senate, Senator Kennedy of
            Massachusetts speaking for the Joint
            Resolution on Nuclear Weapons Freeze and
            Reductions to the Committee on Foreign
            Relations, S.J. Res. 163, 97th Cong., 1st
            sess., Congressional Record (10 March 1982),
            vol. 128, pt. 3, 3832-34.

B.   U.S. Congress. Senate. Senator Kennedy of
            Massachusetts speaking for the Joint
            Resolution on Nuclear Weapons Freeze and
            Reductions to the Committee on Foreign
            Relations. S.J. Res. 163. 97th Cong., 1st
            sess. Congressional Record (10 March
            1982), vol. 128, pt. 3.

PR.   (U.S. Congress, Senate 1982, 3832-34)

RL.   U.S. Congress. Senate. 1982. Senator Kennedy
            of Massachusetts speaking for the Joint
            Resolution on Nuclear Weapons Freeze and
            Reductions to the Committee on Foreign
            Relations. S.J. Res. 163. 97th Cong., 1st
            sess. Congressional record (10 March),
            vol. 128, pt. 3.

PRESIDENTIAL DOCUMENTS

12.13 *The Weekly Compilation of Presidential Documents* publishes in serial form presidential proclamations, executive orders, and such other documents as addresses, letters, vetoes, etc. Presidential proclamations and executive orders are also carried in the *Federal Register*, published daily:

N.   [4]President, Proclamation, "Caribbean
        Basin Economic Recovery Act, Proclamation
        5142, Amending Proclamation 5133," Federal
        Register (4 January 1984) vol. 49, no. 2, p.
        341. Microfiche.

B.   U.S. President. Proclamation. "Caribbean Basin
        Economic Recovery Act, Proclamation 5142,
        Amending Proclamation 5133." Federal
        Register (4 January 1984) vol. 49, no. 2,
        p. 341. Microfiche.

PR.   (U.S. President 1984, 341)

RL.   U.S. President. Proclamation. 1984. Caribbean
        Basin Economic Recovery Act, Proclamation
        5142, amending Proclamation 5133. Federal
        Register (4 January) vol. 49, no. 2.
        Microfiche.

12.14   The public papers of the presidents of the United States are collected in two large works:

N.   [11]J. D. Richardson, ed., Compilation of
        the Messages and Papers of the Presidents,
        1789–1897, 53d Cong., 2d sess., 1907, House
        Miscellaneous Document no. 210 (Washington,
        D.C.: Government Printing Office, 1907), 4:16.

B.   Richardson, J. D., ed. Compilation of the
        Messages and Papers of the Presidents,
        1789–1897. 53d Cong., 2d sess., 1907,
        House Miscellaneous Document no. 210.
        Pts. 1–10, 10 vols. Washington, D.C.:
        Government Printing Office, 1907.

PR.   (Richardson 1907, 4:16)

RL.   Richardson, J. D., ed. 1907. Compilation of
        the messages and papers of the
        presidents, 1789–1897. 53d Cong., 2d
        sess., House miscellaneous document no.
        210. Pts. 1–10, 10 vols. Washington,
        D.C.: Government Printing Office.

N.   [12]U.S., President, Public Papers of the
        Presidents of the United States (Washington,
        D.C.: Office of the Federal Register, National
        Archives and Records Service, 1956), Dwight D.
        Eisenhower, 1956, 222–23.

B.   U.S. President. Public Papers of the
        Presidents of the United States.

Washington, D.C.: Office of the <u>Federal
Register</u>, National Archives and Records
Service, 1953–. Dwight D. Eisenhower,
1956.

PR.   (U.S. President 1956, 222–23)

RL.   U.S. President. 1956. <u>Public papers of the
presidents of the United States</u>.
Washington, D.C.: Office of the <u>Federal
Register</u>, National Archives and Records
Service, 1953–. Dwight D. Eisenhower.

UNITED STATES CONSTITUTION

12.15 The United States Constitution is referred to by article and section (by clause as well, if relevant). Use capital roman numerals
when referring to articles and amendments, and arabic numerals
when referring to sections.

N.   [16]<u>Constitution</u>, art. I, sec. 4.

N.   [17]<u>Constitution</u>, amend. XIV, sec. 2.

In papers using the parenthetical-reference system, citations to
the Constitution are usually given in the text, and it is unnecessary to include Constitutional entries in either bibliographies or
reference lists.

PUBLICATIONS BY GOVERNMENT COMMISSIONS

12.16 Several government commissions, such as the Federal Communications Commission, Federal Trade Commission, and Securities and Exchange Commission, also publish bulletins, circulars,
reports, study papers, and the like. These are often classified as
House or Senate documents.

N.   [1]Securities and Exchange Commission,
<u>Annual Report of the Securities and Exchange
Commission for the Fiscal Year</u> (Washington,
D.C.: GPO, 1983), 42.

B.   U.S. Securities and Exchange Commission.
<u>Annual Report of the Securities and
Exchange Commission for the Fiscal Year</u>.
Washington, D.C.: GPO, 1983.

PR.   (U.S. Securities and Exchange Commission 1983,
42)

RL.   U.S. Securities and Exchange Commission. 1983.
<u>Annual report of the Securities and</u>

Exchange Commission for the fiscal year. Washington, D.C.: GPO.

N.   [2]Congress, Senate, Report of the Federal Trade Commission on Utility Corporations, 70th Cong., 1st sess., 1935, S. Doc. 91, pt. 71A.

B.   U.S. Congress. Senate. Report of the Federal Trade Commission on Utility Corporations. 70th Cong., 1st sess., 1935. S. Doc. 91.

PR.   (U.S. Congress 1935)

RL.   U.S. Congress. Senate. 1935. Report of the Federal Trade Commission on utility corporations. 70th Cong., 1st sess, S. Doc. 91, pt. 71A.

EXECUTIVE DEPARTMENT DOCUMENTS

12.17   Executive department documents consist of reports of executive departments and bureaus, bulletins, circulars, and miscellaneous materials. Many departmental publications are classified in series, and some have personal authors whose names are given in the citations. Authors and authoring agencies should be cross-referenced in bibliographies and reference lists, paralleling current library practice:

N.   [1]Department of the Interior, Minerals Management Service, An Oilspill Risk Analysis for the Central Gulf (April 1984) and Western Gulf of Mexico (July 1984), by Robert P. LaBelle, open-file report, U.S. Geological Survey, 83-119 (Denver, Colo.: U.S. Geological Survey, 1983), lease offerings microform.

B.   U.S. Department of the Interior. Minerals Management Service. An Oilspill Risk Analysis for the Central Gulf (April 1984) and Western Gulf of Mexico (July 1984), by Robert P. LaBelle. Open-file report, U.S. Geological Survey, 83-119. Denver, Colo.: U.S. Geological Survey, 1983. Lease offerings microform.

PR.   (U.S. Department of the Interior 1983)

Or:

PR/CR.   (LaBelle 1983)

RL.   U.S. Department of the Interior. Minerals Management Service. 1983. An oilspill

> risk analysis for the central Gulf (April
> 1984) and western Gulf of Mexico (July
> 1984), by Robert P. LaBelle. Open-file
> report, U.S. Geological Survey, 83-119.
> Denver, Colo.: U.S. Geological Survey.
> Lease offerings microform.

RL/CR.   LaBelle, Robert P. 1983. See U.S. Department
of the Interior. 1983.

N.   [4]Department of Labor, Employment
Standards Administration, Resource Book:
Training for Federal Employee Compensation
Specialists ([Washington, D.C.]: U.S.
Department of Labor, Employment Standards
Administration, 1984), 236.

B.   U.S. Department of Labor. Employment Standards
Administration. Resource Book: Training
for Federal Employee Compensation
Specialists. [Washington, D.C.]: U.S.
Department of Labor, Employment Standards
Administration, 1984.

PR.   (U.S. Department of Labor 1984, 236)

RL.   U.S. Department of Labor. Employment Standards
Administration. 1984. Resource book:
Training for federal employee
compensation specialists. [Washington,
D.C.]: U.S. Department of Labor,
Employment Standards Administration.

TREATIES

12.18 Since 1950, treaties have been published in *United States Treaties and Other International Agreements,* the annual bound volumes of the papers as they were numbered and published by the Department of State in pamphlet form in the series Treaties and Other International Acts (TIAS). Multilateral treaties appear in the Treaty Series of the United Nations, although usually a year or more after their signature. Treaties predating 1950 may be found (depending upon their nature and date) in the Treaty Series of the League of Nations, the Treaty Series and Executive Agreement Series of the Department of State, and in *Statutes at Large.*

N.   [8]Department of State, "Nuclear Weapons
Test Ban," 5 August 1963, TIAS no. 5433,
United States Treaties and Other International
Agreements, vol. 14, pt. 2.

B.   U.S. Department of State. "Nuclear Weapons Test Ban," 5 August 1963. TIAS no. 5433. <u>United States Treaties and Other International Agreements</u>, vol. 14, pt. 2.

PR.   (U.S. Department of State 1963, vol. 14, pt. 2)

RL.   U.S. Department of State. 1963. Nuclear Weapons Test Ban, 5 August 1963. TIAS no. 5433. <u>United States treaties and other international agreements</u>, vol. 14, pt. 2.

N.   [9]U.S., "Naval Armament Limitation Treaty," 26 February 1922, <u>Statutes at Large</u>, (December 1923–March 1925), vol. 43, pt. 2.

B.   U.S. "Naval Armament Limitation Treaty," 26 February 1922. <u>Statutes at Large</u>, (December 1923–March 1925), vol. 43, pt. 2.

PR.   (U.S. 1922)

RL.   U.S. 1922. Naval Armament Limitation Treaty, 26 February 1922. <u>Statutes at large</u>, (December 1923–March 1925), vol. 43, pt. 2.

N.   [10]United Nations, Treaty Series, "Denmark and Italy: Convention concerning Military Service," 15 July 1954, <u>Treaties and International Agreements Registered or Filed or Reported with the Secretariat of the United Nations</u>, vol. 250 (1956), no. 3516, 45.

B.   United Nations. Treaty Series. "Denmark and Italy: Convention concerning Military Service," 15 July 1954. <u>Treaties and International Agreements Registered or Filed or Reported with the Secretariat of the United Nations</u>, vol. 250 (1956), no. 3516.

PR.   (United Nations, Treaties Series 1956, vol. 250, no. 3516, 45)

RL.   United Nations. Treaty Series. 1956. Denmark and Italy: Convention concerning military service, 15 July 1954. <u>Treaties and international agreements registered or filed or reported with the Secretariat of the United Nations</u>, vol. 250, no. 3516.

UNPUBLISHED DOCUMENTS

12.19 Most unpublished documents of the United States government are held in the National Archives in Washington, D.C., or in one of its branches. All materials, including manuscripts and typescript records, films, still photographs, and sound recordings, are cited by record group. They may also have titles and file numbers, which should be included in any citation. *The Chicago Manual of Style,* thirteenth edition (16.158) gives suggestions for ordering the information in citations to such materials. For papers involving many citations to unpublished public documents, use the method of citation that appears below. The adopted method of citation should be used consistently throughout the notes, bibliography, parenthetical references, or reference list of a paper.

N.   [2]Congress, Senate, Committee on the Judiciary, "Lobbying," File 71A–F15, Record Group 46, National Archives, Washington, D.C.

B.   U.S. Congress. Senate. Committee on the Judiciary. "Lobbying." File 71A–F15. Record Group 46. National Archives. Washington, D.C.

PR.   (U.S. Congress, Senate n.d.)

Or:

PR/CR.   (Lobbying n.d.)

RL.   U.S. Congress. Senate. Committee on the Judiciary. n.d. Lobbying. File 71A–F15. Record Group 46. National Archives. Washington, D.C.

RL/CR.   Lobbying. n.d. <u>See</u> U.S. Congress. Senate. n.d.

TECHNICAL REPORT LITERATURE

12.20 Under the category of United States public documents falls an extensive collection of technical report literature readily available through large information services, several of which can be accessed through such computer services as Dialog and Orbit. Many of these reports stem from contracts and grants awarded by federal agencies to universities, specialized consultants, corporations, and professional associations and societies. The National Technical Information Service (NTIS), a federal agency within the Department of Commerce, provides access to scientific and technical reports produced by federal agencies and their contractors, and recovers the costs of this service from sales to users. The NTIS distributes many government and nongovernment printed materials that are not distributed to depository libraries. NTIS also tracks the scientific and technical material available through depository library networks. Another such large information network is the Educational Resources Information Center (ERIC), which makes available education-related materials. For an excellent discussion of technical report literature, its background, and current availability, see chapter 5 of *Introduction to United States Public Documents* by Joe Morehead, third edition (Littleton, Colo.: Libraries Unlimited, 1983), available at the reference desks of most research libraries. Much of the information from these services is available on-line, on paper, or on microfiche. The following examples show how to refer to several kinds of technical report literature:

N.   [8]Barbara Robson, <u>Tanzania: Country Status Report</u> (Washington, D.C.: Center for Applied Linguistics, Language/Area Reference Center, 1984), 7, ERIC, ED 248 700.

B.   Robson, Barbara. <u>Tanzania: Country Status Report</u>. Washington, D.C.: Center for Applied Linguistics, Language/Area Reference Center, 1984. ERIC, ED 248 700.

PR.   (Robson 1984, 7)

RL.   Robson, Barbara. 1984. <u>Tanzania: Country status report</u>. Washington, D.C.: Center for Applied Linguistics, Language/Area Reference Center. ERIC, ED 248 700.

N.   [9]<u>Act of 18 March 1983 on Nuclear Third Party Liability (LRCN)</u> (Paris: French Government, 1983), 6, NTIS, DE84780322.

B.   <u>Act of 18 March 1983 on Nuclear Third Party Liability (LRCN)</u>. Paris: French Government, 1983. NTIS, DE84780322.

PR.   (<u>Act of 18 March 1983</u>, 6)

Or:

PR/CR.   (Nuclear Third Party Liability Act 1983, 6)

RL.   <u>Act of 18 March 1983 on Nuclear Third Party Liability (LRCN)</u>. 1983. Paris: French Government. NTIS, DE84780322.

RL/CR. Nuclear Third Party Liability Act. 1983. <u>See</u>
          <u>Act of 18 March 1983 on Nuclear Third</u>
          <u>Party Liability</u>. 1983.

N.   [10]Bureau of Intelligence and Research,
          <u>Indicators of Comparative East–West Economic</u>
          <u>Strength, 1981</u>, by L. Kornei, 7 December 1982,
          5, NTIS, AD–A145 450/3.

B.   U.S. Bureau of Intelligence and Research.
          <u>Indicators of Comparative East–West</u>
          <u>Economic Strength, 1981</u>. By L. Kornei. 7
          December 1982. NTIS, AD–A145 450/3.

PR.   (U.S. Bureau of Intelligence and Research

          1982, 5)

Or:

PR/CR.   (Kornei 1982, 5)

RL.   U.S. Bureau of Intelligence and Research.
          1982. <u>Indicators of comparative East–West</u>
          <u>economic strength, 1981</u>. By L. Kornei. 7
          December 1982. NTIS, AD–A145 450/3.

RL/CR.   Kornei, L. 1982. <u>See</u> U.S. Bureau of
          Intelligence and Research. 1982.

N.   [11]Frances J. Carter and Raymond C.
          Norris, <u>Quality of Life of Graduate Students:</u>
          <u>Components and Predictors</u>, Paper presented at
          the annual meeting of the American Educational
          Research Association, New Orleans, Louisiana,
          23–27 April 1984, 25, Dialog, ERIC, ED 247
          844.

B.   Carter, Frances J., and Raymond C. Norris.
          <u>Quality of Life of Graduate Students:</u>
          <u>Components and Predictors</u>. Paper
          presented at the Annual Meeting of the
          American Educational Research
          Association, New Orleans, Louisiana, 23–
          27 April 1984. Dialog, ERIC, ED 247 844.

PR.   (Carter and Norris 1984, 25)

RL.   Carter, Frances J., and Raymond C. Norris.
          1984. <u>Quality of life of graduate</u>
          <u>students: Components and predictors</u>.
          Paper presented at the annual meeting of
          the American Educational Research
          Association, New Orleans, Louisiana, 23–
          27 April 1984. Dialog, ERIC, ED 247 844.

STATE AND LOCAL GOVERNMENT DOCUMENTS

12.21   Citations to state and local government documents are in essentially the same form as those to United States government documents:

N.   ¹Illinois Constitution (1848), art. 5, sec. 2.

Ordinarily, the date of a constitution is indicated only when it is not in force. In papers using the parenthetical-reference system, constitutional citations are usually given in the text, and it is unnecessary to include constitutional entries in either bibliographies or reference lists.

N.   ²Revised Statutes, Annotated (Baldwin, 1943).

B.   Kentucky. Revised Statutes, Annotated (Baldwin, 1943).

PR.   (Kentucky 1943)

RL.   Kentucky. 1943. Revised statutes, annotated (Baldwin).

Note 2 above shows the style used in referring to an annotated revision made by William K. Baldwin in 1943.

N.   ³Ohio. Judicial Organization Act, Statutes (1830) 3:1571–78.

B.   Ohio. Judicial Organization Act. Statutes. 1830.

PR.   (Ohio 1830, 3:1571–78)

RL.   Ohio. 1830. Judicial Organization Act. Statutes.

N.   ⁴New York, N.Y., "Good Samaritan" Law, Administrative Code (1965), sec. 67–3.2.

B.   New York, N.Y. "Good Samaritan" Law. Administrative Code. 1965.

PR.   (New York 1965, sec. 67–3.2)

Or:

PR/CR.   ("Good Samaritan" law 1965, sec. 67–3.2)

RL.   New York, N.Y. 1965. "Good Samaritan" law. Administrative code.

RL/CR.   "Good Samaritan" law. 1965. See New York, N.Y. 1965.

BRITISH GOVERNMENT DOCUMENTS

12.22 Citations to British government documents, like those to their counterparts in United States documents, should begin with the name of the authorizing body under which they were issued— Parliament, Public Record Office, Foreign Office, Ministry of Transport, or so on—always preceded by "United Kingdom" (if published since 1801) or "Great Britain" (if published before 1801 and after 1707) or "England" (if dated prior to 1707).

12.23 The most recent edition of *Anglo-American Cataloguing Rules* has recommended that British government publications be listed under United Kingdom (abbreviated "U.K."), although Great Britain (abbreviated "G.B.") has been widely used until recently and is also acceptable, taking into consideration the dates of publication involved (see 12.22).

12.24 The publisher of most government material is Her (His) Majesty's Stationery Office (HMSO) in London.

12.25 More often cited in notes or text than in bibliographical or reference-list entries, English statutes are always cited by name, regnal year of the sovereign (for statutes passed prior to 1963) or year (for statutes passed since 1963), and chapter number (arabic numeral for national statutes, roman for local). The listing of the names of statutes passed prior to the 1850s may present difficulties, because shortened titles of acts were not always designated, as they have been by law since 1892. In the second set of examples below, for instance, the document is simply described in place of a title. In references to English statutes passed prior to 1963, names of sovereigns are abbreviated and arabic numerals are used to indicate regnal year (tables of regnal years are available in many reference works). Since 1963, published statutes have been numbered serially within each calendar year, so these statutes are cited by year and chapter number. Before publication in the *Statutes* or in the *Public General Acts and Church Assembly Measures* (called the *Public General Acts and General Synod Measures* since 1972), statutes are cited as in the first set of examples below. When they are published in one or the other compilation, their citations follow the forms shown in the last two sets of examples.

N.   [1]Laws, Statutes, etc., <u>Coroner's Act, 1954</u>, 2 & 3 Eliz. 2, c. 31.

B. U.K. Laws, Statutes, etc. <u>Coroner's Act, 1954</u>.
    2 & 3 Eliz. 2, c. 31.

PR. (U.K. Laws, Statutes, etc. 1954)

Or:

PR/CR. (<u>Coroner's Act, 1954</u>)

RL. U.K. Laws, Statutes, etc. 1954. <u>Coroner's Act,
    1954</u>. 2 & 3 Eliz. 2, c. 31.

RL/CR. <u>Coroner's Act, 1954</u>. <u>See</u> U.K. Laws, Statutes,
    etc. 1954.

N.   [2]King's General Pardon, 1540, <u>Statutes
   of the Realm</u>, 32 Hen. 8, c. 49.

B. England. King's General Pardon. 1540. <u>Statutes
    of the Realm</u>. 32 Hen. 8, c. 49.

PR. (England, King's General Pardon 1540)

Or:

PR. (England 1540)

RL. England. King's General Pardon. 1540. <u>Statutes
    of the Realm</u>. 32 Hen. 8, c. 49.

N.   [3]<u>Statutes</u>, 31 Vict., c. xiv, 2 April
  1868.

B. U.K. <u>Statutes</u>. 31 Vict., c. xiv. 2 April 1868.

PR. (U.K. 1868)

RL. U.K. 1868. <u>Statutes</u>. 31 Vict., c. xiv. 2
    April.

N.   [4]Laws, Statutes, etc., <u>Police and
  Criminal Evidence Act, 1984</u>, <u>Public General
  Acts and General Synod Measures</u>, 1984, pt. 3,
  c. 60.

B. U.K. Laws, Statutes, etc. <u>Police and Criminal
    Evidence Act, 1984</u>. <u>Public General Acts
    and General Synod Measures</u>, 1984, pt. 3,
    c. 60.

PR. (U.K. Laws, Statutes, etc. 1984)

RL. U.K. Laws, Statutes, etc. 1984. <u>Police and
    Criminal Evidence Act, 1984</u>. <u>Public
    General Acts and General Synod Measures</u>,
    pt. 3, c. 60.

PARLIAMENTARY PAPERS

12.26 The *Parliamentary Papers* are bound annually in two sequences,
each with its own series of volume numbers. In one sequence,

public acts are arranged alphabetically by the official name of
the acts, with related committee proceedings and reports following each bill. In the other sequence, reports, accounts, and papers (sometimes called *Sessional Papers*) are arranged alphabetically by primary subject matter. The *Sessional Index* is a useful
guide to pagination and organization within these two sequences.
Among the Parliamentary Papers discussed above are *Command
Papers,* so named because they are presented by command of
the reigning monarch. For the numbering and abbreviations for
consecutive series of Command Papers, see *The Chicago Manual of Style,* thirteenth edition (16.168). The term *Parliamentary
Papers* also refers to such other publications of the House of
Commons and the House of Lords as their journals, votes, proceedings, and debates (see 12.28).

N.   [7]<u>Report of the Royal Commission on</u>
            <u>Indian Currency and Finance</u>, vol. 2,
            Appendices, Cmd. 2687 (1926).

B.   U.K. <u>Report of the Royal Commission on Indian</u>
            <u>Currency and Finance</u>. Vol. 2, Appendices.
            Cmd. 2687. 1926.

PR.   (U.K. 1926)

RL.   U.K. 1926. <u>Report of the Royal Commission on</u>
            <u>Indian Currency and Finance</u>. Vol. 2,
            Appendices. Cmd. 2687.

N.   [8]<u>The Basic Facility and the Sterling</u>
            <u>Area</u>, Cmnd. 3787 (October 1968), 15–16.

B.   U.K. <u>The Basic Facility and the Sterling Area</u>.
            Cmnd. 3787. October 1968.

PR.   (U.K. 1968, 15–16)

RL.   U.K. 1968. <u>The basic facility and the sterling</u>
            <u>area</u>. Cmnd. 3787. October.

SESSIONAL PAPERS

12.27   The Sessional Papers are a part of the Parliamentary Papers, but
the latter are also sometimes referred to as Sessional Papers.
Though the annual series of Sessional Papers is identified by
year date alone, it is divided into titles, each title having its
individual set of volume numbers, and each being listed as a
publication either of the House of Commons or the House of
Lords. A citation to these Sessional Papers can be deceiving,
since some volumes are made up of separate papers paged individually and arranged either chronologically by day or alphabet-

ically by primary subject. Cite the specific document by its title, with pertinent numbered sections or paragraphs (if the paper is long), and page numbers. The volumes include well-arranged tables of contents and are indexed annually (see also 12.26).

N. [1]Parliament, "Present and Future Role of the Assistant Chief Education Officer," Sessional Papers (Commons), 1982–83, Prison Education, 25 April 1983, vol. 2, par. 9.14, p. 102.

B. U.K. Parliament. "Present and Future Role of the Assistant Chief Education Officer." Sessional Papers (Commons). 1982–83, Prison Education. 25 April 1983.

PR. (U.K. Parliament 1983, vol. 2, par. 9.14, p. 102)

RL. U.K. Parliament. 1983. Present and future role of the Assistant Chief Education Officer. Sessional papers (Commons). 1982–83, Prison education. 25 April.

Parliamentary Debates

12.28   Since 1909 the *Parliamentary Debates* have been published separately for the two houses. The name *Hansard* (for an original printer of the Debates) often does not appear on the title pages of volumes issued since 1908, but it still has official sanction, and the Debates are commonly referred to as Hansard or Hansard's, even though they are now published by HMSO (see 12.24). Use the title as it appears in the volume that is being cited. Series and volume numbers should also be cited:

N. [1]Parliamentary Debates (Lords), 5th ser., vol. 13 (1893), col. 1273.

B. U.K. Parliamentary Debates (Lords). 5th ser., vol. 13 (1893), col. 1273.

PR. (U.K. 1893)

RL. U.K. 1893. Parliamentary debates (Lords). 5th ser., vol. 13, col. 1273.

N. [2]Hansard Parliamentary Debates, 3d ser., vol. 249 (1879), cols. 611–27.

B. U.K. Hansard Parliamentary Debates. 3d ser., vol. 249 (1879), cols. 611–27.

PR. (U.K. 1879)

RL.   U.K. 1879. <u>Hansard parliamentary debates</u>. 3d
ser., vol. 249, cols. 611–27.

N.   [3]Churchill, Speech to the House of
Commons, 18 January 1945, <u>Parliamentary
Debates</u> (Commons), 5th ser., vol. 407 (1944–
45), cols. 425–46.

B.   U.K. Winston Churchill. Speech to the House of
Commons, 18 January 1945. <u>Parliamentary
Debates</u> (Commons). 5th ser., vol. 407
(1944–45), cols. 425–46.

PR.   (U.K. Winston Churchill 1945)

RL.   U.K. Winston Churchill. Speech to the House of
Commons, 18 January 1945. <u>Parliamentary
debates</u> (Commons). 5th ser., vol. 407
(1944–45), cols. 425–46.

BRITISH FOREIGN AND STATE PAPERS

12.29   The *British Foreign and State Papers* are arranged within the
volumes alphabetically by country and, further, by subject:

N.   [1]Foreign Office, "Austria: Proclamation
of the Emperor Annulling the Constitution of
4th March, 1849," <u>British Foreign and State
Papers, 1952–53</u>, 41:1298–99.

B.   U.K. Foreign Office. "Austria: Proclamation of
the Emperor Annulling the Constitution of
4th March, 1849." <u>British Foreign and
State Papers, 1952–53</u>.

PR.   (U.K. Foreign Office 1952–53, 41:1298–99)

RL.   U.K. Foreign Office. 1952–53. Austria:
Proclamation of the Emperor annulling the
constitution of 4th March, 1849. <u>British
foreign and state papers, 1952–53</u>.

12.30   Reports are issued in pamphlet form by the several ministries,
commissions, committees, and the like:

N.   [1]Office of the Minister of Science,
Committee on Management and Control of
Research, <u>Report, 1961</u>, 58.

B.   U.K. Office of the Minister of Science.
Committee on Management and Control of
Research. <u>Report, 1961</u>.

PR.   (U.K. Office of the Minister of Science 1961,

58)

> RL.   U.K. Office of the Minister of Science.
>   Committee on Management and Control of
>   Research. 1961. <u>Report, 1961</u>.

12.31 The early records entitled *Calendar of . . .* are arranged chronologically. In some, numbered items—grants, leases, warrants, pardons, and so on—appear within a "calendar" of no uniform duration. Dates are essential, therefore, in identifying the items, although parenthetical references should be used for these works only when reference lists include adequate cross-references and when as much information as possible is given in the text.

> N.   [1]Public Record Office, "Queen Mother to
>   the Queen," 18 February 1581, <u>Calendar of
>   State Papers, Foreign Series, of the Reign of
>   Elizabeth [I]</u> (January 1581–April 1582)
>   (London: HMSO, 1907), no. 58, 63.

> B.   U.K. Public Record Office. "Queen Mother to
>   the Queen," 18 February 1581. <u>Calendar of
>   State Papers, Foreign Series, of the
>   Reign of Elizabeth [I]</u> (January 1581–
>   April 1582). London: HMSO, 1907.

> PR.   (U.K. Public Record Office 1907)

> RL.   U.K. Public Record Office. 1907. Queen Mother
>   to the Queen, 18 February 1581. <u>Calendar
>   of state papers, foreign series, of the
>   reign of Elizabeth [I]</u> (January 1581–
>   April 1582). London: HMSO. No. 58, 63.

CANADIAN PUBLIC DOCUMENTS

12.32 Canadian government documents are issued by both houses of the Canadian Parliament (Senate and House of Commons) and by the various executive departments. Statutes are published in the *Statutes of Canada* and identified by calendar year and by chapter (c.) number.

> N.   [1]House of Commons, <u>Order Paper and
>   Notices</u>, 16 February 1972, 6.

> B.   Canada. House of Commons. <u>Order Paper and
>   Notices</u>. 16 February 1972.

> PR.   (Canada 1972, 6)

> RL.   Canada. House of Commons. 1972. <u>Order paper
>   and notices</u>. 16 February.

N.   [2]Statutes of Canada, 1919, 10 Geo. 5,
           c. 17.

B.   Canada. Statutes of Canada. 1919. 10 Geo. 5,
               c. 17.

PR.   (Canada 1919)

RL.   Canada. 1919. Statutes of Canada. 10 Geo. 5,
               c. 17.

Unpublished records are housed in the Public Archives of Canada (PAC) and identified by the name of the record group, series, and volume.

N.   [2]Privy Council Office Records, series
           1, vol. 1477, Public Archives of Canada, n.d.

B.   Canada. Privy Council Office Records, series
               1, vol. 1477. Public Archives of Canada.
               n.d.

PR.   (Canada n.d.)

RL.   Canada. Privy Council Office Records. n.d.
               Series 1, vol. 1477. Public Archives of
               Canada.

LEAGUE OF NATIONS AND UNITED NATIONS DOCUMENTS

12.33 For these documents, give the following information, more or less in the order shown, whenever it is available: authorizing body, topic of the paper, series number, place of publication, date, publication number, and page reference when applicable:

N.   [1]League of Nations, Monetary and
           Economic Conference: Draft Annotated Agenda
           Submitted by the Preparatory Commission of
           Experts, II, Economic and Financial, 1933,
           II.Spec.I.

B.   League of Nations. Monetary and Economic
               Conference: Draft Annotated Agenda
               Submitted by the Preparatory Commission
               of Experts. II. Economic and Financial.
               1933. II.Spec.I.

PR.   (League of Nations 1933, II.Spec.I)

RL.   League of Nations. 1933. Monetary and economic
               conference: Draft annotated agenda
               submitted by the Preparatory Commission
               of Experts. II. Economic and Financial.
               II.Spec.I.

N.   [2]United Nations, Secretariat,
        Department of Economic Affairs, <u>Methods of
        Financing Economic Development in
        Underdeveloped Countries</u>, 1951, II.B.2.

B.   United Nations. Secretariat. Department of
        Economic Affairs. <u>Methods of Financing
        Economic Development in Underdeveloped
        Countries</u>. 1951.

PR.   (United Nations 1951, II.B.2)

RL.   United Nations. Secretariat. Department of
        Economic Affairs. 1951. <u>Methods of
        financing economic development in
        underdeveloped countries</u>.

13 Preparing the Manuscript: The Most Effective Use of Computer Systems and Typewriters

RESPONSIBILITIES OF THE WRITER AND OF THE PERSON PREPARING THE MANUSCRIPT

13.1   The writer is responsible for the correct presentation of the paper in its entirety—all the preliminary, illustrative, and reference matter as well as the main body of the text. The person preparing the manuscript, if other than the writer, should be held responsible for an accurate transcription of the copy, the layout of the components as set forth in chapter 14, and the general appearance of the final copy, but not for matters of content.

EQUIPMENT

13.2   Access to only one kind of typewriter, computer system, or photocopier means that the options for preparing a manuscript will be limited by the capabilities of the equipment. At many degree-granting institutions, however, students may select from several kinds of typewriters, software, computer systems, and photocopiers to meet the specifications set by the dissertation office or by a particular department or discipline. To decide what equipment to use for preparing a manuscript, follow this step-by-step process. First, determine in as much detail as possible what the paper will be like in its finished form: the kind of notes it will have, the special characters it will require, and the complexity of formatting it will require (i.e., equations, formulas, illustrations, tables, lengthy footnotes, transcriptions, linguistic trees, computer graphics, music, non-Latin alphabets, etc.). Second, decide on what equipment to use (for example, whether to enter the paper on a computer system or type the paper in its final form) by becoming as familiar as possible with the potentials and limitations of the available equipment. Learn as much as possible about the capabilities of available facilities. In other words, make sure that the equipment being considered is able to produce the desired results.

13.3 For papers prepared on computer systems, select software *before* hardware; then choose hardware that is compatible with the selected software. If feasible, make sure that every piece of hardware is fully compatible with the chosen software by consulting someone knowledgeable.

13.4 Whenever possible, test samples of the kind of work to be done on the proposed system before making a commitment to use that system. This step will also help ensure familiarity with all the stages of development the paper requires and with the computer capabilities needed at each stage. For example, do not take it for granted that a particular printer will meet the specifications of a dissertation office in terms of letter-quality resolution (see 13.34) and the quality of the photocopies that can be made from material printed on it. Be sure that the dissertation secretary or thesis adviser approves the quality of the final printing, duplicate copies, if any, and paper stock used.

13.5 The writer can best determine what kind of equipment suits the paper's requirements. Certain guidelines that apply universally are discussed below.

For computerized word processing, see 13.6–42.
For typing, see 13.43–44.
For materials, see 13.45–50.
For duplicating, see 13.51–52.

COMPUTERIZED WORD PROCESSING

13.6 It is always a good idea before preparing a paper on a computer system to become familiar with the information in the user's manuals for the selected computer system.

ENTERING TEXT

13.7 Text entry does not vary significantly from one computer system to another. Usually the first step in producing a paper on a computer is to enter the text directly, using a standard QWERTY keyboard. Choice of display qualities of a screen is somewhat subjective. The writer should be satisfied with the characteristics of the screen display, for example, the resolution and background color. It is also important to have a computer system that gives the writer complete control over selecting the portion of text to be displayed on the screen and control over positioning of the cursor. The writer should easily be able to position the cursor anywhere in the text.

SPECIAL CHARACTERS

13.8 For papers that require the use of special characters, computer systems offer a major advantage because they can often produce a far greater range of characters than those that appear on the standard keyboard or those available with even the most sophisticated electronic typewriters. Some systems allow one to use function keys or combinations of keys or special codes to enter diacritical marks, non-Latin characters, and math symbols. There are also systems that allow the "remapping" of standard keyboards (alternative keyboard functions) to make it easier to enter text that requires special characters. Such systems may display the alternative keyboard layout on the screen. Not all systems have the capability of displaying exactly the special characters that have been entered, and so some systems display only a limited range of nonkeyboard characters. Sometimes special characters may be represented by combinations of standard characters. Some systems allow the creation of individual special characters and complete fonts.

STORED KEYSTROKES

13.9 If a paper includes a name, a term, or a phrase that will appear often, software that can "store" a sequence of keystrokes on a specific function key may speed text entry and improve accuracy. For example, instead of entering "University" many times in a paper, the individual keystrokes of this word could be "mapped" to a key that when hit once would enter the full word. Optimal word processing programs allow the storage of libraries of such keystrokes. This function can be particularly useful for those using word processors that introduce special characters into the text as combinations of keyboard characters.

EDITING TEXT

13.10 For those who expect to revise a paper significantly or who simply want an efficient means of editing while entering the text, computer systems offer the advantage of modifying text quickly, easily, and accurately. Significant portions of a paper—entire paragraphs, a misspelled word throughout, etc.—can be revised, reformatted, and reprinted without rekeying correct portions and possibly introducing new errors in the process. With most word-processing systems, it is possible to insert and delete text, move it from one location to another, replace sections with other sections, and automatically find text strings and replace them with other text strings.

13.11 To choose the right software for editing a paper, evaluate what each package offers in terms of the requirements of the writing assignment (especially any specifications that are unique) and editing preferences (e.g., composing at the terminal, significantly rewriting while entering, introducing notes early or late in the process). Though many word processors have editing capabilities, individual software packages are distinguished by their power, speed, and flexibility. Certain software restricts some operations (for example, copying, moving) on large segments of the text; other software allows flexible management of segments of relatively unrestricted sizes. Most software packages include search and replace operations: finding any given text string and replacing it with another given text string; changing a text string once or making changes throughout the paper (a "global change"). More sophisticated packages, however, include "wild card" routines, which match strings of any given prefix, suffix, or internal letter combination (e.g., *b*t* would match *bit, bat, bet*, etc.). The more powerful programs make changes based on various specified conditions (e.g., only in lines with a number, only in lines containing the letters *xyz*).

FILE MANAGEMENT

13.12 No matter what type of paper is being processed, it is important to be able to manipulate files easily, to save and retrieve files, name and rename them, generate automatic back-up copies, and delete and merge files. Long papers should be saved in several files; for example, one for each chapter (if about thirty pages). If the software generates lists, tables of contents, and other parts of the paper, it may be necessary to combine copies of the text files, save the composite file, and then process the paper as a whole. It is important to name files carefully in order to determine which generation of a particular component is being displayed on the screen or printed.

BACKING UP FILES

13.13 No matter what software or hardware is used to prepare a manuscript, it is necessary to save copies of the work in progress. Preferably, printed and on-line copies should be saved and dated so that there are at all times paper and electronic media backups (diskette or tape) of every part of the paper at each stage of composition. Those who do not do so run the risk of losing material that cannot be replaced.

FORMATTING TEXT

13.14 Formatting refers to the process of positioning text for display, such as laying it out correctly for printing on an 8½-by-11-inch page, as specified in chapter 14. Some powerful formatting software can perform special functions, such as generating tables of contents and lists; managing headers and footers; controlling orphan lines; paginating; changing variable fields in the paper to text strings; producing computer graphics; positioning and numbering footnotes, tables, and illustrations at the appropriate place in the text; and controlling the flow of text around such special components as equations, tables, and illustrations.

13.15 There are two primary ways of formatting text, as a sequence of *page images* and as a *coded text stream*. In general, text-stream systems are used for longer, more complicated papers, while page-image systems are used for shorter ones.

PAGE-IMAGE FORMATTING

13.16 Page-image formatting is a process that automatically positions text as it is being entered, usually for printing on an 8½-x-11-inch page. The writer first defines the page-image format, for example, by answering menu prompts or using a displayed ruler to set top and bottom margins, line length, page length, tab markers, etc. Entry and formatting are almost simultaneous processes, and the screen displays a full or partial view of the page almost as it would appear if printed. When the text being entered reaches the "end" of the page, a page break is automatically entered; as words reach the right margin, words are "wrapped" to the next line and hyphenated when necessary. Automatic hyphenation routines require careful proofreading of the text, because they are not always correct (see 3.37).

TEXT-STREAM FORMATTING

13.17 Long, complicated papers may require the capabilities of a text-stream formatting system. With such a system, the text is entered as a totally unformatted sequence of words, without regard to margins, pages, footnote placement, etc. Formatting codes, or "control words," are entered simultaneously with the text or after the text has been completed. For a sample of unformatted text with coding such as that used on the University of Chicago's dissertation-formatting program TREATISE, see 14.50.

13.18 Formatting is a separate processing step. The text-stream file containing the codes is processed by a formatting or composing program, and a second file is created. This second file is usually a page-image file that can be displayed on the screen or printed. Sample 14.51 shows the formatted version of the text in sample 14.50.

13.19 *Text coding scheme.* The text coding scheme, the key element to this type of formatting process, gives layout information to the formatter. There are two general categories of coding schemes, those using *procedural tags* and those using *declarative tags*.

13.20 *Procedural tags.* Procedural tags indicate precise formatting information, for example, <SP> for leaving a blank line, <IN 2> for indenting two character positions, <PA> for starting a new page.

13.21 *Declarative tags.* Declarative tags simply identify components of the paper, for example, <CHAPTER>, <SECTION>, <FOOTNOTE>. This procedure usually makes use of resources called *document-specification libraries,* which are predefined layouts, or document format descriptions (e.g., the layout necessary for a dissertation). With such a system, the same text could be processed through different formatters to conform to different requirements, such as those for a dissertation, a manuscript being distributed for review, a manuscript being sent to a publisher, or a book being published independently.

13.22 *Revising a paper using a text-stream formatting system* may be done in two ways, depending upon the kind of revisions that are necessary. If many changes must be made, the changes should be made to the unformatted copy, which then can be reformatted as many times as necessary. Some changes, however, can only be made on the formatted copy (e.g., adjusting incorrect hyphenation produced in the formatting process). On some larger computers, it may save time and cost to make minor changes when possible on the formatted copy, such as replacing one word string with another of the same length, replacing a whole line (especially in unjustified text), and adding or deleting lines at the tops and bottoms of pages or in footnotes.

Transferring Text

13.23 At some point in the processing of a paper, it may be necessary to transfer the text from one processing system to another. In general, text created on one computer system cannot easily be transferred to another without losing formatting information. This can be true with regard to transfers between different computers, operating systems, versions of operating systems, word-processing programs, and even versions of word-processing programs. Before attempting any text transfers, be sure that all the necessary steps are clearly understood. Generally, it is easiest to transfer documents coded with declarative tags (see 13.21).

Entering Footnotes on a Computer System

13.24 Those who are considering preparing a paper with footnotes would be well advised to read the software documentation carefully before selecting the software itself and then once again before beginning to enter the text and notes. At the very least, a program should be able to introduce superscript numbers at the ends of referenced words and single-space and double-space on the same page, so that notes at the bottom of the double-spaced text can be single-spaced, with a blank line between notes. Some sophisticated programs completely automate the process of arranging footnotes within the text, placing them on the proper pages and assigning them consecutive numbers. The more sophisticated a software's treatment of footnotes, the easier it will be to revise the paper, inserting new footnotes or rearranging them as the paper reaches each stage of composition.

Of course, papers that do not use footnotes but rely instead on parenthetical references or endnotes can be revised more easily at any stage of composition when using many standard word-processing programs, since footnote placement would not be a major consideration.

EQUATIONS AND FORMULAS

13.25 Only the most sophisticated word-processing packages are able to produce equations more complex than simple linear equations. Usually it is necessary to create equations or formulas by using adjunct software. Complex equations may be difficult to produce on microcomputers. The task is made somewhat easier by following the guidelines of the American Mathematical Society's *Manual for Authors of Mathematical Papers,* which suggests ways of keeping equations simple (see the bibliography at the end of this manual). It may be necessary to introduce equations and formulas as artwork (see 7.27–32).

TABLES

13.26 Some software packages offer the capabilities necessary to create tables, such as the ability to produce multiple tabs, to make columnar adjustments, and to perform spread-sheet management functions. Vertical as well as horizontal rules are often options, though these may also be added by hand (see chapter 6 for instructions on compiling tables and treating the artwork in them). Some powerful programs position tables within the text in proximity to references to them; position tables correctly on individual pages; automatically number the tables and adjust the numbering throughout revisions, including table numbers used in cross-references; and generate a list of tables for the preliminaries. Footnotes for tables, however, usually must be entered at the keyboard rather than generated and placed within tables automatically.

13.27 Many parts of a paper, such as footnotes, tables, and illustrations, are numbered. Some word-processing programs allow the automatic cross-referencing of such components, eliminating the need to update cross-references manually whenever numbered components of the paper are inserted or deleted.

COMPUTER GRAPHICS

13.28   If a paper includes bar graphs, line graphs, and pie charts, it may be advantageous to use computer software for creating such graphics. Computers can also be used to create and manipulate line art, that is, line drawings. Graphics created on a computer are usually vector graphics, which are created from coordinate points that can be interpreted (connected to form images) by display devices, printers, and plotters.

13.29   Graphics that do not originate on a computer, such as photographs or hand drawings, can be "scanned" into the machine with a device ("scanner") that transforms the image into a digital representation called a bit map. Software exists for transforming vector graphics into bit maps. Graphics can also be entered with specially adapted cameras ("digital-input cameras").

13.30   Depending upon the capabilities of the computer system, once computer graphics are generated, they can be merged with the text or inserted as illustrations (see chapter 7).

PRINTING

13.31   Printing is an important consideration in the process of preparing the paper by means of a computer system. When ascertaining the requirements for the preparation process, give special consideration to printing needs. Be sure that all printing requirements are understood and that the required capabilities are available. Take into consideration printer compatibility with software, printing speed, printer resolution, and the capability for printing graphics, equations, and special characters. Only after the characteristics that constitute acceptable printing for a particular application have been ensured by testing, should the manuscript be entered on a computer system.

PRINTER AND SOFTWARE INTERFACE

13.32   Among the most important considerations of the printing process are the printer and software interfaces that link the word-processing program to the printer. For example, there are two major types of ports (parallel and serial), and individual cable configurations vary. Software support for a printer should receive special attention. Remember, not all software programs support all printers. Software should have capabilities for adjusting the mode of signals sent to the printer and for altering individual signals. Printers should be designed to allow easy control such as adjusting the interface signals using front panel controls instead of internal switches. The system used should be able to print only a part of the paper (e.g., one page with a revision on it), print while editing (it can take up to several hours for some printers to print a paper), and to pause while printing (to change paper or daisywheels or to fix jams).

SPECIAL FEATURES

13.33 The formatted version of a paper prepared on a computer system should have only those characteristics that the printer is able to reproduce. For example, daisywheel printers do not print italics as readily as they underline or print boldface characters. In choosing a printer, consider the following features and how they apply to the specific needs of the paper: underlining, using boldface or italics, shadowing, superscripting, typing special characters, variable feeding, color printing, providing variable type styles and pitch, and computer graphics. Other special features have to do with spacing between characters, words, and lines.

RESOLUTION

13.34 All term papers, theses, and dissertations must meet requirements set forth by degree-granting institutions. Most institutions will accept only those theses and dissertations printed on letter-quality daisywheel or laser printers; but dot matrix printers, which are often faster and less expensive to operate, may be used for working drafts of a paper and graphics. Dot matrix printers frequently feature three modes: draft, medium resolution, and "near-letter-quality." The term "near-letter-quality" in this context, however, does not refer to what most advisers and dissertation secretaries mean when they refer to a manuscript prepared on a letter-quality printer. Thesis advisers and dissertation secretaries usually specify what constitutes a letter-quality manuscript, which almost invariably means a paper printed by a daisywheel or laser printer on acid-free paper. Even very high resolution dot matrix printing is usually unacceptable. The final copy must be on acid-free paper stock or must reproduce well on it using available photocopying equipment.

SPEED

13.35   Speed can be a major consideration in choosing a printer. Some printers can type more characters per second (cps) than others (e.g., 12–18 cps, 25–35 cps, 36–60 cps, 80–120 cps, 200 cps). Dot matrix printers are sometimes faster than daisywheel or laser printers, but they offer the lowest resolution and do not include many of the features listed in 13.33. Note that the rated speeds for printers, which may be cited in accompanying literature, may reflect optimum conditions. It is advisable, before selecting a printer, to determine how long the printer would take to print a paper of a given length. This would make it possible to anticipate how much preparation time would be needed for printing drafts.

PRINTING THE FINAL COPY

13.36   While draft copies may be printed on pin-fed paper, dissertation offices usually require cut-sheet paper or the type of form-fed paper that will not leave ragged edges when separated. It is usually advantageous when using cut-sheet paper stock to print a long research paper to use a sheet feeder. It is sometimes more economical to print only one final version of a research paper and then photocopy it onto acid-free paper stock, if photocopies are acceptable.

COMPUTER HARDWARE

13.37   Most computers have some type of word-processing capabilities. Several general categories, distinguished primarily by computing power and flexibility, are microcomputers, word processors, minicomputers, and mainframes. The potentials and limitations of each vary with the type of word-processing facilities and the requirements of the paper being produced. With regard to word processing, bigger is not necessarily better. On the other hand, word-processing facilities on larger computers can be powerful and sophisticated.

WORD PROCESSORS

13.38   Word processors are microprocessor-based machines designed primarily for producing documents. The keyboard of a word processor contains function keys labeled with common editing operations, such as those for deletions and insertions. Word processors, however, tend to be expensive and sometimes cannot handle extremely complex formatting requirements, like equations.

MICROCOMPUTERS

13.39 Microcomputers were designed not specifically for word processing but for a variety of computer applications, such as programming, data storage and retrieval, and numerical analysis. With a good word-processing program, a microcomputer may, however, be as effective as a word processor in handling many types of documents. The key element is the power of the word-processing program.

MINICOMPUTERS

13.40 Minicomputers can be especially useful when a paper's format is complex or when a paper requires very elaborate graphics, tables, or equations. A number of popular word-processing programs are available for minicomputers.

MAINFRAMES

13.41 Although word-processing programs are available on mainframes, mainframes are sometimes best used as resources for more complex applications, such as producing dissertations with hundreds of statistical tables. Mainframes are also very useful for certain types of composition, especially with regard to complex graphics. Many mainframes also provide sophisticated word-processing capabilities combined with advanced features for special processing, for example, equation setting and programs specifically tailored for formatting dissertations.

13.42 This chapter has dealt only with computerized word processing as it relates to writers of term papers, theses, and dissertations, which must be produced as finished texts. For instructions on how to prepare such papers for use by publishers, see the *Chicago Guide to Preparing Electronic Manuscripts* (Chicago: University of Chicago Press, 1987).

TYPING

13.43   Though any kind of typewriter can meet the specifications set forth in this manual, most typists of research papers now use self-correcting electric typewriters with typing elements and automatic carriage returns; self-correcting electronic typewriters with daisywheels and special features, including memories and spellers; or electronic transfer typewriters, which also use daisywheels but operate quietly and use self-correcting carbon ribbons instead of white correcting tape. If an institution requires carbon copies rather than photocopies of a paper, only manual, electric, and electronic typewriters with daisywheels may be used.

13.44   Either pica or elite type, or one of the types available on newer typewriters, is satisfactory for typing most papers. Some institutions specify either pica or elite for theses or dissertations, and some will not accept other available type sizes and styles. A typist who expects to do a considerable amount of typing of theses, dissertations, or other research papers—particularly those designed for submission to publishers—would be well advised to use a specially equipped typewriter, preferably with variable type sizes, proportional spacing, special characters, and italics and boldface as well as underlining. The typewriter should be able to single- and double-space, and the accurate half-space turn of the roller is a great convenience in the typing of superscripts and subscripts. For papers that require different type styles and sets of special characters, electric typewriters have typing elements, and electronic typewriters have daisywheels, designed for easy removal and replacement. In addition, some electronic typewriters are designed to interface with computer systems and serve as printers (see 13.31–36).

RIBBON

13.45   Whether the paper is typed or printed on a daisywheel printer, the final copy must be made with a very good carbon ribbon that will provide evenness of resolution and result in acceptable photocopies on acid-free paper stock. Those using manual typewriters should use a good fabric ribbon and replace it frequently.

CORRECTING AND ERASING

13.46   All corrections and erasures must be invisible. Since theses and dissertations now may usually be accepted as photocopies and as typed or printed manuscripts on acid-free paper, several kinds of corrections and erasures are permissible.

CORRECTING AND ERASING ON TYPEWRITTEN MANUSCRIPTS

13.47 Thorough cover-ups using correcting papers, fluids, or self-correcting typewriter tapes are acceptable. Deletion or insertion of more than one character should be made by retyping. Many typewriters now include a half-spacing function for inclusion of missing characters. All such corrections should be made before the paper is removed from the typewriter whenever possible.

CORRECTING AND ERASING ON MANUSCRIPTS TO BE PHOTOCOPIED

13.48 All of the above-mentioned methods would apply, with the addition of the use of white correcting tape for covering lines and joining portions of pages, since many photocopiers do not reproduce this tape. Manuscripts with extensive revisions of this kind may have to be fed into the photocopier one page at a time instead of automatically. These manuscripts must be photocopied onto acid-free paper, but this paper does not flow as smoothly through automatically feeding copiers as lower quality paper stock, which is recommended over acid-free paper for drafts to be reproduced via this process.

CORRECTING ON PHOTOCOPIES

13.49 To erase unwanted specks and unwanted characters on a line that would not have to be rekeyed to meet the standard, always use correcting fluid designed especially for use on photocopies.

PAPER STOCK

13.50 Whether a paper is typed or entered on a computer system, it should reach its final form as a correctly formatted text on the paper stock specified by the degree-granting institution. In the absence of such a directive, for archival purposes the American Library Association has established guidelines in which it recommends the use of acid-free paper. Acid-free paper is 20-pound weight, neutral-pH paper that is advertised either as "buffered" or as having a minimum 2 percent alkaline reserve. Photocopies and carbon copies should also be made on this type of paper. Some but not all types of paper referred to as "dissertation bond" meet these requirements.

DUPLICATING

13.51 It may be cost effective to reproduce the manuscript using offset printing when over ten copies of a thesis or dissertation are needed.

13.52 In using photocopiers to duplicate manuscripts, it is important to remember the following points: (1) ask to have the machine cleaned before the paper is copied; (2) use only acid-free paper stock that has not been removed from its package or wrapper until immediately before use, as the moisture on long-opened paper can create feeding problems in the photocopy process; (3) when copying from acid-free paper to acid-free paper, feed the pages one by one to prevent feeding problems; (4) if the paper stock is photocopy paper or somewhat lighter weight typewriting paper, feed it into large photocopiers fifty or fewer pages at a time; (5) check every copied manuscript to be sure that all copies are uniform and that no pages are missing; and (6) check for distortions, such as those having to do with the 2 percent enlargement created by each photocopy generation in art work.

14 Formats of Component Parts and Sample Layouts

14.1   This chapter discusses the correct layout of words on the page (see 14.2–24), giving directions for typists and those preparing papers on computer systems. These directions assume the use of monotype spacing and type of a size equivalent to pica or elite. The samples in 14.25–51 are reproduced pages of dissertations and other scholarly publications, with specifications for the layout of pages written in script within the sample page or spelled out in print above each sample. For further information on equipment and materials to be used in preparing a manuscript, see chapter 13 or consult the index.

BASIC DIRECTIONS FOR LAYING OUT THE TEXT

MARGINS

14.2   Leave a margin of at least one inch on each of the four sides of the sheet. Some institutions require more than this, particularly on the left, since binding reduces the margin. The only margin that may be shortened by one or two lines is the bottom margin, where an extra line of text may be permitted to avoid beginning the next page with a very short line.

14.3   In general, a ragged right margin is preferable to a justified margin. Justifying right margins should be done only if this can be achieved without leaving large gaps of white spaces, or "rivers,'' on the printed page. When lines are automatically justified by a computer, all hyphenation must be proofread carefully and adjusted to the standards set forth in chapter 3.

INDENTION

14.4   Indent paragraphs six to eight spaces, unless other specific regulations are made. Indent a block quotation four spaces from the left margin, and indent the beginning of a paragraph in a block quotation another four spaces. Only block quotations of poetry may be centered on the page with respect to the length of a line of text and the longest line of poetry cited. Follow the same scheme of indention consistently.

SPACING

14.5   The text should be double-spaced, except for block quotations, notes, captions, legends, and long headings, which should be single-spaced with a space between items. This means that any computer system suitable for use in preparing manuscripts of research papers must have the capability of double-spacing and single-spacing on the same page.

PAGINATION

14.6   Assign a number to every page of the paper except blank pages and dedication and epigraph pages, which are not counted in the pagination of the paper. On the title page, pages facing large illustrations and carrying captions, and part-title pages, if any, the numbers are not shown, but the pages are counted in the pagination.

14.7   For the preliminaries, number with small roman numerals (ii, iii, iv, etc.) centered at the bottom of the page on the seventh line above the edge. The numbering begins with "ii." The title page counts as page i, unless there is a frontispiece, which becomes page i, making the title page page ii. But these numbers do not appear; that is, they are not typed on the pages.

14.8   Number the remaining parts, including text, illustrations, appendix, notes, and reference list or bibliography with arabic numerals centered at the top of the page on the seventh line below the edge, except that on every page with a major heading (e.g., the first page of a chapter, of the bibliography, etc.), place the number at the foot of the page, centered on the seventh line above the edge. Begin the numbering of the main body of the paper with "1" and run consecutively to the end.

14.9 An alternate scheme of pagination in the text and reference matter is that of numbering all pages in the upper right-hand corner—excepting of course the first pages of chapters, of appendixes, of reference lists, and of bibliographies, where the numbers should be centered below the text.

MAJOR HEADINGS

14.10 Generic headings (e.g., CHAPTER 2) as a rule begin two inches from the top of the paper (i.e., begin typing on the thirteenth line), centered and in uppercase followed by a number or letter (see 1.35). After a blank line, the title follows centered in uppercase. The text begins on the third line below the heading and title, if any, with a six- to eight-space indention for the new paragraph, or with a subheading. If the title is longer than forty-eight spaces, set it in two (or more) double-spaced lines, in inverted-pyramid form. Use no punctuation at the ends of lines.

SUBHEADINGS

14.11 A *centered subheading* of more than forty-eight spaces should be divided into two or more single-spaced lines, in inverted-pyramid form. A *side heading* of more than a half-line should be divided more or less evenly into two (or more) single-spaced lines, the runovers beginning at the margin. *Paragraph headings* should be underlined and should end with a period. All other subheadings should omit punctuation at the ends of lines. For capitalization and style of subheadings, see 1.36–37.

14.12 All subheadings begin on the third line below the preceding text. If two (or more) subheadings appear together (i.e., without intervening text), a blank line should be left between them, and a blank line should also be left between the subheading and the text following.

LAYING OUT FOOTNOTES ON THE PAGE

SPACING, INDENTION, PLACEMENT OF FOOTNOTE NUMERALS

14.13 Separate text and footnotes with a twenty-space rule—that is, strike the key for underlining twenty times, beginning at the left-hand margin on the first line beneath the text. The first line of footnote material is on the second line below this (the third line under the text). Indent the first line of each footnote the same number of spaces as the paragraph indention in the text (consistently either six, seven, or eight spaces throughout the paper). Type the footnotes single-space, but use double-space between individual notes.

14.14 Place the footnote numeral slightly above the line (never a full space above). There should be no punctuation after the numeral and no extra space between it and the first word of the note:

    [2]Gabriel Marcel, <u>The Mystery of Being</u>, 1:42.

Since most typewriters lack the numeral one, the small "el"—1—is used in its place, in footnotes and elsewhere. The capital "eye"—I—should be used only for the roman numeral one, never for the arabic 1. If the computer system used to prepare a paper with notes is not able to produce superscript numbers, these numbers may be typed into the text using a typewriter with a typeface compatible with that used to produce the rest of the manuscript on the computer system.

ESTIMATING SPACE FOR TEXT AND FOOTNOTES

14.15 To place the footnote directly on the page and maintain the proper margin at the foot of the page, a *guide sheet* should be used. A special carbon paper may be used or a sheet may be made of firm, light-weight wrapping paper. Cut it the same length as the typing paper and one-half inch wider. Measure off top and bottom margins to correspond with those used on the typed page, insert the paper into the typewriter or printer, and beginning with "1" on the line, number down the extreme right-hand edge of the guide sheet to the line opposite that of the last line of typed matter. It is helpful also to indicate in the top and bottom margins of the guide sheet the point opposite which the page number should appear.

14.16 Before rolling the paper and guide sheet into the typewriter or printer, place the guide sheet beneath the bottom sheet of typing paper, align the top and left-hand edges of paper, carbon paper, and guide sheet so that the numbered edge of the guide sheet extends beyond the typing paper; then roll the stacked paper into the typewriter or printer. It may be necessary to adjust the top edges after the paper is placed in the machine.

14.17 When the first footnote number appears in the text, stop and count the number of lines in the corresponding footnote, add two to allow for the line of separation, and deduct this total from the total number of typed lines as shown on the guide sheet. The difference between the two figures will give the number of the line at the end of which to stop typing text in order to allow proper space for the footnote. As each succeeding footnote number appears in the text, add the number of lines in the corresponding footnote, allowing one extra for the blank line between notes, and again determine the number of text lines to be typed.

14.18 All will go according to plan, and the bottom margin will be the proper depth unless a footnote number occurs in the last line of text after all available footnote space has been allotted. Make it a habit to look ahead so as to discover such a difficulty in advance, and avoid the necessity of retyping the page by omitting the last line, even though this will result in a bottom margin deeper than usual.

FOOTNOTES THAT RUN ONTO THE NEXT PAGE

14.19 A similar difficulty arises when a footnote number shows the corresponding footnote to be longer than can be accommodated in the space remaining on the page. This calls for a division of the footnote.

14.20 Begin the note on the page where reference to it appears in the text and type as much as the page will allow, taking care to break the note within a sentence. Carry the remainder into the footnote area of the next page, where it precedes the footnotes for that page, if any (see 14.43). To indicate the continuation of a footnote by such a statement as "Continued on the next page" is bad form.

ARRANGEMENT OF SHORT FOOTNOTES

14.21 To avoid the unattractive appearance and the waste of space which result from the placement of many short footnotes, each on a line by itself and separated from its fellows by extra space above and below, it is advisable to let such short notes follow each other on the same line. There must, however, be at least three spaces between the end of one note and the beginning of another, and *all the notes on one line must be complete:*

[1]Kirke, <u>Keats</u>, 37.   [2]Ibid., 42.   [3]Ibid.

It is not permissible to carry over to the next line a part of the last such short note. Similarly, it is not permissible to utilize the blank space following a note of more than one line length to insert a short note.

Wrong:

> [1]Duff, <u>Literary History of Rome</u>, 2.   [2]Ibid,
>   180.

Right:

> [1]Duff, <u>Literary History of Rome</u>, 2.
>
> [2]Ibid., 180.

Wrong:

> [1]Gabriel Marcel, <u>The Mystery of Being</u>
> (Chicago: Henry Regnery Co., 1960).   [2]Ibid.,
>   1:6.

Right:

> [1]Gabriel Marcel, <u>The Mystery of Being</u> (Chicago:
> Henry Regnery Co., 1960).
>
> [2]Ibid., 1:6.

ARRANGEMENT OF FOOTNOTES ON A SHORT PAGE

14.22 When the end of a chapter covers less than a whole page, any footnotes applicable to the page should be arranged in the usual style after the space and separating line, *immediately* below the text.

ARRANGEMENT OF FOOTNOTES IN A QUOTATION

14.23 When a single-spaced, indented quotation itself includes one or more footnotes that form part of the block quotation, the corresponding footnotes should be placed beneath the quotation, separated from the last line of the quotation by an eight-space rule (i.e., striking the key for underlining eight times). The reference indexes and the footnotes should follow exactly the form used in the original (see 9.4). References added by the writer of the paper should be numbered in sequence with the paper's notes, and the footnotes placed at the bottom of the page.

14.24 Some word-processing software can number footnotes, place them on the correct page, and adjust the spacing of text around them automatically. For information on computerized word processing and the footnote method of citation, see 13.27.

SAMPLE PAGES

TITLE PAGE

14.25 Note that when this model is used, spacing may vary slightly depending upon the number of lines in the title, etc. But space A′ should always be equal to or greater than space A, B′ should always equal space B, and C′ should equal space C.

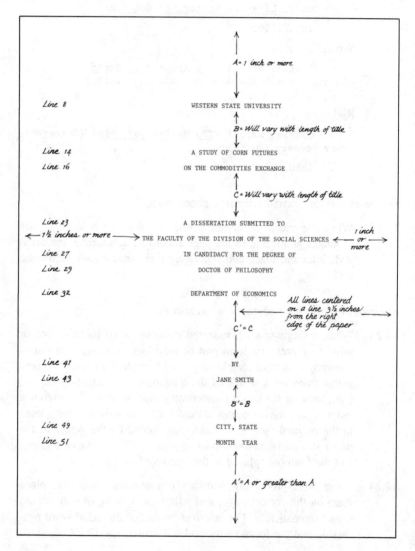

14.26 See 1.10–17 for an extensive discussion of how to design a table of contents. Note that some computer programs can generate tables of contents automatically (see 13.26–27).

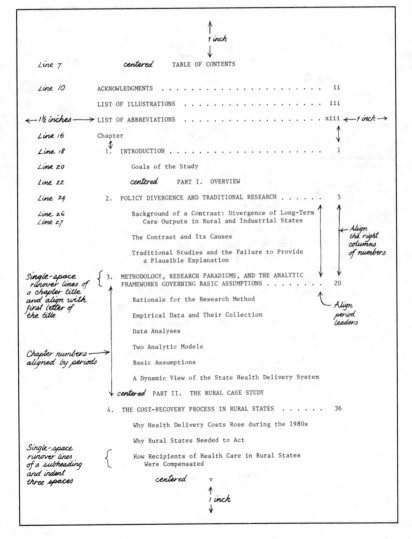

1 inch

Line 7   *centered*   TABLE OF CONTENTS

Line 10   ACKNOWLEDGMENTS ii

LIST OF ILLUSTRATIONS iii

←—1½ inches—→ LIST OF ABBREVIATIONS . . . . xiii ←—1 inch—→

Line 16   Chapter

Line 18   1. INTRODUCTION 1

Line 20   Goals of the Study

Line 22   *centered*   PART I. OVERVIEW

Line 24   2. POLICY DIVERGENCE AND TRADITIONAL RESEARCH 5

Line 26 / Line 27   Background of a Contrast: Divergence of Long-Term Care Outputs in Rural and Industrial States

       The Contrast and Its Causes   ←— Align the right columns of numbers

       Traditional Studies and the Failure to Provide a Plausible Explanation

Single-space runover lines of a chapter title and align with first letter of the title   3. METHODOLOGY, RESEARCH PARADIGMS, AND THE ANALYTIC FRAMEWORKS GOVERNING BASIC ASSUMPTIONS 20

       Rationale for the Research Method   ←— Align period leaders

       Empirical Data and Their Collection

       Data Analyses

       Two Analytic Models

Chapter numbers aligned by periods   Basic Assumptions

       A Dynamic View of the State Health Delivery System

    centered PART II. THE RURAL CASE STUDY

   4. THE COST-RECOVERY PROCESS IN RURAL STATES 36

       Why Health Delivery Costs Rose during the 1980s

       Why Rural States Needed to Act

Single-space runover lines of a subheading and indent three spaces   How Recipients of Health Care in Rural States Were Compensated

     centered   v

1 inch

14.27 See 1.10–17 for an extensive discussion of how to design a table of contents. Note that some computer programs can generate tables of contents automatically (see 13.26–27).

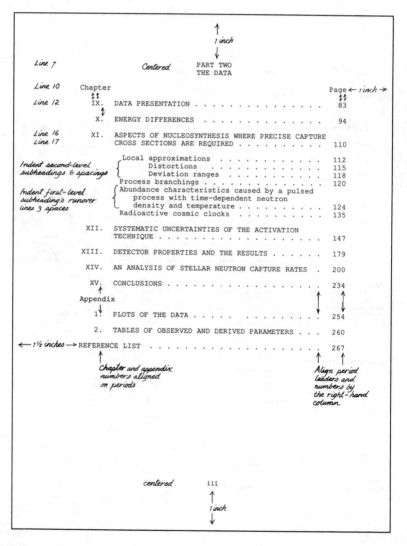

14.28   See 1.18 for a discussion of how to design a list of illustrations, and see chapter 7 for greater detail concerning illustrations in a paper and how to prepare them.

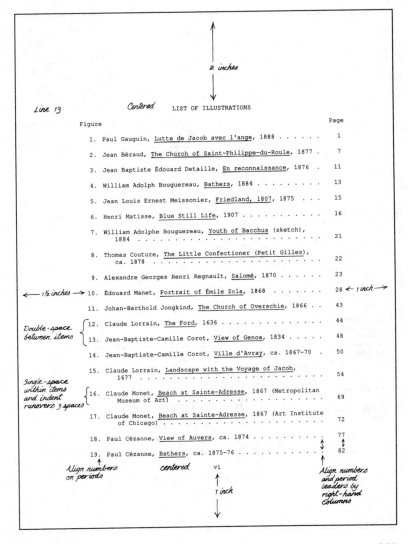

14.29   Leave at least three lines above or below the text if the illustration is set at the bottom or at the top of a page.

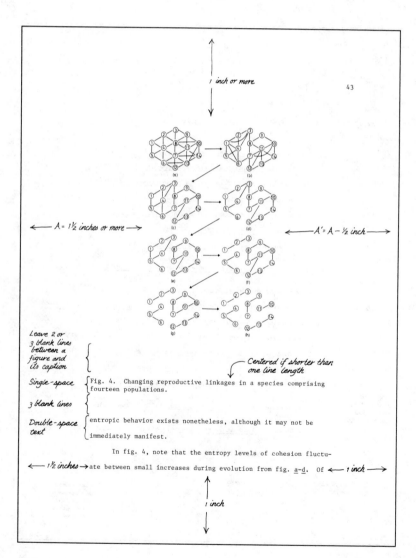

14.30   See chapter 7 for greater detail concerning illustrations in a paper and how to prepare them.

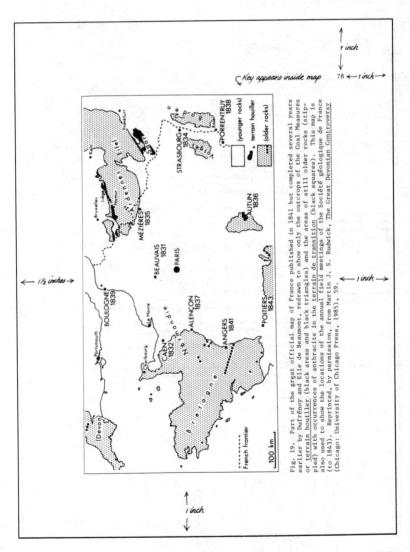

Fig. 19. Part of the great official map of France published in 1841 but completed several years earlier by Dufrénoy and Elie de Beaumont, redrawn to show only the outcrops of the Coal Measures or terrain houiller (black areas and black triangles) and the areas of still older rocks (stippled) with occurrences of anthracite in the terrain de transition (black squares). This map is also used to show the locations of the annual field meetings of the Société géologique de France (to 1843). Reprinted, by permission, from Martin J. S. Rudwick, *The Great Devonian Controversy* (Chicago: University of Chicago Press, 1985), 59.

14.31   See also 1.23 and 13.26–27.

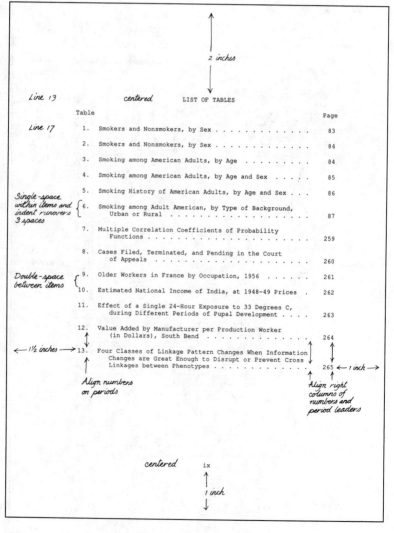

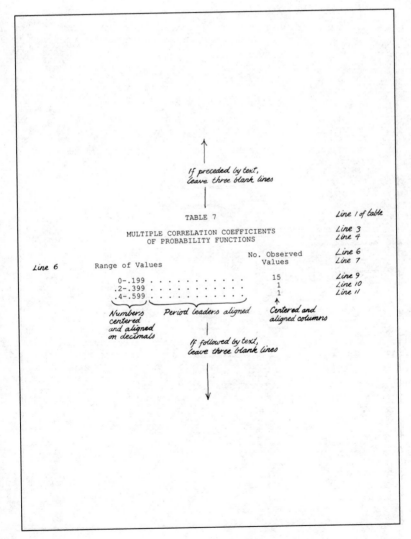

If preceded by text,
leave three blank lines

TABLE 7 — Line 1 of table

MULTIPLE CORRELATION COEFFICIENTS — Line 3
OF PROBABILITY FUNCTIONS — Line 4

	No. Observed	
	Values — Line 6 / Line 7	
Line 6 Range of Values		
0-.199	15	Line 9
.2-.399	1	Line 10
.4-.599	1	Line 11

Numbers centered and aligned on decimals   Period leaders aligned   Centered and aligned columns

If followed by text,
leave three blank lines

259

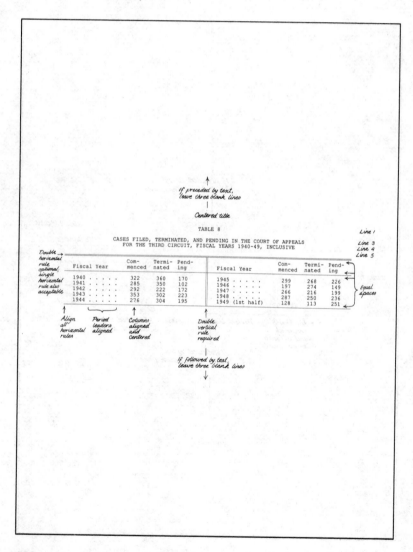

If preceded by text, leave three blank lines

Centered title

TABLE 8

CASES FILED, TERMINATED, AND PENDING IN THE COURT OF APPEALS
FOR THE THIRD CIRCUIT, FISCAL YEARS 1940-49, INCLUSIVE

Line 1
Line 3
Line 4
Line 5

Double horizontal rule optional; single horizontal rule also acceptable

Fiscal Year	Com-menced	Termi-nated	Pend-ing		Fiscal Year	Com-menced	Termi-nated	Pend-ing
1940	322	360	170		1945	299	268	226
1941	285	350	102		1946	197	274	149
1942	292	222	172		1947	266	216	199
1943	353	302	223		1948	287	250	236
1944	276	304	195		1949 (1st half)	128	113	251

Equal spaces

Align all horizontal rules

Period leaders aligned

Columns aligned and centered

Double vertical rule required

If followed by text, leave three blank lines

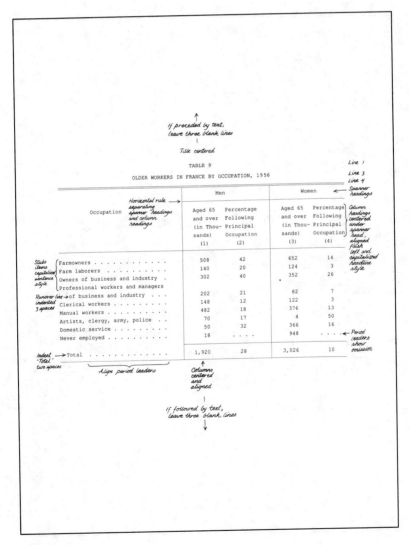

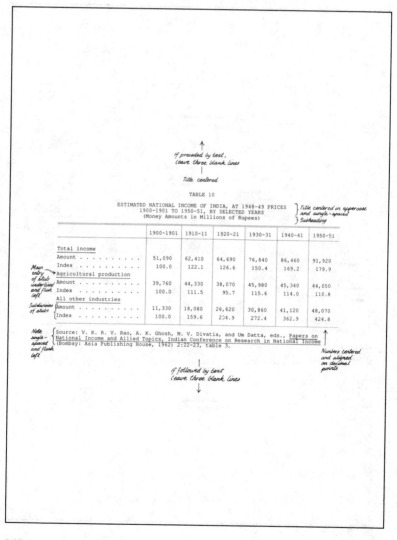

*If preceded by text,
leave three blank lines*

Title centered

TABLE 10

ESTIMATED NATIONAL INCOME OF INDIA, AT 1948-49 PRICES
1900-1901 TO 1950-51, BY SELECTED YEARS
(Money Amounts in Millions of Rupees)

*Title centered in uppercase
and single-spaced
Subheading*

	1900-1901	1910-11	1920-21	1930-31	1940-41	1950-51
Total income						
Amount	51,090	62,410	64,690	76,840	86,460	91,920
Index	100.0	122.1	126.6	150.4	169.2	179.9
Agricultural production						
Amount	39,760	44,330	38,070	45,980	45,340	44,050
Index	100.0	111.5	95.7	115.6	114.0	110.8
All other industries						
Amount	11,330	18,080	26,620	30,860	41,120	48,070
Index	100.0	159.6	234.9	272.4	362.9	424.8

Main entry of stub underlined and flush left

Subdivisions of stubs

Note single-spaced and flush left

Source: V. K. R. V. Rao, A. K. Ghosh, M. V. Divatia, and Um Datta, eds., Papers on
National Income and Allied Topics, Indian Conference on Research in National Income
(Bombay: Asia Publishing House, 1962) 2:22-23, table 3.

*Numbers centered
and aligned
on decimal
points*

*If followed by text
leave three blank lines*

TABLE WITH DECKED HEADS

14.36 See also sample 14.34.

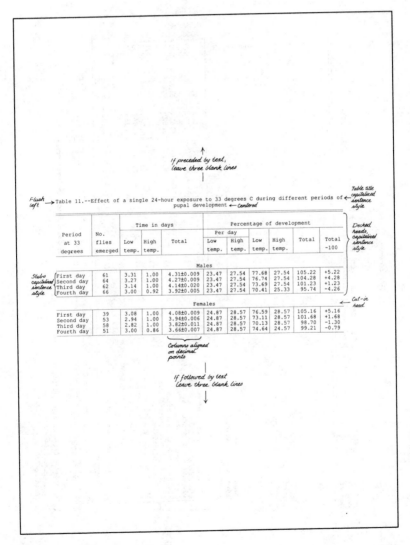

Table 11.--Effect of a single 24-hour exposure to 33 degrees C during different periods of pupal development

Period at 33 degrees	No. flies emerged	Time in days			Percentage of development					
					Per day					
		Low temp.	High temp.	Total	Low temp.	High temp.	Low temp.	High temp.	Total	Total -100
Males										
First day	61	3.31	1.00	4.31±0.009	23.47	27.54	77.68	27.54	105.22	+5.22
Second day	64	3.27	1.00	4.27±0.009	23.47	27.54	76.74	27.54	104.28	+4.28
Third day	62	3.14	1.00	4.14±0.020	23.47	27.54	73.69	27.54	101.23	+1.23
Fourth day	66	3.00	0.92	3.92±0.005	23.47	27.54	70.41	25.33	95.74	-4.26
Females										
First day	39	3.08	1.00	4.08±0.009	24.87	28.57	76.59	28.57	105.16	+5.16
Second day	53	2.94	1.00	3.94±0.006	24.87	28.57	73.11	28.57	101.68	+1.68
Third day	58	2.82	1.00	3.82±0.011	24.87	28.57	70.13	28.57	98.70	-1.30
Fourth day	51	3.00	0.86	3.66±0.007	24.87	28.57	74.64	24.57	99.21	-0.79

14.37   See 6.22. Note that when a table is placed broadside, its caption is at the binding and its notes, if any, are at the bottom of the table.

Title centered

TABLE 12

VALUE ADDED BY MANUFACTURER PER PRODUCTION WORKER (IN DOLLARS), SOUTH BEND STANDARD METROPOLITAN AREA AND SEVEN SELECTED STANDARD METROPOLITAN AREAS, 1947

Census Group and Code Number	South Bend	South Bend Rank among Selected Standard Metropolitan Areas	Chicago	Indianapolis	St. Louis	Detroit	Toledo	Grand Rapids	Milwaukee
20. Food & kindred products	9,183	5	9,340	8,585	8,777	8,296	7,600	7,709	11,932
23. Apparel & related products	3,797	11	5,397	5,017	4,588	5,170	4,495	5,081	4,732
24. Lumber & products, except furniture	5,629	2	5,503	3,700	4,464	7,569	5,124	5,168	5,262
26. Paper & allied products	7,111	6	6,605	7,286	5,781	6,491	6,629	7,858	7,804
27. Printing & publishing industries	9,767	4	9,125	10,040	8,660	11,528	10,350	8,990	7,888
32. Stone, clay & glass products	4,033	11	6,558	6,058	5,663	6,563	10,284	6,049	6,383
33. Primary metal industries	6,397	4	6,689	4,321	5,599	5,600	6,668	5,263	6,453
34. Fabricated metal products	5,351	10	6,534	5,037	5,687	6,569	5,759	5,884	6,928
35. Machinery, except electrical	6,048	10	6,656	5,502	5,756	6,847	7,298	7,022[a]	6,368
36. Electrical machinery	6,613	6	6,682	6,614	6,054	6,862	5,823[a]		6,243
39. Miscellaneous manufactures	4,755	7	6,042	5,521	4,760	5,825	4,608	5,239	4,642

Source: U.S. Department of Commerce, Bureau of the Census, Census of Manufactures: 1947, vol. 3, Statistics by States (Washington, D.C.: Government Printing Office, 1948), 205-9, 308-18, 343-50, 479-81, 483, 648-49.

[a] Complete figures are not provided by the Census.

Marginal annotations: Centered and single-spaced · Centered single-spaced over stub (Census Group and Code Number) · Numbered stub items single-spaced flush left · Double-space between notes · Notes single-spaced flush left · 124

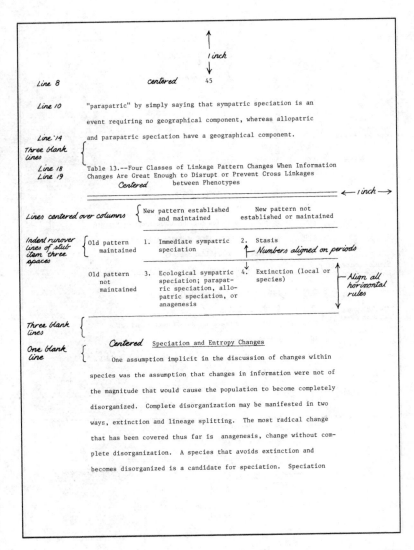

1 inch

Line 8   centered   45

Line 10   "parapatric" by simply saying that sympatric speciation is an

event requiring no geographical component, whereas allopatric

Line 14   and parapatric speciation have a geographical component.

Three blank lines

Line 18   Table 13.--Four Classes of Linkage Pattern Changes When Information

Line 19   Changes Are Great Enough to Disrupt or Prevent Cross Linkages

Centered   between Phenotypes

← 1 inch →

Lines centered over columns

New pattern established and maintained	New pattern not established or maintained

Indent runover lines of stub item three spaces

Old pattern maintained	1. Immediate sympatric speciation	2. Stasis
Old pattern not maintained	3. Ecological sympatric speciation; parapatric speciation, allopatric speciation, or anagenesis	4. Extinction (local or species)

Numbers aligned on periods

Align all horizontal rules

Three blank lines

One blank line

Centered   Speciation and Entropy Changes

      One assumption implicit in the discussion of changes within

species was the assumption that changes in information were not of

the magnitude that would cause the population to become completely

disorganized. Complete disorganization may be manifested in two

ways, extinction and lineage splitting. The most radical change

that has been covered thus far is anagenesis, change without com-

plete disorganization. A species that avoids extinction and

becomes disorganized is a candidate for speciation. Speciation

LIST OF ABBREVIATIONS

14.39 See 1.24 and chapter 2.

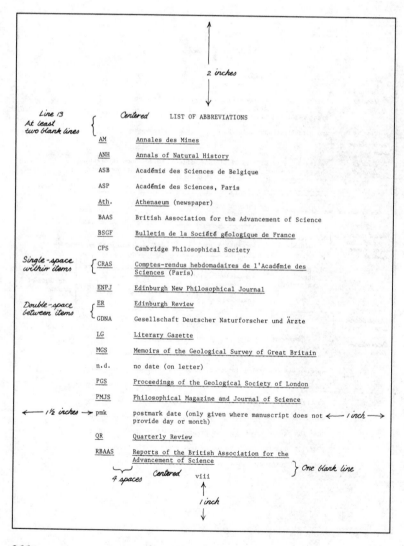

Line 13
At least
two blank lines

Centered   LIST OF ABBREVIATIONS

AM   Annales des Mines

ANH   Annals of Natural History

ASB   Académie des Sciences de Belgique

ASP   Académie des Sciences, Paris

Ath.   Athenaeum (newspaper)

BAAS   British Association for the Advancement of Science

BSGF   Bulletin de la Société géologique de France

CPS   Cambridge Philosophical Society

Single-space
within items
CRAS   Comptes-rendus hebdomadaires de l'Académie des
          Sciences (Paris)

ENPJ   Edinburgh New Philosophical Journal

Double-space
between items
ER   Edinburgh Review
GDNA   Gesellschaft Deutscher Naturforscher und Ärzte

LG   Literary Gazette

MGS   Memoirs of the Geological Survey of Great Britain

n.d.   no date (on letter)

PGS   Proceedings of the Geological Society of London

PMJS   Philosophical Magazine and Journal of Science

1½ inches → pmk   postmark date (only given where manuscript does not ← 1 inch →
          provide day or month)

QR   Quarterly Review

RBAAS   Reports of the British Association for the
          Advancement of Science   } One blank line

4 spaces   Centered   viii

1 inch

14.40 See 1.25. The content of this example is taken, with some revisions, from the glossary in *Lithic Illustration: Drawing Flaked Stone Artifacts for Publication* by Lucile R. Addington (Chicago: University of Chicago Press, 1986).

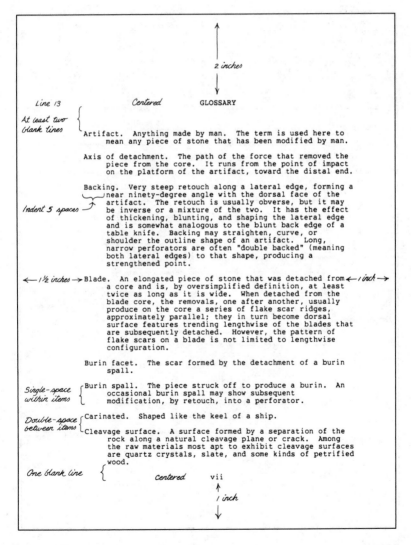

2 inches

Line 13   *Centered*   GLOSSARY

At least two blank lines

Artifact. Anything made by man. The term is used here to mean any piece of stone that has been modified by man.

Axis of detachment. The path of the force that removed the piece from the core. It runs from the point of impact on the platform of the artifact, toward the distal end.

Indent 5 spaces

Backing. Very steep retouch along a lateral edge, forming a near ninety-degree angle with the dorsal face of the artifact. The retouch is usually obverse, but it may be inverse or a mixture of the two. It has the effect of thickening, blunting, and shaping the lateral edge and is somewhat analogous to the blunt back edge of a table knife. Backing may straighten, curve, or shoulder the outline shape of an artifact. Long, narrow perforators are often "double backed" (meaning both lateral edges) to that shape, producing a strengthened point.

← 1½ inches → Blade. An elongated piece of stone that was detached from *← 1 inch →* a core and is, by oversimplified definition, at least twice as long as it is wide. When detached from the blade core, the removals, one after another, usually produce on the core a series of flake scar ridges, approximately parallel; they in turn become dorsal surface features trending lengthwise of the blades that are subsequently detached. However, the pattern of flake scars on a blade is not limited to lengthwise configuration.

Burin facet. The scar formed by the detachment of a burin spall.

Single-space within items

Burin spall. The piece struck off to produce a burin. An occasional burin spall may show subsequent modification, by retouch, into a perforator.

Double-space between items

Carinated. Shaped like the keel of a ship.

Cleavage surface. A surface formed by a separation of the rock along a natural cleavage plane or crack. Among the raw materials most apt to exhibit cleavage surfaces are quartz crystals, slate, and some kinds of petrified wood.

One blank line   *Centered*   vii

1 inch

14.41   See also 13.25 for a discussion of computerized word processing and special features such as equations and formulas.

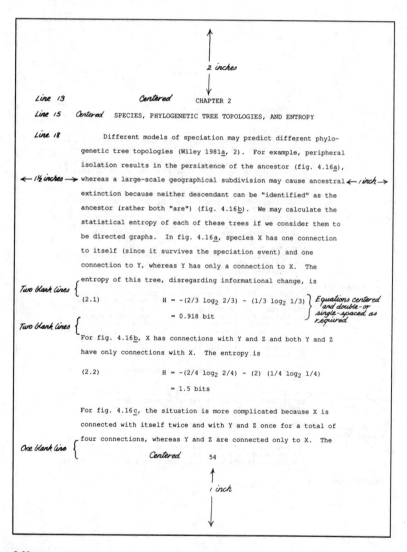

2 inches

Line 13   Centered   CHAPTER 2

Line 15   Centered   SPECIES, PHYLOGENETIC TREE TOPOLOGIES, AND ENTROPY

Line 18   Different models of speciation may predict different phylogenetic tree topologies (Wiley 1981a, 2). For example, peripheral
isolation results in the persistence of the ancestor (fig. 4.16a),

←1½ inches→ whereas a large-scale geographical subdivision may cause ancestral ←1 inch→
extinction because neither descendant can be "identified" as the
ancestor (rather both "are") (fig. 4.16b). We may calculate the
statistical entropy of each of these trees if we consider them to
be directed graphs. In fig. 4.16a, species X has one connection
to itself (since it survives the speciation event) and one
connection to Y, whereas Y has only a connection to X. The
entropy of this tree, disregarding informational change, is

Two blank lines {

(2.1) $H = -(2/3 \log_2 2/3) - (1/3 \log_2 1/3)$ } Equations centered
                                                                        and double- or
               $= 0.918$ bit   single-spaced as
                                                                        required
Two blank lines {

For fig. 4.16b, X has connections with Y and Z and both Y and Z
have only connections with X. The entropy is

(2.2) $H = -(2/4 \log_2 2/4) - (2) (1/4 \log_2 1/4)$

               $= 1.5$ bits

For fig. 4.16c, the situation is more complicated because X is
connected with itself twice and with Y and Z once for a total of
four connections, whereas Y and Z are connected only to X. The

One blank line {   Centered   54

1 inch

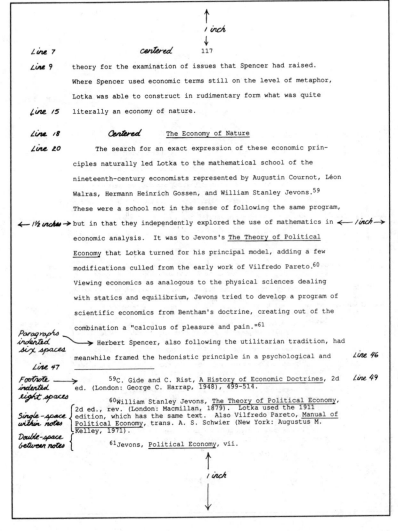

1 inch

Line 7   *centered*   117

Line 9   theory for the examination of issues that Spencer had raised.

Where Spencer used economic terms still on the level of metaphor,

Lotka was able to construct in rudimentary form what was quite

Line 15   literally an economy of nature.

Line 18   *Centered*   The Economy of Nature

Line 20   The search for an exact expression of these economic prin-

ciples naturally led Lotka to the mathematical school of the

nineteenth-century economists represented by Augustin Cournot, Léon

Walras, Hermann Heinrich Gossen, and William Stanley Jevons.[59]

These were a school not in the sense of following the same program,

← 1½ inches → but in that they independently explored the use of mathematics in *← 1 inch →*

economic analysis. It was to Jevons's The Theory of Political

Economy that Lotka turned for his principal model, adding a few

modifications culled from the early work of Vilfredo Pareto.[60]

Viewing economics as analogous to the physical sciences dealing

with statics and equilibrium, Jevons tried to develop a program of

scientific economics from Bentham's doctrine, creating out of the

combination a "calculus of pleasure and pain."[61]

Paragraphs indented six spaces → Herbert Spencer, also following the utilitarian tradition, had

meanwhile framed the hedonistic principle in a psychological and   *Line 46*

Line 47

Footnote indented eight spaces →   [59]C. Gide and C. Rist, A History of Economic Doctrines, 2d   *Line 49*
ed. (London: George C. Harrap, 1948), 499–514.

Single-space within notes   [60]William Stanley Jevons, The Theory of Political Economy,
2d ed., rev. (London: Macmillan, 1879). Lotka used the 1911
edition, which has the same text. Also Vilfredo Pareto, Manual of
Political Economy, trans. A. S. Schwier (New York: Augustus M.
Kelley, 1971).

Double-space between notes   [61]Jevons, Political Economy, vii.

1 inch

14.43 See also 14.19–20.

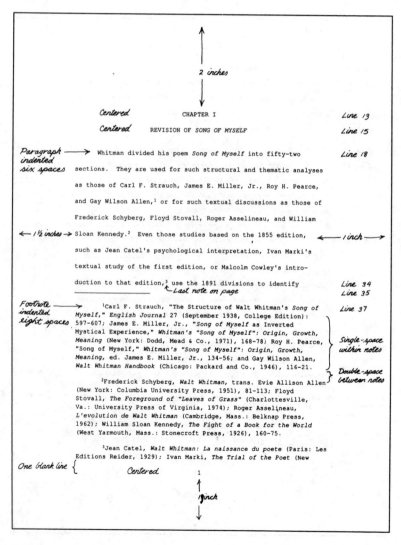

2 inches

Centered CHAPTER I   *Line 13*

Centered REVISION OF *SONG OF MYSELF*   *Line 15*

Paragraph indented six spaces → Whitman divided his poem *Song of Myself* into fifty-two   *Line 18*

sections. They are used for such structural and thematic analyses

as those of Carl F. Strauch, James E. Miller, Jr., Roy H. Pearce,

and Gay Wilson Allen,[1] or for such textual discussions as those of

Frederick Schyberg, Floyd Stovall, Roger Asselineau, and William

← *1½ inches* → Sloan Kennedy.[2] Even those studies based on the 1855 edition, ← *1 inch* →

such as Jean Catel's psychological interpretation, Ivan Marki's

textual study of the first edition, or Malcolm Cowley's intro-

duction to that edition,[3] use the 1891 divisions to identify   *Line 34*
      ↳ Last note on page   *Line 35*

Footnote indented eight spaces → [1]Carl F. Strauch, "The Structure of Walt Whitman's *Song of Myself*," *English Journal* 27 (September 1938, College Edition):   *Line 37*
597–607; James E. Miller, Jr., "*Song of Myself* as Inverted Mystical Experience," *Whitman's "Song of Myself": Origin, Growth, Meaning* (New York: Dodd, Mead & Co., 1971), 168–78; Roy H. Pearce,   *Single-space within notes*
"Song of Myself," *Whitman's "Song of Myself": Origin, Growth, Meaning*, ed. James E. Miller, Jr., 134–56; and Gay Wilson Allen, *Walt Whitman Handbook* (Chicago: Packard and Co., 1946), 116–21.   *Double-space between notes*

     [2]Frederick Schyberg, *Walt Whitman*, trans. Evie Allison Allen (New York: Columbia University Press, 1951), 81–113; Floyd Stovall, *The Foreground of "Leaves of Grass"* (Charlottesville, Va.: University Press of Virginia, 1974); Roger Asselineau, *L'evolution de Walt Whitman* (Cambridge, Mass.: Belknap Press, 1962); William Sloan Kennedy, *The Fight of a Book for the World* (West Yarmouth, Mass.: Stonecroft Press, 1926), 160–75.

     [3]Jean Catel, *Walt Whitman: La naissance du poete* (Paris: Les Editions Reider, 1929); Ivan Marki, *The Trial of the Poet* (New

One blank line {   *Centered*   1

1 inch

1 inch

Line 7   2 ← *1 inch →*

← 1½ inches → passages that in the 1855 text were divided only by spaces between   *Line 9*

line groups. Interpretations that strive to show Whitman's

reliance on Hindu texts, such as those of T. R. Rajasekhavaiah,

Som P. Raucham, and V. K. Chari,[4] use the numbering to indicate

lines while asserting that "the numerical division . . . scarcely

adds anything" to the poem.[5]

Paragraph indented six spaces   Analyses of technique compare the poem's structure to that

of a symphony,[6] an example of oratory,[7] the ocean,[8] and "a series

of spells evoking all the senses of man,"[9] each relying on the

fifty-two sections in order to identify passages. Discussions of

the formal poetics of *Song of Myself* focus on the resemblances of

Whitman's prosody to English translations of the Bible, on the

Line 33 poem's language, on the rhetoric of the catalogues, on linguistic

Line 34

Line 36 _____

York: Columbia University Press, 1976); Malcolm Cowley, ed.,
Complete Poetry and Prose of Walt Whitman (New York: Pellegrini &
Cudahy, 1948), 3-39.

Footnote indented eight spaces →   [4]T. R. Rajasekhavaiah, *The Roots of Whitman's Grass*
(Madison, N.J.: Farleigh Dickinson University Press, 1970), 386-
88; Som P. Raucham, *Walt Whitman and the Great Adventure with Self*
(Bombay: Manaktalas, 1967), 2-25; and V. K. Chari, *Whitman in the
Light of Vedantic Mysticism* (Lincoln, Nebr.: University of
Nebraska Press, 1964), 120-30.   *Single-space within notes*

[5]Rajasekhavaiah, 386.   *Double-space between notes*

[6]Basil De Selincourt, "The Form," *Walt Whitman, a Critical
Study* (London: M. Secker, 1914), 94-115.

[7]Allen, 241.

[8]F. O. Matthiessen, "Only a Language Experiment," ed.
Edwin Haviland Miller, *A Century of Whitman Criticism*
(Bloomington, Ind.: Indiana University Press, 1969), 172-86.

[9]Henry Seidel Canby, *Walt Whitman an American* (Boston:
Houghton Mifflin Co., 1943), 110.

1 inch

Line 7

Line 9   117 ← *1 inch* →

← *1½ inches* → By examining sectional divisions, we can show that 1891 revisions

underscore the function of each section as a unit of meaning

governed by its own rhythm within what Roger Mitchell calls

Line 15 Whitman's "group size pattern":

Line 17
Line 18

*Indent block
quotation
4 spaces*

> Whitman is doing more than simply distributing a pattern of
> groups in some sensible fashion over the lines of a poem,
> creating what I am calling a group/line pattern. He is also
> conscious of the size of his groups and of their progression in
> terms of size through the poem, a phenomenon which I refer to as
> the group size pattern. . . . The pull of these two patterns
> against one another lends rhythmical force to the statement.

Line 25   (Mitchell 1969, 1608)

Line 27 Such an analysis demonstrates the method governing Whitman's

treatment of stanzas and sections in the 1891 version, and suggests

certain principles Whitman had in mind when he scrutinized the

line-group and sectional divisions of the 1888 version of Leaves of

Grass. He did not hesitate to make even very significant changes.

In Song of Myself, he separated one line group into two, combined

stanzas in three sections, and changed a sectional division,

between sections 21 and 22. In the 1888 version, the sections were

Line 41 divided as follows:

Line 43
Line 44

> Prodigal, you have given me love--therefore I to you give
>   love!
> O unspeakable passionate love.

*Indent this
runover line
8 spaces*

                   22   *Centered over text of poem*

*Poetry already
indented 4 spaces
as block
quotation*

> You sea! I resign myself to you also--I guess what you mean,
> I behold from the beach your crooked inviting fingers,
> I believe you refuse to go back without feeling of me,
> We must have a turn together, I undress, hurry me out of sight
>   of the land

In the 1891 version, Whitman divided the sections two lines later,

placing more time between the speaker's invitation from the sea and

his immersion, adding greater emphasis. This revision suggests

1 inch

Notes

14.45 As it is more common for endnotes to be used in a book than in a research paper, this model is taken from Wayne Booth's *Critical Understanding: The Powers and Limits of Pluralism* (Chicago: University of Chicago Press, © 1979 by University of Chicago), 353. It serves as a good example of a content note, the only kind of endnote recommended for use in papers, and then only in papers using parenthetical references (see 8.20).

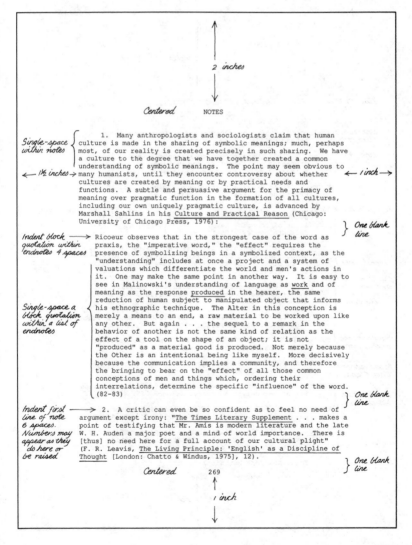

2 inches

Centered NOTES

Single-space within notes · *1½ inches* · *1 inch*

1. Many anthropologists and sociologists claim that human culture is made in the sharing of symbolic meanings; much, perhaps most, of our reality is created precisely in such sharing. We have a culture to the degree that we have together created a common understanding of symbolic meanings. The point may seem obvious to many humanists, until they encounter controversy about whether cultures are created by meaning or by practical needs and functions. A subtle and persuasive argument for the primacy of meaning over pragmatic function in the formation of all cultures, including our own uniquely pragmatic culture, is advanced by Marshall Sahlins in his <u>Culture and Practical Reason</u> (Chicago: University of Chicago Press, 1976):

One blank line

Indent block quotation within endnotes 4 spaces · *Single-space a block quotation within a list of endnotes*

> Ricoeur observes that in the strongest case of the word as praxis, the "imperative word," the "effect" requires the presence of symbolizing beings in a symbolized context, as the "understanding" includes at once a project and a system of valuations which differentiate the world and men's actions in it. One may make the same point in another way. It is easy to see in Malinowski's understanding of language as <u>work</u> and of meaning as the response <u>produced</u> in the hearer, the same reduction of human subject to manipulated object that informs his ethnographic technique. The Alter in this conception is merely a means to an end, a raw material to be worked upon like any other. But again . . . the sequel to a remark in the behavior of another is not the same kind of relation as the effect of a tool on the shape of an object; it is not "produced" as a material good is produced. Not merely because the Other is an intentional being like myself. More decisively because the communication implies a community, and therefore the bringing to bear on the "effect" of all those common conceptions of men and things which, ordering their interrelations, determine the specific "influence" of the word. (82-83)

One blank line

Indent first line of note 6 spaces. Numbers may appear as they do here or be raised

2. A critic can even be so confident as to feel no need of argument except irony: "<u>The Times Literary Supplement</u> . . . makes a point of testifying that Mr. Amis is modern literature and the late W. H. Auden a major poet and a mind of world importance. There is [thus] no need here for a full account of our cultural plight" (F. R. Leavis, <u>The Living Principle: 'English' as a Discipline of Thought</u> [London: Chatto & Windus, 1975], 12).

One blank line

Centered 269

1 inch

14.46   See 8.21–33. Note the use of initials for the first and second given names of authors, which is acceptable when followed consistently in a reference list and when accepted by the dissertation secretary or thesis adviser. In a reference list, several works by one author are arranged by date of publication, not alphabetically.

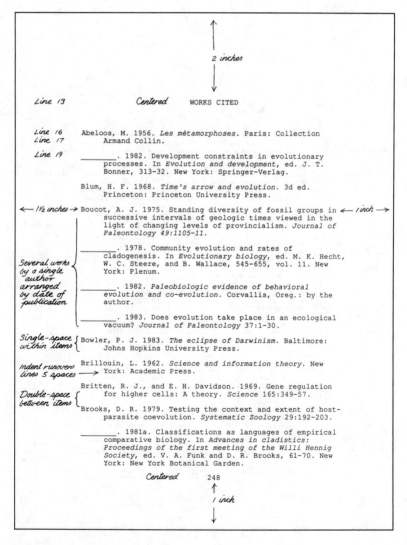

↑

2 inches

↓

Line 13   *Centered*   WORKS CITED

Line 16   Abeloos, M. 1956. *Les métamorphoses*. Paris: Collection
Line 17   Armand Collin.

Line 19   _____. 1982. Development constraints in evolutionary
                 processes. In *Evolution and development*, ed. J. T.
                 Bonner, 313-32. New York: Springer-Verlag.

              Blum, H. F. 1968. *Time's arrow and evolution*. 3d ed.
                 Princeton: Princeton University Press.

← *1½ inches* → Boucot, A. J. 1975. Standing diversity of fossil groups in ← *inch* →
                 successive intervals of geologic times viewed in the
                 light of changing levels of provincialism. *Journal of
                 Paleontology* 49:1105-11.

              _____. 1978. Community evolution and rates of
                 cladogenesis. In *Evolutionary biology*, ed. M. K. Hecht,
Several works   W. C. Steere, and B. Wallace, 545-655, vol. 11. New
by a single   York: Plenum.
author
arranged   _____. 1982. *Paleobiologic evidence of behavioral
by date of   evolution and co-evolution*. Corvallis, Oreg.: by the
publication   author.

              _____. 1983. Does evolution take place in an ecological
                 vacuum? *Journal of Paleontology* 37:1-30.

Single-space { Bowler, P. J. 1983. *The eclipse of Darwinism*. Baltimore:
within items   Johns Hopkins University Press.

Indent runovers Brillouin, L. 1962. *Science and information theory*. New
lines 5 spaces → York: Academic Press.

              Britten, R. J., and E. H. Davidson. 1969. Gene regulation
Double-space {   for higher cells: A theory. *Science* 165:349-57.
between items
              Brooks, D. R. 1979. Testing the context and extent of host-
                 parasite coevolution. *Systematic Zoology* 29:192-203.

              _____. 1981a. Classifications as languages of empirical
                 comparative biology. In *Advances in cladistics:
                 Proceedings of the first meeting of the Willi Hennig
                 Society*, ed. V. A. Funk and D. R. Brooks, 61-70. New
                 York: New York Botanical Garden.

                          Centered   248
                                          ↑
                                        1 inch
                                          ↓

REFERENCE LIST ARRANGED ALPHABETICALLY, CITING MANY
WORKS BY ONE AUTHOR

14.47 See 8.21–33. Note that in this format all the works by one author are first arranged by date, then alphabetically by title.

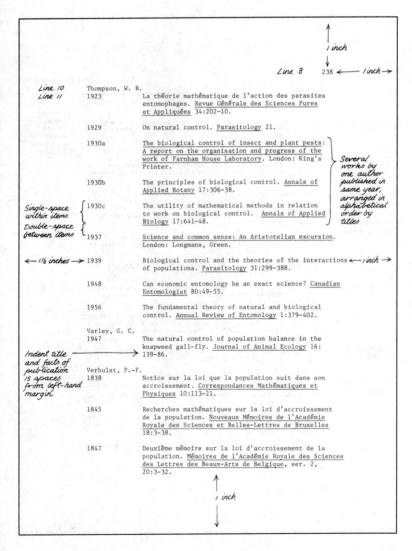

BIBLIOGRAPHY IN WHICH SEVERAL WORKS BY ONE AUTHOR ARE ARRANGED CHRONOLOGICALLY

14.48

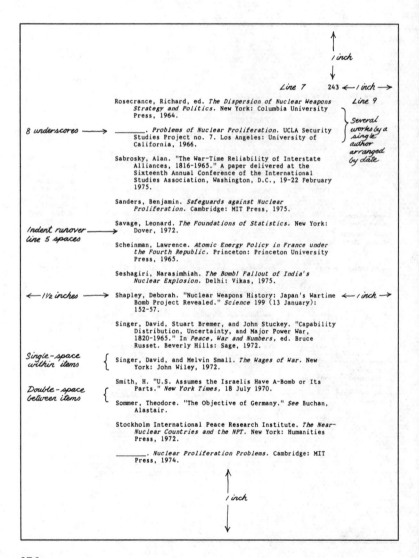

Line 7   243 ←—1 inch—→

Rosecrance, Richard, ed. *The Dispersion of Nuclear Weapons Strategy and Politics*. New York: Columbia University Press, 1964.

———. *Problems of Nuclear Proliferation*. UCLA Security Studies Project no. 7. Los Angeles: University of California, 1966.

8 underscores

Sabrosky, Alan. "The War-Time Reliability of Interstate Alliances, 1816-1965." A paper delivered at the Sixteenth Annual Conference of the International Studies Association, Washington, D.C., 19-22 February 1975.

Sanders, Benjamin. *Safeguards against Nuclear Proliferation*. Cambridge: MIT Press, 1975.

Savage, Leonard. *The Foundations of Statistics*. New York: Dover, 1972.

Indent runover line 5 spaces

Scheinman, Lawrence. *Atomic Energy Policy in France under the Fourth Republic*. Princeton: Princeton University Press, 1965.

Seshagiri, Narasimhiah. *The Bomb! Fallout of India's Nuclear Explosion*. Delhi: Vikas, 1975.

Shapley, Deborah. "Nuclear Weapons History: Japan's Wartime Bomb Project Revealed." *Science* 199 (13 January): 152-57.

←—1½ inches—→

Singer, David, Stuart Bremer, and John Stuckey. "Capability Distribution, Uncertainty, and Major Power War, 1820-1965." In *Peace, War and Numbers*, ed. Bruce Russet. Beverly Hills: Sage, 1972.

Singer, David, and Melvin Small. *The Wages of War*. New York: John Wiley, 1972.

Single-space within items

Smith, H. "U.S. Assumes the Israelis Have A-Bomb or Its Parts." *New York Times*, 18 July 1970.

Double-space between items

Sommer, Theodore. "The Objective of Germany." *See* Buchan, Alastair.

Stockholm International Peace Research Institute. *The Near-Nuclear Countries and the NPT*. New York: Humanities Press, 1972.

———. *Nuclear Proliferation Problems*. Cambridge: MIT Press, 1974.

276

14.49 When using computerized word processing, variable spacing often results in more than one space being left after periods separating elements in reference lists or bibliographies, as in the example below.

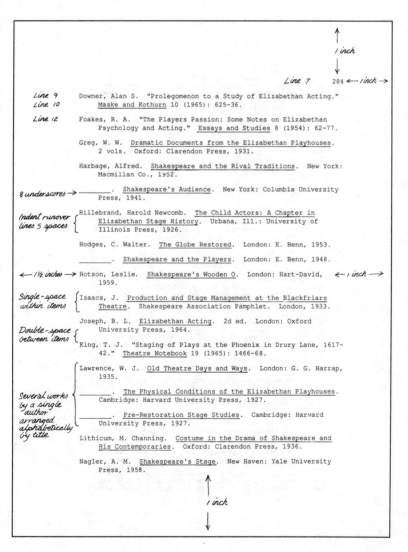

Line 7   284 ← *1 inch* →

Line 9
Line 10

Downer, Alan S. "Prolegomenon to a Study of Elizabethan Acting."
Maske and Kothurn 10 (1965): 625-36.

Line 12

Foakes, R. A. "The Players Passion: Some Notes on Elizabethan
Psychology and Acting." Essays and Studies 8 (1954): 62-77.

Greg, W. W. Dramatic Documents from the Elizabethan Playhouses.
2 vols. Oxford: Clarendon Press, 1931.

Harbage, Alfred. Shakespeare and the Rival Traditions. New York:
Macmillan Co., 1952.

8 underscores →

————. Shakespeare's Audience. New York: Columbia University
Press, 1941.

*Indent runover
lines 5 spaces*

Hillebrand, Harold Newcomb. The Child Actors: A Chapter in
Elizabethan Stage History. Urbana, Ill.: University of
Illinois Press, 1926.

Hodges, C. Walter. The Globe Restored. London: E. Benn, 1953.

————. Shakespeare and the Players. London: E. Benn, 1948.

← *1½ inches* → Hotson, Leslie. Shakespeare's Wooden O. London: Hart-David, ← *1 inch* →
1959.

*Single-space
within items*

Isaacs, J. Production and Stage Management at the Blackfriars
Theatre. Shakespeare Association Pamphlet. London, 1933.

*Double-space
between items*

Joseph, B. L. Elizabethan Acting. 2d ed. London: Oxford
University Press, 1964.

King, T. J. "Staging of Plays at the Phoenix in Drury Lane, 1617-
42." Theatre Notebook 19 (1965): 1466-68.

Lawrence, W. J. Old Theatre Days and Ways. London: G. G. Harrap,
1935.

*Several works
by a single
author
arranged
alphabetically
by title*

————. The Physical Conditions of the Elizabethan Playhouses.
Cambridge: Harvard University Press, 1927.

————. Pre-Restoration Stage Studies. Cambridge: Harvard
University Press, 1927.

Lithicum, M. Channing. Costume in the Drama of Shakespeare and
His Contemporaries. Oxford: Clarendon Press, 1936.

Nagler, A. M. Shakespeare's Stage. New Haven: Yale University
Press, 1958.

1 inch

14.50 This page, which shows unformatted copy, was produced on TREATISE, a text-stream dissertation-formatting program on a mainframe computer. See 13.17–22.

```
 1.    .im treatise
 2.    .im symgr
 3.    .chapter 'PROGRAM SIZE AND PROLIFERATION'
 4.       The choice between one bomb and, say, seven bombs
 5.    a year is based more on symbolics and psychology than
 6.    on economic or military analysis.  Many students of
 7.    proliferation have come to the conclusion that:
 8.    .quote begin
 9.    the danger of proliferation today is the emergence
10.    of what might be called the primitive nuclear powers
11.    with a
12.    .xit limited
13.    stock of untested nuclear weapons [emphasis
14.    .footnote 'added].'
15.    P. L. Olgaard, "The Soviet-American Draft Nonproliferation
16.    Treaty: Will it Work?"
17.    in
18.    .xit Preventing the Spread of Nuclear Weapons,
19.    by C. F. Barnaby (New York: Humanities Press, 1969), 219.
20.    .footend
21.    .quote end
22.    .restore
23.    .quote begin
24.    One must be careful to consider thoughts about physical
25.    realities, as well as the realities themselves.  Even
26.    if physical developments pose no
27.    .xit real
28.    problem, the fears they bring about can take on a life
29.    of their own [emphasis
30.    .footnote 'added].'
31.    George Quester,
32.    .xit The Politics of Nuclear Proliferation
33.    (Baltimore: Johns Hopkins University Press, 1973), 210.
34.    .footend
35.    .quote end
36.    .restore
37.    So, in this sense:
38.    .quote begin
39.    even a minimum size, inefficient and unreliable "bomb"
40.    could result in a local disaster and an international
41.    crisis of immense
42.    .footnote 'proportions.'
43.    Richard J. Barber Associates, Inc.,
44.    .xit on
45.    LDC Nuclear Power Prospects, 1975-1990: Commercial,
46.    Economic and Security Implications
47.    .xro on
48.    (Washington, D.C.: Barber Associates, 1975).
49.    .footend
50.    .quote end
51.    .restore
52.       A one-bomb-a-year program also seems to drive those
53.    studies of nuclear proliferation that concentrate on the
54.    "diversion option"--that is, a country "goes nuclear"
55.    by diverting spent reactor fuel from a power reactor,
56.    reprocessing it, and using the plutonium to manufacture
57.    an atomic bomb.  In this context the range of assay
58.    (safeguards) techniques generally available can ensure
59.    accountability within a few percentage points of total
60.    inventory.  In other words, if a typical power reactor
```

TREATISE FORMATTED VERSION OF THE FIRST PAGE OF A CHAPTER (FROM SAMPLE 14.50)

14.51   This page, which shows the formatted version of the unformatted copy in 14.50, was produced on TREATISE, a text-stream dissertation-formatting program on a mainframe computer. See 13.17–22.

CHAPTER 2

PROGRAM SIZE AND PROLIFERATION

The choice between one bomb and, say, seven bombs a year is based more on symbolics and psychology than on economic or military analysis. Many students of proliferation have come to the conclusion that

> the danger of proliferation today is the emergence of what might be called the primitive nuclear powers with a *limited* stock of untested nuclear weapons [emphasis added].[1]

> One must be careful to consider thoughts about physical realities, as well as the realities themselves. Even if physical developments pose no *real* problem, the fears they bring about can take on a life of their own [emphasis added].[2]

So, in this sense,

> even a minimum size, inefficient and unreliable "bomb" could result in a local disaster and an international crisis of immense proportions.[3]

A one-bomb-a-year program also seems to drive those studies of nuclear proliferation that concentrate on the "diversion option"--that is, a country "goes nuclear" by diverting spent reactor fuel from a power reactor, reprocessing it, and using the plutonium to manufacture an atomic bomb. In this context the range of assay (safeguards) techniques generally available can ensure accountability within a few per-

---

[1]P. L. Olgaard, "The Soviet-American Draft Nonproliferation Treaty: Will it Work?" in *Preventing the Spread of Nuclear Weapons*, by C. F. Barnaby (New York: Humanities Press, 1969), 219.

[2]George Quester, *The Politics of Nuclear Proliferation* (Baltimore: Johns Hopkins University Press, 1973), 210.

[3]Richard J. Barber Associates, Inc., *LDC Nuclear Power Prospects, 1975-1990: Commercial, Economic and Security Implications* (Washington, D.C.: Barber Associates, 1975).

17

Selected Bibliography by Discipline

BIOLOGICAL SCIENCES

Council of Biology Editors. CBE Style Committee. *CBE Style Manual: A Guide for Authors, Editors, and Publishers in the Biological Sciences*. 5th ed., rev. and exp. Bethesda, Md.: Council of Biology Editors, 1983.

ENGINEERING

American Institute of Chemical Engineers. *Guide for Writers and Speakers*. New York: American Institute of Chemical Engineers, [1978].

Institute of Electrical and Electronics Engineers. "Information for IEEE Authors." *IEEE Spectrum* 2 (August 1965): 11–15.

Society of Mining Engineers. *Author's Guide*. Littleton, Colo.: Society of Mining Engineers/AIME, 1983. Includes supplement entitled "Suggestions to Authors of Papers Intended for Society of Mining Engineers Publications."

GEOPHYSICAL SCIENCES

Cochran, Wendell, Peter Fenner, and Mary Hill, eds. *Geowriting: A Guide to Writing, Editing, and Printing in Earth Science*. Alexandria, Va.: American Geological Institute, 1984.

HUMANITIES

Gibaldi, Joseph, and Walter S. Achtert, eds. *MLA Handbook for Writers of Research Papers*. 2d ed. New York: Modern Language Association of America, 1984.

"LSA Style Sheet." *LSA Bulletin*, no. 106 (December 1984): 50–58.

LAW AND POLITICS

Brightbill, George D., and Wayne C. Maxson. *Citation Manual for United States Government Publications*. Philadelphia: Center for Study of Federalism, Temple University, 1974.

Selected Bibliography by Discipline

Garner, Diane L., and Diane H. Smith. *The Complete Guide to Citing Government Documents: A Manual for Writers and Librarians*. Bethesda, Md.: Congressional Information Service, 1984.

Morehead, Joe, Jr. *Introduction to United States Public Documents*. 3d ed. Littleton, Colo.: Libraries Unlimited, 1983.

Pemberton, John E. *British Official Publications*. 2d rev. ed. Oxford: Pergamon Press, 1973.

Rodgers, Frank. *A Guide to British Government Documents*. New York: H. W. Wilson Company, 1980.

A Uniform System of Citation. 13th ed. Cambridge: Harvard Law Review Association, 1981.

U.S. Government Printing Office Style Manual. Rev. ed. Washington, D.C.: Government Printing Office, 1984.

MATHEMATICS

American Mathematical Society. *A Manual for Authors of Mathematical Papers*. 7th ed. Providence, R.I.: American Mathematical Society, 1980.

PHYSICAL SCIENCES

Dodd, Janet S., ed. *The ACS Style Guide: A Manual for Authors and Editors*. Washington, D.C.: American Chemical Society, 1986.

Hathwell, David, and A. W. Kenneth Metzner, eds. *Style Manual*. 3d ed. New York: American Institute of Physics, 1978.

SOCIAL SCIENCES

American Psychological Association. *Publication Manual of the American Psychological Association*. 3d ed. Washington, D.C.: American Psychological Association, 1983.

GENERAL GUIDES

Achtert, Walter S., and Joseph Gibaldi, eds. *The MLA Style Manual*. New York: Modern Language Association of America, 1985.

Howell, John Bruce. *Style Manuals of the English-Speaking World: A Guide*. Phoenix, Ariz.: Oryx Press, 1983.

University of Chicago Press. *The Chicago Manual of Style*. 13th ed. Chicago: University of Chicago Press, 1982.

Walker, Mellisa. *Writing Research Papers: A Norton Guide*. New York and London: W. W. Norton & Company, 1984.

Webster's Standard American Style Manual. Springfield, Mass.: Merriam-Webster, 1985.

Weidenborner, Stephen, and Domenick Caruso. *Writing Research Papers: A Guide to the Process*. New York: St. Martin's Press, 1982.

Zweifel, Frances W. *A Handbook of Biological Illustration*. Chicago: University of Chicago Press, 2d ed., 1988.

Index

Alphabetizing (*continued*)
 as editor, 9.41, 10.28, 10.30
 where initial varies, 10.23
 with religious title, 10.25
 as translator, 10.28, 10.30
Chinese names, 10.20
 chronological order in, 10.27
 compound family names, 10.17
 in glossaries, 1.25
 Hungarian names, 10.22
 Japanese names, 10.21
 letter-by-letter, 10.14
 list of abbreviations, 1.24
 Mac, 10.15–16
 non-Western names, 10.22
 optional style of, 10.16
 pseudonyms, 10.26
 reference list, 8.3, 8.21–22
 Saint, 10.15–16
 samples of, 10.15, 14.39–40, 14.46–49
 Spanish names, 10.18
 Sr. and *Jr.,* reversed names with,
  10.24
 succession of works by same author,
  10.27–34
 titles, 10.27
 words that resemble author's name,
  10.32
 works by unknown author, 10.31
A.M., 2.57
Annotating of bibliography, 10.36
Apostrophe
 with plurals, 3.6
 with possessives, 3.7–11
Appendix, 1.38–43, 5.14, 6.14, 9.3
Appositives, 3.73
Arabic names, 10.19
Arabic numerals. *See also* Illustrations;
  Numbers; Roman numerals
 for chapter numbers, 1.16, 1.35
 classical work, citing of, 9.105
 columns of a table, numbering, 6.35
 endnotes, 1.45
 enumeration, 2.70–73
 figure number, 1.18, 7.13
 generic heading of chapter, 1.35
 note numbering, 9.6
 pagination of
  appendix, 1.43
  introduction, 1.33
  reference matter, 1.3, 14.8
  text, 1.3, 14.8
 part numbers, citing of, 2.44
 scriptures, citing of, 2.20
 tables, numbering, 6.13
 unpublished materials, citing of, 2.47
 volume number, citing of, 9.82

Art
 with computer graphics, 13.29
 works of, 9.128, 11.63–64
Article. *See* Encyclopedia; Journal;
  Magazine; Newspaper; Periodical
Asterisk, in notes, 6.58
Author, corporate, 9.34, 11.10
Author-date citation. *See* Parenthetical
  references; Reference list
Author's name. *See also* Alphabetizing;
  Bibliography; Note; Reference list
 brackets in, use of, 9.25
 with coauthors, 9.32, 11.5
 comma in, 9.25–35
 with editor, translator, or compiler,
  9.39–41
 initials in, 9.25
 in note, 9.25–35
 of preface, foreword, or introduction,
  9.42
 with pseudonym, 9.26–27
 in shortened reference, 9.134–39

Backing up computer files, 13.13
Back matter. *See* Reference matter
Bar graph, 13.28
BASIC. *See* Computer program
B.C., 2.56
B.C.E., 2.56
Biblical citations. *See* Scriptural citations
Bibliography
 alphabetizing of, 10.14–34
 annotating of, 10.36
 author's names reversed in, 10.9–10
 classification of, 10.3–6
 entries compared with note entries,
  10.7–13
 footnote, 10.6
 foreign title in, 10.35
 format of, 10.8
 with multiple references in notes, 11.65–
  66
 page reference in, 10.12–13
 parentheses in, 10.11
 periods in, 10.11
 purpose of, 10.7
 quotation marks in, 10.34
 samples of, 14.48–49
 subheading in, 10.5
 underlining in, 10.33
 volume number in, 10.11
Bill. *See* Public documents
Bit map, with computer graphics, 13.29
Blank page, 1.7, 1.10, 14.6
Block quotation
 with computerized word processing, 5.5

286 / Index

Facts of publication (*continued*)
  name of city, 9.51, 9.52
  n.p., use of, 9.55
  in reference list, 8.33
Family name. *See* Alphabetizing; Author,
    name of; Bibliography, alphabetizing
    of
Figure. *See* Illustration
Figure number, 7.12–15
  with caption within an illustration, 7.10
  position of, 7.12
  with respect to margins, 7.7
  with two or more illustrations on a page,
    7.8
File management, with computerized word
    processing, 13.12
Film. *See* Motion picture
Final copy, with computerized word
    processing, 13.36
First, or full, reference. *See* Note
Folding of illustration, 7.44–46
Footers, with computerized word
    processing, 13.14
Footnote, with any part of paper, 1.4. *See*
    Note
Foreign language. *See* Foreign words and
    phrases
Foreign words and phrases, 4.28–33
  in bibliography, 10.35
  capitalizing titles, 4.10–12
  classical work, 9.99, 9.103–11
  English name of foreign city in note,
    9.53
  name of foreign city with newspaper
    title, 9.93–95
  in name of publishing agency, 9.64
  omission in, 5.29
  quotation in, 5.29
  shortened title for foreign newspaper,
    9.95
Foreword, in a note, 9.42, 11.24
Formatting text, with computerized word
    processing, 13.25
Formula, 13.2, 13.25
Forthcoming, for date of publication,
    9.68
FORTRAN. *See* Computer program
Fraction
  in currencies, 2.40
  hyphenation of, 3.19
  number in, 2.39
Fragment, 2.48. *See also* Unpublished
    materials; Quotation; Numbering
Frontispiece, in pagination, 14.7
Front matter. *See* Preliminaries
Function keys, with computerized word
    processing, 13.8

Generic heading, 14.10
  of acknowledgments, 1.8
  of appendix, 1.40
  of bibliography, 10.2
  of chapter, 1.35
  of chapter in table of contents, 1.16
  of introduction, 1.33
  of list of abbreviations, 1.24
  of list of illustrations, 1.18
  of part
    with spelled out number, 1.16
    in table of contents, 1.16
    with uppercase roman numeral, 1.16
  vertical spacing of, 14.5
Geographical name, 2.13–15
German, 4.10
Glossary, 1.25–27,, 14.40
Government. *See* Public documents
Graph, 7.30
Greek, 4.11, 7.7, 9.103–11. *See also*
    Classical works; Foreign words and
    phrases

Hardware, 13.2–5, 13.44
Headers, with computerized word
    processing, 13.44
Homonym, spelling of, 3.34
Hyphenation, 2.67, 3.12–53. *See also*
    Compound word; Word division
  of abbreviation, 3.50
  with *able* or *ible,* 3.44
  with adjectival compound, 3.28
  with *all,* 3.26
  authoritative spelling guides, 3.1
  with *better, best, ill, lesser, well,* etc.,
    3.23
  in classical citation, 2.46
  of compound word, 3.12–34
  with computerized word processing,
    3.37, 13.16, 13.22, 14.3
  in continued numbers, 2.67
  with *elect,* 3.17
  in foreign language, 3.53
  of fraction, 3.19
  of homonym, 3.34
  with *ing* or *ed,* 3.40–41
  of initials, 3.49–50
  with like nouns, 3.14
  at line end, 3.36
  in medieval citation, 2.46
  for missing letters, 3.96
  for missing words, 3.97
  with *odd,* 3.30
  for omission in a table, 6.45
  with participle, 3.24
  with phrase, 3.27
  of prefix compound, 3.34